Contemporary Photography and Theory

Contemporary Photography and Theory

Concepts and Debates

Sally Miller

BLOOMSBURY VISUAL ARTS
LONDON • NEW YORK • OXFORD • NEW DELHI • SYDNEY

BLOOMSBURY VISUAL ARTS
Bloomsbury Publishing Plc
50 Bedford Square, London, WC1B 3DP, UK
1385 Broadway, New York, NY 10018, USA

BLOOMSBURY, BLOOMSBURY VISUAL ARTS and the Diana logo are trademarks of Bloomsbury Publishing Plc

First published in Great Britain 2020

Cover design by Eleanor Rose | Cover photograph: *Dark Pacific Sun*, 2014. © Mohini Chandra and Christopher Stewart. Courtesy of the artists

A catalogue record for this book is available from the British Library.

A catalogue record for this book is available from the Library of Congress.

ISBN: HB: 978-1-3500-0332-3
PB: 978-1-3500-0331-6
ePDF: 978-1-3500-0334-7
eBook: 978-1-3500-0333-0

Typeset by Deanta Global Publishing Services, Chennai, India
Printed and bound in India

To find out more about our authors and books visit www.bloomsbury.com and sign up for our newsletters.

Contents

Figures

Acknowledgements

This book came out of a conversation with Davida Forbes about photography, books and teaching in which I said that I thought a text for students in their second and third years would be a good thing. Davida's suggestion that I should write it myself was something I was less sure of, however, I am now grateful for the suggestion. I would also like to thank Molly Beck, Nick Bellorini, Margaret Michniewicz, Sophie Tann, Louise Baird-Smith and Alexander Highfield from Bloomsbury for their support as well as the many artists who generously gave permission for their works to be reproduced, and the reviewers who provided such valuable comments and suggestions.

I must additionally thank my BA(Hons) Photography students past and present for their questions, thoughts and occasional perplexed silences which have all directed me in writing this book. I am also grateful to Stephen Bull, Daniel Campbell-Blight, Rachel Gillies, Fergus Heron, Francis Hodgson, Åsa Johannesson, Joanna Lowry, Aaron Schuman, Christopher Stewart and Esther Teichmann for sharing their thinking and ideas on photography over the years.

Finally, I must thank Craig for his infinite patience and Ursula for the immense chaos and joy she has bought into our lives. This book is dedicated to my family.

Introduction

The relationship between photography and theory is complex, and for students, the essay is often regarded as an arduous obstacle to the otherwise enjoyable experience of taking photographs and making work. This book does not remedy that. However, I hope that by offering a series of essays on contemporary photography and theory the complexity of their relationship may at least become more thought provoking. By providing an extended analysis of a range of case studies from established and emerging artists and incorporating new thinking from other disciplines, this text aims to enable students to develop and expand their thinking about photography.

There are many ways of thinking through the work made by contemporary photographers and I have, of course, not been able to cover all the artists, topics, theorists and debates that I wished to. The examples chosen are not always those by the most recognized artists – in fact sometimes these have been deliberately avoided to allow different aspects of established theory to come through. The examples are composed of those that are popular with students, those that I have found useful from pedagogic point of view and some personal favourites – it is not definitive, and there are many other examples. I hope you enjoy finding and interpreting them using some of the ideas explored in this book.

To briefly explain the structure of the book, the book contains five parts, each of which offers an introduction to some of the key areas of debate in contemporary photography: 'Photography and Identity'; 'Photography, Landscape and Place', 'Photography, Performance and the Politics of Representation', 'Photography and Psychoanalysis'; and 'Photography and the Event'. Within each part, there are three chapters which offer a different approach to the section topic. The purpose of each chapter is to offer an overview of a particular concept and develop an analysis through an extended example or set of examples. Each chapter or part can be read independently; indeed, the book can be approached as a set of fifteen essays. However, there is a progression through each section with further and more complex ideas being introduced. This progression is often also historical; though this should not be taken to mean that newer works are more complex, it is simply a way of tracing the debates that have occurred and deepening the application of theory as the key terms and ideas become familiar. Together, the individual chapters and parts support the integration of a range of key thinkers and theorists into an understanding of contemporary photographic practice.

Part One, 'Photography and Identity', addresses the relationship between photography and identity from the early use of photography as a new technology to produce honorific images of wealthy sitters to its contemporary use as a way of sharing representations of the self via social media. In this section writings on subjectivity will be examined in order to demonstrate how particular kinds of 'self' are constructed through the discursive framework of the photographic portrait. Considering the portrait in relation to writings on subjectivity can help us to understand what links works by artists such as Eileen Perrier, Bettina von Zwehl and Hasan Elahi. This section will introduce the writings of a number of theorists including Michel Foucault, Allan Sekula and Julian Stallabrass. Though these writers and their work may be familiar to many students, it is presented here as a means of introducing some of the key ideas that will be developed throughout the book.

Chapter 1, 'The Honorific and the Subjugated Photographic Portrait', considers the portrait through the categories of the honorific and the subjugated portrait by reading these through a contemporary example by Eileen Perrier. Chapter 2, 'The Blank Portrait and the Intimate Record', looks at how two contemporary genres of portraiture – the blank portrait and the intimate record – comment upon and extend these early categories of photographic portraiture. To conclude this section, Chapter 3, 'The Portrait and the Contemporary Self', will examine the impact of digital technology on the understanding and meaning of photographic representations of the self.

Part Two, 'Photography, Landscape and Place', expands upon some of the ideas explored in relation to the portrait in order to look at landscape as a discursive construction – a way in which we assign meaning and significance to land. Like the self, landscape is not natural but a cultural construction. How artists have chosen to photograph land reflects different historical and social values, hopes and fears. To begin, Chapter 4, 'The Politics of Place', will consider the picturesque and the sublime. Photography inherited certain ways of framing nature from landscape painting, and as such, aesthetic categories such as the 'picturesque' and the 'sublime' have often dominated our ideas about what a landscape is and how we look at it. However, a number of contemporary artists and photographers have challenged and reworked these categories to ask us to consider our relationship to a range of issues including colonialism, national identity and technology. We will consider the work of Mohini Chandra and Christopher Stewart, Sally Mann, Justin James King and Thomas Albdorf. Chapter 5, 'Non-Place and New Topologies', will explore some of the new approaches to landscape photography that have been developed in order to engage with emerging categories of place. To begin, we will look at Marc Augé's writings in relation to works by Andreas Geffler and Roger Eberhard. In the second part of this chapter Trevor Paglen's work will be discussed in relation to writings on the topological landscape and the politics of the secret. Finally, Chapter 6, 'Ruins and the

Anthropocene', will consider the meaning of the ruined landscape as a means of reflecting upon the social, economic and political conditions of neoliberalism. Examples discussed will include Joel Meyerowitz, Tong Lam, Joanna Zylinska and Matthew Buckingham.

Part Three, 'Photography, Performance and the Politics of Representation', addresses the way in which a number of contemporary photographers have used performance as a means of challenging traditional codes of representation. In particular, we will address how performance has emerged as a way of engaging with the post-identity politics of the neoliberal era. To begin, Chapter 7, 'Performances of Gender', introduces the understanding of gender as performative that is elaborated in Judith Butler's seminal book *Gender Trouble*. We will consider Amalia Ullman's *Excellences & Perfections* as a way of exploring contemporary discourses of femininity such as the girl and 'the perfect'. Chapter 8, 'Race, History and Time', will consider artists who use atemporal performances to challenge the understanding of race as an ahistorical, essential category. We will look at works by Shadi Ghadirian, Omar Victor Diop and Nona Faustine. To conclude this section, Chapter 9, 'Performativity and Disability', will address how artists such as Laura Swanson, Sam Taylor-Johnson and Hannah Laycock have used a strategy of performance to draw attention to the way in which disability is a culturally and socially organized subjectivity.

Part Four, 'Photography and Psychoanalysis', introduces psychoanalytic theory as a means of understanding the unconscious fears, fantasies and pleasures at stake in looking at photographs. To begin, Chapter 10, 'Psychoanalysis, Representation and Desire', will consider the work of Lucas Blalock in relation to the Lacan's concept *objet a*. In Chapter 11, 'Psychoanalysis, Spectatorship and the Gaze', we will compare the work of Jemima Stehli and Laurel Nakadate as a way of exploring Lacan's writings on the gaze, sexual difference and fantasy. To conclude, in Chapter 12, 'The Politics of Enjoyment', we will discuss Richard Prince's series *New Portraits* in relation to writings on psychoanalysis, ideology and the Lacanian concept of *jouissance*.

Part Five, 'Photography and the Event', considers the way in which photography has served as a social tool to shape and give meaning to traumatic events and addresses questions about the value and limits of the photographic image. In Chapter 13, 'Photography, Memory, History', the concepts of postmemory and multidirectional memory will be used to theorize the role that photography might play in mediating our relationship to past events of which we have no direct experience. The artists discussed in this chapter will be David Levinthal, Alan Schechner and Marc Adelman. Chapter 14, 'Post-Photojournalism and Contemporary Images of Conflict', will address how a number of new aesthetics have emerged as photographers seek to engage with current events outside of the often sensational images that dominate mainstream press representations of conflict. We will look at the work of Christoph Bangert, Richard Mosse and Antonio Denti. Finally, Chapter

15, 'Photography, Empathy and Responsibility', will address the aftermath and the debates that have taken place around the 'late photograph'. The examples considered in this chapter will be by Simon Norfolk, Rosemary Laing, Heungsoon Im, Ahlam Shibli and Rineke Dijkstra.

The discussion throughout this book is underpinned by the understanding that the photograph, as John Tagg expresses it, 'has no identity' and its 'history has no unity. It is a flickering across a field of institutional spaces. It is this field we must study, not photography as such.'[1] As Tagg's writings show, we cannot analyse photography outside of its political, cultural and historical context. For many theorists writing on the contemporary historical period, neoliberalism is a key term.

Neoliberalism is a slippery and much contested term often used to describe the actions, thinking and rhetoric associated with a set of economic and political practices that have occurred in tandem. These include, but are not limited to, the deregulation of markets, reductions in progressive taxation and the privatization, centralization and reduction of public services. These changes have been ushered in under a rhetoric that argues for the 'common sense' of economically based thinking and competitive and entrepreneurial modes of relation across all sectors.

However, neoliberalism is not just an economic project. In 'What Kind of Thing Is "Neoliberalism"?' Jeremy Gilbert draws attention not only to the 'sheer regularity and similarity' of the basic elements of neoliberal policy such as privatization, centralization and deregulation but also to the 'extent to which a range of significant cultural phenomena seems clearly to share and work to reproduce the basic presuppositions of neoliberal thought and the long-term social objectives of neoliberal policy'.[2] The extended reach of contemporary neoliberalism means that there is a distinction to be made between the historical roots of the term in the thinking of liberal theorists such as Friedrich Hayek and Ludwig von Mises and the writings of contemporary theorists who are concerned with what Gilbert calls 'actually existing neoliberalism'.[3]

Actually existing neoliberalism is 'both a specifically economic process and a broader reconfiguration of society'.[4] This is why Henry Giroux has proposed that neoliberalism is best described as a 'political-economic-cultural project'.[5] Giroux traces the way in which neoliberalism functions as a regulative force, a mode of rationality and a form of public pedagogy. We are perhaps most familiar with thinking of neoliberalism as a regulative force where it 'organizes a range of flows, including people, capital, knowledge, and wealth'.[6] However, Giroux argues that this is supported by neoliberalism as a mode of rationality which 'enables and legitimates the practices of managerialism, deregulation, efficiency, cost-benefit analysis, expanding entrepreneurial forms, and privatization'.[7] Finally, it is as a mode of public pedagogy that neoliberal ideology is able to be 'produced, and disseminated from many institutional and cultural sites'.[8]

Critics such as Gilbert and Giroux argue that the crucial task for those who wish to challenge the hegemony of neoliberalism is not only to locate its forms but also to explore ways of thinking otherwise. Throughout this book we will be exploring works that seek to address the present historical moment, to show us how we might perceive it more clearly and, potentially, *see* otherwise. Let's begin.

Part One

Photography and identity

We understand and negotiate the significance of photographs of the self on a daily basis: the portrait is perhaps the most popular form of vernacular and professional photography. However, what does it mean when fine art photographers engage with the genre of portrait photography? The chapters in this section consider how photographic history and writings on subjectivity can help us to understand what connects works by a diverse range of artists including Eileen Perrier, Zoe Strauss, Bettina von Zwehl, Hasan Elahi and Vivian Fu.

Chapter 1 considers the portrait through the categories of the honorific and the subjugated portrait alongside writings on subjectivity to demonstrate how particular kinds of 'self' are constructed through these categories. Chapter 2 looks at how two contemporary genres of portraiture – the blank portrait and the intimate record – comment upon and extend these early categories of photographic portraiture. To conclude this section, Chapter 3 will examine the impact of digital technology on the production, dissemination and meaning of photographic representations of the self.

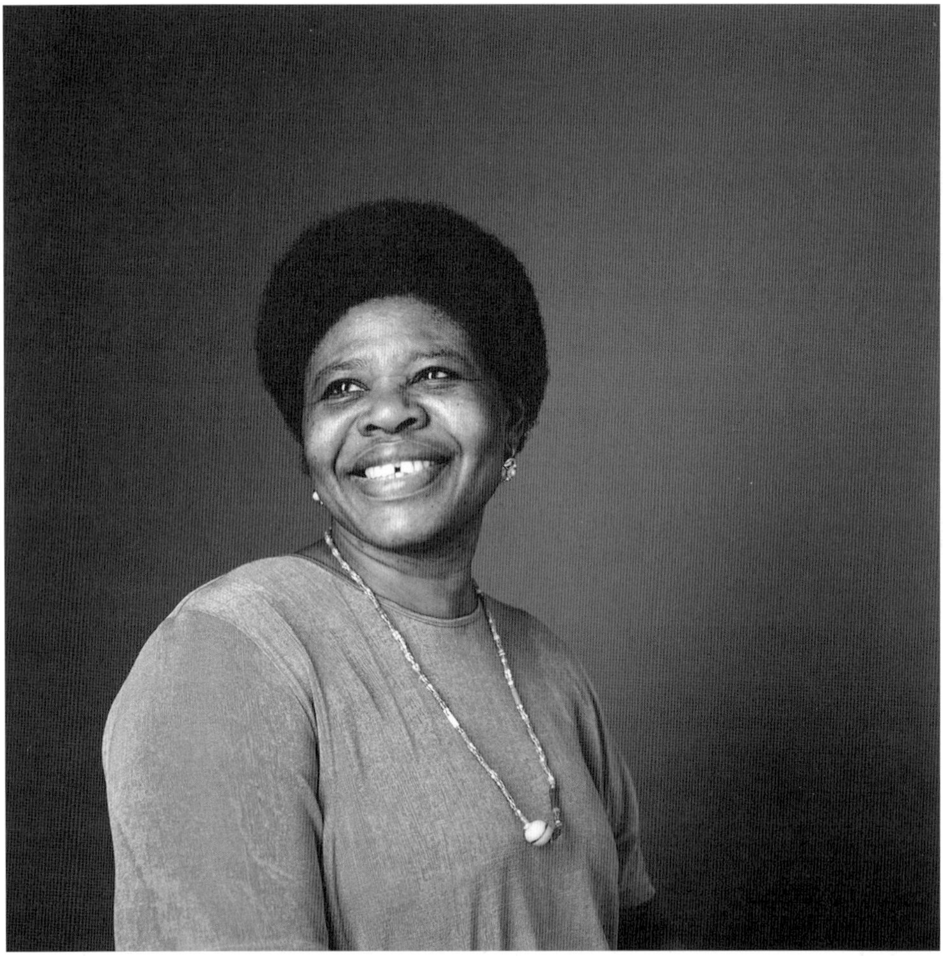

Figure 1.1 Eileen Perrier, *Grace,* 2000. © Eileen Perrier. Courtesy of Eileen Perrier.

1

The honorific and the subjugated portrait

Grace (2000) by Eileen Perrier is a series of twelve colour photographs. The images are all head-and-shoulders portraits taken in a studio with a neutral blue background and soft, flattering lighting. The subjects are posed; they are all seated with their body at a slight angle, their head is turned to the side and they gaze over their shoulder, above and to the left and of the camera. They are all smiling (Figures 1.1 and 1.3a-d).

This simple description belies these images' engagement with the complex history of photographic representations of the self. As outlined in the Introduction, the history and meaning of photography is not singular. As such, photography is best understood by examining the interconnected discourses that give a range of analogue and digital technologies concerned with recording and producing images social, cultural and historical meaning. These discourses are constantly being written and rewritten, with new meanings forged and others abandoned. Many artists who work with photography are not concerned with refining or consolidating these meanings, but commenting upon or contesting them.

Perrier's work is a good example of this. While, at first, *Grace* seems to be easily readable within the genre of portraiture – in particular, in relation to the honorific codes descended from painting that have dominated the formal photographic studio portrait since its invention – it does not simply reproduce these conventions but quotes them as a means of commenting upon them. In order to better understand the nature of Perrier's interventions we need to explore the history of the photographic portrait.

The photographic portrait

Historically, portraiture was a privilege that belonged to the few who could afford to commission a painted likeness. However, the invention of photography allowed for the mass production of portraits. As such, the advent of photography is often seen as a technological development through which the privilege of portraiture was democratized. For example, in *The Genius of Photography* Gerry Badger writes that 'everyone, thanks to photography, was given an identity – the daguerreotype portrait was a magical proof of existence'.[1] However, the way in which the photograph was able to function as 'proof of existence' is complex. While the indexical nature of photography means that it does indeed attest to the physical existence of the subject of photograph. The meaning of the self that is produced through photographic representation is far from straightforward. In short, the identity 'given' by the photographic portrait was not the same as that bestowed by the painted portrait. Photography, through its distinct social, cultural, political and economic uses and meanings, offered a new kind of identity to its sitters.

Although the photographic portrait was popular and sought after, the new experience of the self produced by seeing one's photographic likeness gave rise to a range of responses from excitement and wonder to ambivalence, dissatisfaction and fear. For some, the pleasure of owning a photographic portrait was sufficient in itself. This can be seen in the account of a portrait photographer who overcame the problem of impatient customers by giving them photographs of previous sitters. He testified that although some demanded another sitting, others were 'entirely satisfied with the substitute'.[2] For others, being photographed was a more fraught process: Robert Louis Stevenson remarked of his – yet to be taken – portrait that he dreaded that 'it will not be like me'.[3] On seeing his photographic portrait Nathaniel Hawthorne wrote, 'I was really a little startled at recognising myself so apart from myself'.[4] While the actor Charles MacReady suggested an ingenious solution to this problem of photographic likeness: he would send his portrait in oils to be photographed.[5]

Thus, we can see that photographic likeness, so naturalized in discussions of photography as an indexical medium, is complex: we must learn to recognize ourselves – and others – in photographs.[6] As such, rather than 'magically' making the privileges of the portrait available to all, photography transformed the understanding of the self that had been the subject of the painted portrait.

The *carte de visite*

The *carte de visite* was patented by the French photographer André Adolphe Eugène Disdéri in 1854. The *carte* consisted of a small albumen print, usually a studio portrait, mounted on a card approximately 2½ × 4 inches in size. Unlike the daguerreotype, which was expensive and unique, the *carte* was affordable, mass produced and easily distributed among friends and visitors. Thus, for many historians of photography it is with the *carte* that the true democratization of portraiture arrived: 'The egalitarian eye of the camera … matched by the uniformity of the *carte* as an object.'[7]

However, it was not only access to the privilege of portraiture that produced the democratizing effect of the *carte* but the way in which the 'material culture' of privilege, the dress, gesture, posture and settings of the upper class, became available to everyone in the form of studio backdrops and props. The dispersal of the signs of privilege produced an anxious discussion around class for in the photographers' studio previously rigid social boundaries suddenly appeared to be little more than 'a combination of costumes and stage properties that could easily be simulated'.[8]

Also significant was the way in which the *cartes* themselves were a part of commodity culture. *Cartes* were usually purchased by the dozen, with the explicit intention of exchange, and it is estimated that 300 to 400 million *cartes* were sold in England every year from 1861 to 1867.[9] In addition to your own portrait, it was possible to buy a vast array of *cartes* of public figures and celebrities. Displayed in photographic shop windows, these attracted crowds who were eager to see photographs of politicians, royalty, actresses and courtesans. This was a new pleasure, and several articles at the time drew attention to the disconcerting effect that the display of these disparate collections had. For example, a commentator in *Art Journal* noted that 'the most curious contrasts may be drawn and the most startling combinations effected ... when even the most hurried of passing glances reveals to us the facsimile of Lord Shaftesbury and Cardinal Wiseman, and of the French Emperor and Sims Reeves side-by-side'.[10] As Rachel Teukolsky has noted, in the photographic shop window the 'rigidly divided and stratified Victorian social world became an alarming jumble'.[11]

The way in which the *carte* circulated is also key to understanding its significance. Previously, portraits either had a limited circulation among acquaintances who had a personal knowledge of each other or were located in specific settings in which the sitter already had an established role. The practices of sharing and consuming central to the culture of the *carte* meant that the photographic portrait began to circulate beyond the boundaries of personal knowledge or professional context. This meant that there was no certain way of distinguishing between the *carte* given by the sitter as a token of friendship, affection or esteem and the *carte* that was purchased. Furthermore, the studio settings and props common to all sittings meant that there was 'little to distinguish between the cartes de visite of the anonymous and the eminent'.[12] In short, 'as a highly mobile, standardized commodity, carte portraits easily slipped the leash of their intended functions to then take on ambiguous and potentially disturbing new meanings'[13] and precipitate 'novel social encounters'.[14]

Central to these novel social encounters was a new kind of public visibility in which 'people began to report the curious phenomenon of a person being preceded by their photograph'.[15] As such, Annie Rudd has argued that 'cartes de visite were associated less with a personal, domestic conception of likeness than with a distinctly public one'.[16] Here the 'cartes' semiotic complexity – their status as both objectified likeness and industrially produced commodity'[17] is key. As Rudd notes the *carte* was printed on a card that gave the name of the studio rather than the sitter, as such the *carte* might be seen to be emblematic not the democratization of portraiture but of 'the transformation of one's face into a commercial product'.[18] While the use of clothing and props in the photographic studio challenged the understanding of the 'natural' superiority of the upper class, it was the performance of the self as a commodified individual that allowed the middle class to emerge as a unique social group. However, the middle class was not the only social group that photography played a key role in establishing.

The subjugated portrait

In his seminal article 'The Body and the Archive,' Allan Sekula argues that the use of photography by institutions, such as the police, that sought to observe, categorize, archive and control meant that 'photographic portraiture began to perform a role no painted portrait could have'.[19] Sekula proposes that photography is 'a double system of representation capable of functioning both *honorifically* and *repressively*'.[20] In the judiciary and medical uses of photography that emerged during the nineteenth century, the sitter is presented without the flattering or idealizing goals of traditional portraiture. As John Tagg has described the repressive or subjugated portrait, 'The format varies hardly at all … workers, vagrants, criminals, patients, the insane, the poor, the colonised races – are taken one by one: isolated in a shallow contained space; turned full face and subjected to an unreturnable gaze; illuminated, focused, measured, numbered and named; forced to yield to the minutest scrutiny of gestures and features'.[21] This directs us to an important caveat in the understanding of the photographic portrait as a democratization of privilege: the identity offered by the photographic portrait is not always desirable.

In order to better understand the subject-effects of the photographic portrait, we need to turn to the writings of the philosopher and historian Michel Foucault. Although Foucault's writings encompass a wide range of subjects and themes, one of his primary concerns was demonstrating what we regard to be permanent truths about human nature and history change. This includes our conception of the self. Departing from traditional philosophical interrogations of the nature of the self, Foucault's writings are concerned with subjectivity – the way in which we come to understand ourselves as particular kinds of self, how certain understandings of the self become dominant and why certain ways of being are privileged at different times. Foucault argues that subjectivity, rather than a unique quality of individuals, is a product of social, cultural and historical context.

Of particular interest to photographic theorists who are concerned with the early history of photography are Foucault's writings on power. Or, more specifically power/ knowledge, for Foucault argues that the emergence of new forms of power must be considered in relation to the field of knowledge that accompanies and sustains them.

In describing how contemporary forms of power/knowledge came into being, Foucault argues that in eighteenth-century Europe there was a shift in the focus of government where population, rather than simply territory, came to be understood as the object of political rule. As a result, the power and stability of the state was no longer seen to reside in the sovereign and their court, but in the people whose health, strength and happiness was now seen to be the true measure of successful rule.

What emerged to cope with this new objective was a new form of government. This particular form of government, sometimes expressed as 'government at a distance', occurred through institutions such as schools, workplaces and hospitals. Foucault calls these institutions that are connected to, but distinct from, centralized government the 'carceral network'. The practices of government that occurred through the carceral network required a new set of technologies that would enable every person to become visible to those institutions newly charged with governing the population. Foucault uses the term 'governmentality' to describe the ensemble of techniques and procedures that are used to govern individuals and their conduct.

Through practices such as the examination and the confession the people who made up the population came to be 'known' in extensive details. The details sought were not just information such as their age and occupation but their state of health, beliefs and habits. A key development here is the emergence of the human sciences, in particular those sciences with the prefix 'psy' such as psychology and psychiatry. It is to the language, practices and concepts advanced by the 'psy' sciences that we owe our contemporary understanding of the self. As Nikolas Rose has summarized, 'The birth and history of the knowledges of subjectivity and intersubjectivity are intrinsically bound up with programmes which, in order to govern subjects, have found that they need to know them.'[22]

A Foucauldian approach asks us to invert our common-sense understanding of the self: the self is not a discrete, timeless entity; rather the understanding of the self as a unitary and ultimately knowable subject is an understanding that was produced through the project of knowing the population as an object of rule. Thus, we can see that the self so naturalized in many discussions of photographic portraiture is a relatively recent invention. Of particular interest to photographic theorists is the key role that photography played in producing these new forms of knowledge about the self.

Although the photographic archive produced during this time was vast, it is important to note that photographic records were only a part of an assemblage of techniques and technologies that were marshalled towards the project of describing, categorizing and storing information about the human subject. The photographs acquired their meaning only by being embedded within medical and scientific narratives. As David Green reminds us, 'Their intelligibility does not reside in their correspondence with a reality of appearances but in their relation to a variety of other discourses, representations and significations – a corporeal semiotics – which specified the "body" as the nexus of a network of scientific practices and new modes of surveillance and documentation.'[23]

Physiognomy is an example of one of the scientific narratives that gave these photographs meaning and coherence. The idea that it is possible to 'read' a person's character from their body, in particular, the face, can be traced to antiquity. However, in the late eighteenth century these beliefs were formalized by Johan Kaspar Lavater in his *Essays on Physiognomy* (1772). What distinguishes this text over previous understandings of the connection between exterior appearance and characteristics such as intelligence, morality and dishonesty is the way in which the classification and identification of individuals is formulated in scientific language. Lavatar saw physiognomy as an empirical science in which human character could be determined through the objective reading of facial configurations. However, as many critics have observed,[24] the physiognomic categorization of particular bodies as 'normal' and others as 'deviant' was rooted in social and cultural prejudices which were then formalized as scientific fact. In this way, bodily differences and the social distinctions that arose from them were constructed as necessary, rational and scientific.

Sciences such as physiognomy were incredibly popular and their ideas widely disseminated among a growing population through consumer products such as the physiologies': pocket-size books depicting social types that 'served as guidebooks, as elementary reader for "respectable citizens" of city life'.[25] As Sekula has noted,

> In claiming to provide a means for distinguishing the stigmata of vice from the shining marks of virtue, physiognomy and phrenology offered an essential hermeneutic service to a world of fleeting and often anonymous market transactions. Here was a method for quickly assessing the character of strangers in the dangerous and congested spaces of the nineteenth-century city. Here was a gauge of the intentions and capabilities of the other.[26]

There are two figures who are seen to be key examples of the way in which photography was used to make visible the distinctions being drawn between different 'types' of people at this time: Alphonse Bertillon and Francis Galton.

Alphonse Bertillon and Francis Galton

Alphonse Bertillon was a French criminologist and anthropologist who developed the first criminal identification system to use photography in conjunction with anthropometric and statistical methods. Although police forces were already using photography to produce 'rogues' galleries', these were vast and unorganized collections of criminal portraits. In order to standardize the way in which information on offenders was produced and stored, Bertillon developed a system that he called 'Bertillonage'. The system used the front and side profile photograph that remains the standard 'mugshot' to this day. However, as we have seen photographic likeness is 'slippery' and was not capable of securing the identity of its sitter adequately. Therefore, these photographs were supplemented by verbal, anthropometric and statistical measures. Each Bertillon card contained detailed measurements of eleven different body parts and a brief verbal description of any distinguishing features alongside two photographs. In this way, Bertillon was able to produce what he called a *portrait parle* or 'speaking likeness'. Using Adolphe Quetelet's concept of the average man,[27] the Bertillon cards were then organized within a filing system.

It is important to note that Bertillon utilizes photography in relation to already existing systems of knowledge and organization. The camera is not used in isolation, but put to use within 'a larger ensemble: a bureaucratic-clerical-statistical system of "intelligence"'.[28] It was the effective organization of the records within a system from which they could be retrieved quickly that was key to the success of the Bertillon card. Indeed, Sekula has argued that, for all its importance, 'the central artifact of this system is not the camera but the filing cabinet'.[29]

Nonetheless, Bertillon's system should not be understood as simply a more efficient method of storage and retrieval: the way in which he organized and categorized the records was 'absolutely central to its knowledge effect'.[30] In Bertillion's system individuals acquire their meaning – their individuality – only in relation to others. The organization of the photographic portrait within an archive is paradoxically what allows for the subject to emerge as a unique individual. And the way in which individual's individuality – their difference – was organized was not neutral. In Bertillon's use of Quetelet's concept of the average man, the mean or normal point in statistical analysis is conflated with social 'norms' such that there is a 'slippage from a purely statistical to a discriminatory social law of averages'.[31]

The concept of the average man brings us to our second example: Francis Galton. Galton is known for developing the technique of composite portraiture. In this process negatives of different subjects are combined through repeated partial exposures to produce a single image. Like Bertillon, Galton was influenced by the work of Quetelet. However, rather than seeking to identify the unique features of an individual body in order to secure a definitive, unique identification, Galton sought to produce a visual record of the characteristics common to a particular group. Indeed, the composites that Galton produced of criminality, health and disease are not of people at all. As Shawn Michelle Smith has noted, 'Galton's "typical" portraits represent only imaginary beings, mathematical averages of actual people. They are

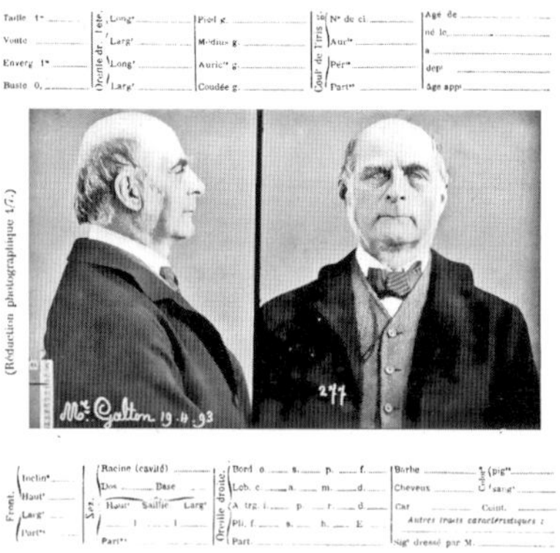

Figure 1.2 Bertilllon card of Francis Galton created upon Galton's visit to Bertillon's laboratory in 1893.

not likenesses, material referents for individual bodies, but portraits of an abstract type, representations that supposedly reveal the "essence" of a biologically determined group.'[32]

What is particularly troubling about Galton's work is the way in which his interest in social Darwinism led him to advocate eugenics. In Galton's writings on heredity the unemployed, the criminal and the insane as well as the accomplished, the intelligent and the good are understood as biological categories which he proposed should be controlled through selective breeding. However, as David Green has stressed, it is important to see Galton's ideas in relation to the emergence of the middle class: 'Insofar as eugenics proposed the reordering of society in accordance with the distribution of mental abilities and cognitive skills amongst the population, it placed a high value on those whose contribution to society was based upon intellectual expertise rather than the ownership of capital or the supply of labour.'[33] The composite portrait thus served a particular social function obscured by the scientific language in which it was described: it used photography as evidence of the innate superiority of the emergent middle class. Here the argument for the 'born' degeneracy of the criminal went hand in hand with establishing the 'natural' intellectual and moral superiority of the middle classes. Such that 'the professional middle class was to be clearly differentiated from both the bourgeoisie and the proletariat'.[34]

As an example, one need only look at the portrait of Galton created during his visit to Bertillon's laboratory in France (Figure 1.2). The portrait takes the form of a Bertillon card. However, the exclusion of any of the anthropometric measurements and the use of 'M. Galton' mitigate the meaning of the portrait: the photograph does not depict Galton as a criminal. As Susan Bailey has observed of this portrait, 'The photograph, with its halo of numbers, is both *homo statisticus*, the supplement to statistician Quetelet's "average man," and a portrait of the scientist dispassionately submitting his body to measurement.'[35] As such, the portrait mobilizes honorific and subjugated conventions together in order to present Galton as a subject emblematic of the emerging middle classes: a modern man of science.

As Sekula reminds us, it is only 'on the basis of mutual comparison, on the basis of the tentative construction of a larger, "universal" archive, that zones of deviance and respectability could be clearly demarcated'.[36] Thus, we can see how both the honorific and the subjugated portrait

> presupposed a certain kind of individual that preceded any shot of a particular individual. The differences in terms of which modern individuals could be said to belong to one or more categories were bestowed on those individuals, not by any particular photograph, ... but by the generic protocols for classifying, posing, shooting, and naming subject matter that transformed virtually anyone and anything into a classifiable image.[37]

Eileen Perrier: *Grace*

To conclude, let's return to Eileen Perrier's *Grace*. If we consider the images of the series individually (Figures 1.3 a-d), they each conform to the conventions of the honorific image. The subject is elevated through the use of flattering lighting, the low position of the camera and the pose: the three-quarter profile in which the subject gazes into distance is one that is frequently adopted by politicians to suggest a sense of purpose and destiny. However, *Grace* is a series of portraits that uniformly uses these elements. The repetition of the same conditions: background, lighting, camera angle and pose, is something that is associated with the subjugated portrait. The uniformity of the portraits directs us away from reading them as 'individual' portraits towards seeking out a connection between the people pictured, to speculate about why they have been photographed in this way.[38]

However, our inquiry is disrupted by two elements: the sheer range of subjects pictured, different sexes, ages and ethnicities, and the fact that they are smiling. The smile is not commonly found in any of the types of portraiture we have discussed so far. However, it is a common feature of vernacular photography. Indeed, David Bate has speculated that the smile 'emerged in photography as a popular convention precisely to signify the willing – "happy" – participation of the sitter "to-be-photographed"'.[39] In Perrier's series, the smile is also what directs us to what unites these subjects: they all have diastema, a gap tooth. Diastema has signified differently across cultures and historical periods. In the Middle Ages a gap tooth was regarded as a sign of a strongly sexed nature. In Ghana, Namibia and Nigeria diastemata are considered a sign of beauty and fertility, while, in France, history has furnished diastema with a different meaning: they are called 'dents du bonheur' (lucky teeth). This expression is purported to have originated in Napoleon's time. As perfect front

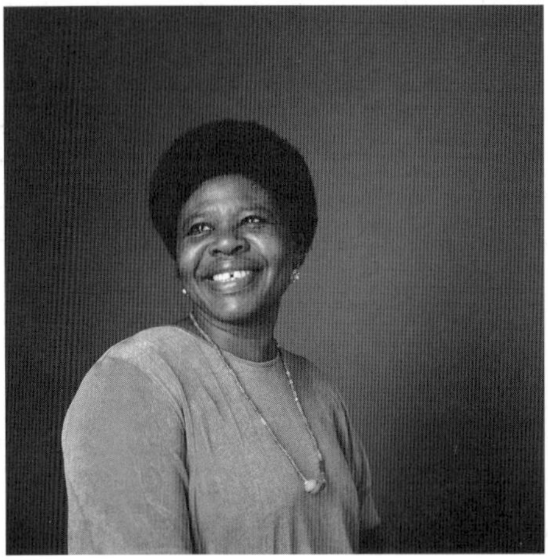

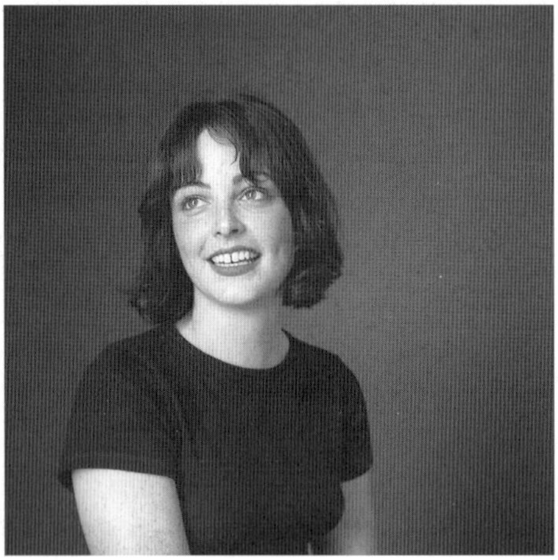

teeth were required to open the powder magazine used in rifles, those with diastema were – luckily – classified as unfit to fight. Diastema has thus been understood as a sign of vice, of beauty, of fertility and of luck. In addition, because diastema occurs naturally in children, for many they recall the innocence of childhood. In *Grace*, elements such as the use of the colour blue for the background and clothing of the sitters are reminiscent of the school portrait and evoke the latter meaning. However, the other meanings and associations are not excluded by these elements. Similarly, the title does not serve to secure a particular meaning, but offer a further set of associations. Grace is a name, a quality and a religious blessing. In Perrier's work it carries an additional meaning. The first photograph in the series is of Perrier's mother, Grace. However, what does the repetition of 'Grace' as a title for the other portraits mean? Here, grace functions in relation to an interior quality. That the subjects possess grace is also signalled by the 'halo' effect produced by careful lighting of the backdrop. In this way, Perrier builds a new set of meanings: the conventions of the subjugated portrait are used in relation to the scientific understanding of diastema as an inherited flaw. However, through the conventions of the honorific portrait Perrier links diastema to both Grace and grace in order to pay tribute to her inheritance.

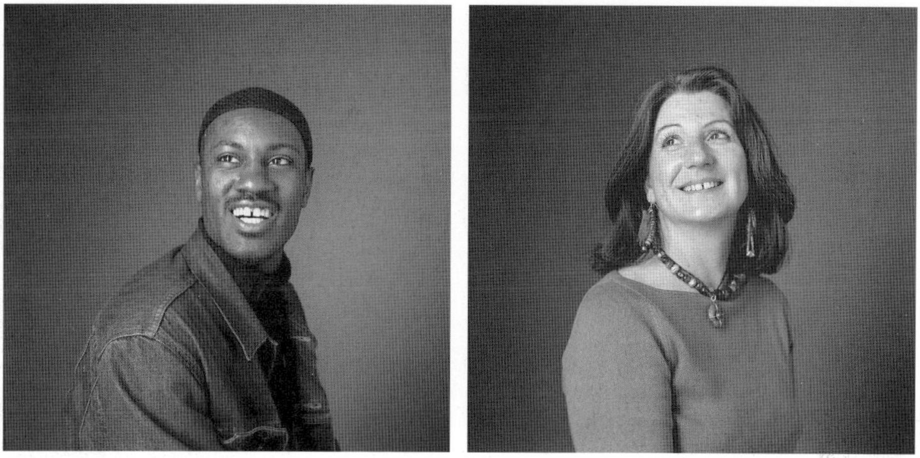

Figure 1.3a,b,c,d Eileen Perrier, *Grace,* 2000. © Eileen Perrier. Courtesy of Eileen Perrier.

2

The blank portrait and the intimate record

The portrait remains a dominant genre of photography, and many contemporary artists working with photography continue to turn to the portrait form to address questions around identity and subjectivity. In this chapter we will be considering two photographers: Bettina von Zwehl and Zoe Strauss. Both of these artists use the photographic portrait as a means of exploring modes of subjectivity specific to neoliberalism. Despite their similar concerns, the kind of engagement the viewer has with the work of these two photographers is quite different. One way of understanding these works and the contrasting effect they have on the viewer is by contextualizing them in relation to two different approaches to the subject that are taken in contemporary art photography. These two approaches have been described in a number of ways. In this chapter we will be using the terms 'blank' and 'intimate' to describe the concerns that differentiate our two examples.

Bettina von Zwehl: *Untitled I*

A young woman looks at the camera with an ambivalent yet compelling expression. The harsh flash and plain background recall the photobooth portrait, but the framing, proportions of the image (which indicate the use of a 5 × 4 camera), the larger than life-size proportions of the print and its location in the gallery suggest that it is not intended to be used for formal purposes of identification. How then should we read this portrait (Figure 2.1)?

In 'What's in a Face? Blankness and Significance in Contemporary Art Photography',[1] Julian Stallabrass identifies the 'blank' style we see used in von Zwhel's work as a prevalent style in contemporary photographic practice. In this genre of portraiture, the subject is typically placed centrally in the frame against a neutral backdrop and faces the camera directly. Titles and any accompanying text tend to be

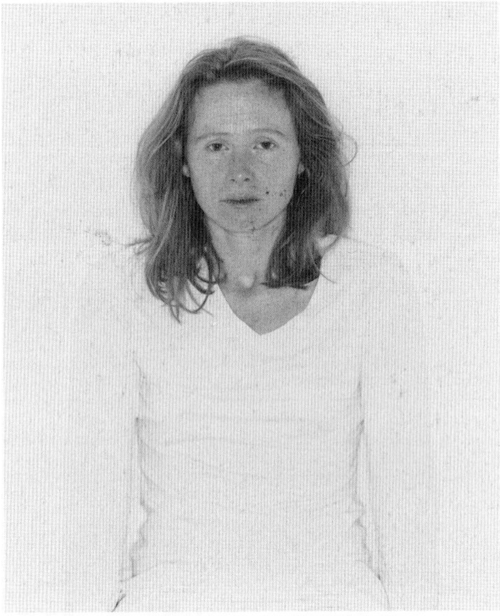

Figure 2.1 Bettina von Zwehl, *Untitled I*, 1998, #1 (series of 7). © Bettina von Zwehl. Courtesy of Bettina von Zwehl.

functional giving brief, factual details such as name, date of the photograph and/or its location. Key elements such as background, lighting and composition are consistent across what are often extended series of photographs, as a means of directing the viewer's attention to 'the particularities of the subject'.[2]

Presenting the subject in a standardized frame is an approach that we might recognize from Chapter 1 as belonging to the bureaucratic uses of photography by institutions such as the police. Stallabrass notes that the return by contemporary practitioners to this approach is surprising given the critique that it has been subjected to by theorists such as John Tagg and Allan Sekula. However, Stallabrass argues that while works by contemporary photographers might share a similar aesthetic to nineteenth-century institutional uses of the photograph, they are informed by a very different understanding of the human subject. Indeed, rather than reproducing the camera's early function as a tool of subjugation, these works seem to be seeking to comment upon some of the contradictions that have arisen from the use of photography as a tool of *both* subjugation and identity formation. That is to say, Stallabrass argues that we should read such works as a critical response to the historical use of photography as a means of classifying individuals.

There are a number of ways in which contemporary artists working in this mode signal their departure from the subjugated portrait.[3] First, the subjects are not strongly differentiated from the photographer or their likely viewers. That is to say, the subject is not marked as 'other' but 'like'. Stallabrass does, however, caution that this alone is not sufficient to mitigate against the objectifying effects of the camera and notes that the subject is still presented to the viewer to be 'read': 'While such photography may offer a critique of the classifying impulse that lay behind imperial ethnographic photography at home and abroad, it is not one that impedes the guilty pleasure of viewing these contemporary subjects as mere image.'[4] Indeed, the use of large format cameras, flash, fine-grain film and life-size or larger than life-size prints means that the opportunities that are presented to examine the subject in these works might be seen to *exceed* what was offered by their ethnographic predecessors.

The meaning of scale in these works has attracted a range of interpretations. For example, Alison Dean counters Stallabrass's reading by proposing that because these large prints cannot be held in the hand, but must be encountered on the wall, they 'have the effect of resisting the viewer's possession',[5] while Norman Bryson argues that scale operates *both* honorifically and repressively in such works: 'Scale gives the subjects and the artworks themselves the power to allure; but it also makes them vulnerable and ready specimens for inspection. … The sitter has the privilege of being in the picture, enlarged to a towering status, and we have the power of looking back, getting intrusively close, cataloguing how and why we are different.'[6]

Our encounter with these works is disturbed not just by their use of scale but by the way in which they borrow codes from other photographic genres, in particular fashion and documentary. This blending of photographic genres further thwarts our ability to assign definitive meaning to the subjects we are presented with. In the absence of sufficient cues, the viewer oscillates between reading the photographs as a record of a type of person and a portrait of an individual. As Stallabrass expresses it, 'There is an interplay of stereotype and the palpable presence of an individual, so that the viewer is encouraged to place the individual within the stereotype but also to perturb the stereotype with the individual.'[7]

The complexity of our encounter with this style of photographic portraiture is furthered by the fact that, although we are given a large amount of visual detail, the textual information given does not indicate a discourse – such a physiognomy – that would allow us to make sense of this detail. Instead of a scientific study of the subject, this disjuncture between information and knowledge is a critical strategy that asks us to reflect upon the 'instability of identity'.[8] What is sought in these images is not knowledge of particular type of subject but an interrogation of subjectivity through the photographic recording of a particular act that contemporary neoliberal subjects must engage in: that of self-presentation.

The large format cameras favoured by photographers working in this genre acquire a further significance here. While contemporary subjects are accustomed to being photographed for a range of reasons, the plate camera and its theatrical paraphernalia of large tripod, camera release and focusing cloth coupled with long set-up and exposure times produce a novel kind of photographic encounter characterized by an extended and ambiguous space in which the subject must compose themselves. Confronted with an unfamiliar technology and often given only sparse or anomalous directions from the photographer,[9] the subjects of these images are forced to organize their bodies and expression in service of an unknown purpose. What is remarkable is that, while there are variations in pose, the expression of the subjects is remarkably consistent. The expression seen in these images is 'the face required by a job application form, a reception desk, a library card, a driver's license'[10] and the passport photograph.

The passport photograph

With the passing of the British Nationality and Status of Aliens Act in 1914, the British passport required a photograph of the bearer. This might be seen as an extension of the system of criminal identification developed by Alphonse Bertillon during the 1880s[11] with the passport allowing for the monitoring of individuals to be extended beyond those who had committed crimes to all citizens. As such, the passport portrait marks the emergence of a new visual discourse of the individual as a subject of the state.

The passport photograph does not simply serve to identify the holder – indeed, everyone always remarks on how little they look like their passport photograph, but asks us to present ourselves as a citizen. As Lily Cho's has noted of the expression required for the passport photograph, 'The "acceptable" facial expressions reveal no emotion. They are natural only insofar as they are completely emotionally neutral. That is, they are not natural at all. They expose a citizen-subject caught and composed for identification purposes.'[12] Cho's argument proposes that we should read the demand for emotional neutrality in passport photographs not in relation to its purported function – ease of identification – but in relation to discourses about citizenship. Here, 'The injunction against emotion in the passport photograph telegraphs the way in which the ideal citizen, in the eyes of the state, is an emotionally neutral one.'[13] As anyone who has sat for a passport photograph knows, it is difficult to form a 'neutral' face. The requirements of the passport photograph are not that we look 'like ourselves', but that we surrender our uniqueness and present ourselves as a particular type of person – a citizen. We can now see how the blankness of the passport photograph relates to a particular type of affective engagement; however, what is its purpose in the work of von Zwhel?

Exacting photography

In 'Exacting Photography: Self-Imaging and Its Frustration in Contemporary Art Photography'[14] Ben Burbridge documents the way in which a number of contemporary artists use exacting physical or psychological conditions – from ambiguous directions to extreme physical circumstances – to bring forth fleeting emotional states and capture them. Burbridge notes that this represents a distinct change in the role of the portrait: 'Where the value of the portrait was once defined by the artist's ability to visually consolidate the self of the portrayed, such projects propose an alternative criteria – their interest or "authenticity" founded on an ability to disrupt and undermine such performances, to seek out aspects of behaviour which fall outside the subject's conscious control.'[15]

Von Zwehl's practice is a notable example of a body of work that takes the capture of interior states as its theme. Von Zwehl's mock-scientific approach and detached style produce a space in which ambiguous and ephemeral emotions are made visible. In the series from which our example is taken, von Zwehl woke her subjects in the middle of the night to photograph them as they were still emerging from sleep. The harsh burst of light produced by her use of flash serves to both surprise her subjects and capture their response in detail. Despite her severe methods, there is something intimate captured in these photographs. As Joanna Lowry has observed, von Zwehl's photographs 'suggest a hard-won and elusive zone in which the subject might become visible';[16] but who is the subject here? What kind of subject becomes visible when the individual is photographed under exacting conditions? Once more we need to turn to the early history of photography to better understand the ways in which photography and subjectivity are intertwined.

Photography, hysteria and the unconscious

The Salpêtrière hospital was a vast establishment that housed some 5,000 female patients. In 1870, the restructuring of the Salpêtrière's wards led to women who had been diagnosed as epileptic being placed in the same ward as those who had been diagnosed as hysteric. The neurologist Jean-Martin Charcot took charge of the ward and became interested in distinguishing between these two diseases by conclusively defining hysteria.

The variability of hysteria's symptoms had led Charcot's contemporary Charles Lasègue to declare hysteria to be 'the wastebasket of medicine';[17] however, Charcot sought to lift the diagnosis and treatment of hysteria out of superstition and speculation and into the scientific realm. What is significant to us is the way in which he used photography to do this.

Under Charcot, the Salpêtrière became the first hospital in Europe to establish an in-house department of photography. Charcot used photography not only to record the hysterical attack but also as a means of countering the suspicion with which the symptoms of hysteria were met: the photograph serving to 'exteriorize, make visible, and arrest the hysterical symptom in a way that would allow for a clean separation between this symptom and the patient's alleged intention'.[18]

In Chapter 1 we examined the ways in which the camera was used to record physical features, the meaning of which was 'read' through sciences such as physiognomy, to reveal traits such as character, aptitude and degeneracy. Here we again see an understanding of 'the human body in its entirety and in its parts as a source of data that could be extracted through measurement, comparison, and analysis'.[19] However, in the work of Charcot, and later Sigmund Freud, there is a significant difference in the understanding of the relationship between the subject and the body. Freud's psychoanalytic practice of free association and Charcot's visual discourse of hysteria both sought to make present that which 'escapes' the subject, that which is beyond conscious control. Here we arrive at an understanding of the body not as a register of character but as an 'archive of unconscious meanings'.[20]

We are now in a better position to understand von Zwehl's practice. In our example, we see a similar concern with producing those conditions under which the camera can capture something elusive about the subject. However, rather than seeking the essence of hysteria, von Zwehl seeks out those fleeting moments between subjective states. What does the desire to capture these moments tell us about contemporary subjectivity?

The rewriting of relation between the social and the economic that takes place under neoliberalism has precipitated significant shifts not only in culture but also in subjectivity. As Jeremy Gilbert has observed, 'What defines the regularity of neoliberalism as a discursive formation is precisely the persistence of an individualistic conception of human selfhood and of the idea of the individual both as the ideal locus of sovereignty and the site of governmental intervention.'[21] Or, as Wendy Brown expresses it, 'All conduct is economic conduct; all spheres of existence are framed and measured by economic terms and metrics, even when those spheres are not directly monetized. In neoliberal reason and in domains governed by it, we are only and everywhere *homo oeconomicus,* which itself has a historically specific form.'[22] How does von Zwhel's work relate to this complex, emergent form of subjectivity? A clue might be found in Jonathan Crary's book *24/7: Late Capitalism and the Ends of Sleep.* As Crary writes,

> Most of the seemingly irreducible necessities of human life – hunger, thirst, sexual desires, and recently the need for friendship – have been remade into commodified or financialized forms. Sleep poses the idea of a human need and interval of time that cannot be colonized and harnessed to a massive engine of profitability, and thus remains an incongruous anomaly. ... The stunning, inconceivable reality is that nothing of value can be extracted from it.[23]

Thus, we might see that what is significant about these moments captured by von Zwehl as subjects wake from sleep, rest after exercise or simply hold their breath is that these 'pauses' are states that cannot be put to use by capitalism. In seeking to document those 'aspects of behaviour and appearance which appear to resist commodification',[24] von Zwehl asks us to critically reflect not only on the history of photograph but also upon contemporary subjectivity.

Zoe Strauss: *10 Years*

Zoe Strauss is best known for her work collected under the title *10 Years*.[25] Starting in 2001, every year on the first Sunday in May, Strauss would display a selection of her photos on the pillars underneath a bridge on the I-95 highway in Philadelphia. The exhibition lasted just three hours. Inkjets of photos were available for $5 during the show, and at the end of the afternoon the prints on the columns could be taken for free.

In contrast to the approach taken by von Zwehl, Strauss's work is associated with a group of photographers including Nan Goldin, Larry Clark and Mark Morrisroe who privilege an 'intimate' approach to their subjects. Alison Dean has proposed that the term 'intimacy' 'is in many ways constitutive of photographic history'.[26] Dean gives the photographer Nadar (Gaspard-Félix Tournachon) who famously championed what he called the 'instant understanding'[27] that allows the good portrait photographer to produce a convincing and sympathetic likeness as an example of the long-standing association between intimacy and the photographic encounter. Dean argues that photography's relation to indexicality makes it particularly suited to discourses of intimacy and proposes that the 'language of intimate portraiture' can still be found in the work of contemporary photographers.

While an intimate approach has been praised for its sympathetic engagement with its subjects – characteristics that are seen to be lacking from the 'blank' style of portraiture – it has also attracted charges of voyeurism. For example, writing on Goldin's work, Liz Kotz has drawn attention to the way in which an aesthetic of intimacy is used to 'naturalize' the photographic encounter between Goldin and her subjects. Kotz is critical of the way in which this aesthetic of intimacy is taken at face value by some critics and used to produce a reading of Goldin's work that 'allows us to ignore everything we know about the history of photography',[28] in particular, its 'problematic enmeshment with histories of social surveillance and coercion'.[29] Kotz cautions that such a reading 'ignores the extraordinary power of the photographic language employed: a language with a history and an inscribed structure of power relations that cannot be easily evaded by the spontaneous performance before the lens'.[30]

The unflinching and intimate approach taken by Strauss to her, often vulnerable, subjects has divided critics and revived long-standing debates about the photographic portrait and power relations. Although Strauss has been praised for her 'clear-sighted empathy, which allows the viewer to feel like part of the exchange between photographer and subject',[31] others have seen in her work 'a relentless reification of her subjects, a tireless exploitation that turns them into objects of our spectatorship'.[32] Central to these discussions is the position of the photographer. As Orvell succinctly states, 'Where the photographer is standing makes all the difference.'[33]

A useful essay to consider here is 'Inside/Out' by Abigail Solomon-Godeau. In this essay Solomon-Godeau takes up the inside/out binary that is frequently invoked when discussing the position of the photographer in relation to their subject. In these debates, the insider position is usually considered to be the 'good' position. While the outsider position is seen to be characterised by an alienated voyeurism, the insider position is 'understood to imply a position of engagement, participation, and privileged knowledge'.[34]

Although Strauss is a part of the neighbourhood she photographs and her status as an 'insider' has been invoked by some in defence of her work, for others, this does not serve to mitigate the subjugating effects of the work. For these critics, Strauss's work is naïve and uniformed by critiques of representation and thus serves as an example of what Solomon-Godeau has described elsewhere as 'victim photography' in which there is a 'double act of subjugation': 'First, in the social world that has produced its victims; and second, in the regime of the image produced within and for the same system that engenders the conditions it then represents.'[35]

The concern that dominant social relations are reproduced and reinforced by the act of photographic representation is foremost in Miles Orvell's review. Although Orvell acknowledges that Strauss comes from inside the working-class culture that she photographs, and concedes that this 'gives her work a seeming authenticity, as if there is little distance between the photographer and her subject',[36] he argues that Strauss's treatment 'leaves them marginalized, exploiting them as spectacles, transforming them into objects for middle-class visual delectation, caricatures of their visible markings and surfaces'.[37] Of particular concern to Orvell is Strauss's focus on markers of bodily difference. For Orvell, Strauss's depiction of tattoos, piercings, scars, obesity and amputations is such that 'the human presence in each image becomes erased under the more powerful impact of the scar, the tattoo, the red hair, the stump arm, showing us a world seen through the narrow channel of social class and body image'.[38] As such, for Orvell, Strauss's work only reinforces the marginalization of her subjects.

While also observing the 'feverish intensity' with which Strauss's work shows a multitude of scars and wounds, Sally Stein offers a different reading. Noting that Strauss does not give an account of these injuries that seem to be attributable to a range of causes (freak accidents, good or bad medical care, wartime service, domestic violence and self-inflicted), Stein argues that this is a strategy which asks viewers to 'decide whether [Strauss's] omission of information about the sources of such scars attests to her lack of interest in systematic diagnosis or to her belief that the sources are too complex to be oversimplified by the naming of a single agent or event'.[39]

Beth Uzwiak's reading of Strauss's work draws attention to the way in which the inclusion of images of architecture alongside store signs and graffiti serves to locate Strauss's subjects in both a geographical context of urban deprivation and a historical context that includes two wars, environmental disasters and the largest economic crisis since the Great Depression.[40] Uzwiak proposes that the scarred and wounded bodies that appear in Strauss's work should be read not individually, but in relation to a social context. For Uzwiak, it is not individual pathology but economically predicated, systemic violence that is written on the bodies of Strauss's subjects. Thus, Uzwiak argues that Strauss's photographs not only 'raise long-standing questions about the *intimacies* of photographic encounters: what do we take away from photographs – especially images of presumed suffering or violence'[41] but also ask us to engage with 'the intimacies of uncertainty and contingency that characterize contemporary life in the U.S.'[42]

Intimacy

Intimacy is often presented as an 'antidote' to voyeurism; however, a number of writings on intimacy have drawn attention to the way in which categories such as the 'intimate' and the 'private' are striated with power relations. As Nikolas Rose states in the opening pages of his book *Governing the Soul: The Shaping of the Private Self*,

> Our mental states, subjective experiences and intimate relationships offer themselves as perhaps the only place where we can locate our real private selves. There is, no doubt, much comfort to be afforded by such a belief. But it is profoundly misleading. … Our personalities, subjectivities, and 'relationships' are not private matters, if this implies that they are not the objects of power. … Thoughts, feelings and actions may appear as the very fabric and constitution of the intimate self, but they are socially organised and managed in minute particulars.[43]

Lauren Berlant has similarly argued that 'the inwardness of the intimate is met by a corresponding publicness'.[44] Like Rose, Berlant is interested in the way in which disciplinary power is mobilized by affects such as intimacy. Berlant argues that intimacy has a normalizing force: it makes some relationships and feelings towards people seem personal and natural rather than socially produced. Berlant thus asks us to recognize the way in which discourses of intimacy reverberate with the violence of social exclusion.[45]

r, Berlant argues that in addition to 'personalizing' the hegemonic ideals lic sphere, intimacy can repel these ideals and create new forms of . As such, intimacy offers a way of exploring affective ties that exist beyond those of the heterosexual nuclear family and traditional political affiliations. In describing those attachments that have 'no designated place ... the glances, gestures, encounters, collaborations, or fantasies that have no canon'[46] Berlant proposes an aesthetics of 'minor intimacies'.[47] This is where we might usefully situate Strauss's work. As Uzwiak argues, 'Against the silence that normalizes social suffering for some and not for others, Strauss presents everyday living in its own terms. With suffering and pain live beauty, survival, and intimacies that defy normative codes.'[48]

One of the most famous images from Struass' series is 'Monique Showing Black Eye'. In this photograph a young woman looks at the camera with a gaze that is both confrontational and apprehensive as she holds back her hair to show the extent of the bruising that covers the left-hand side of her face. As Clare Raymond has written, 'the phrase "black eye" does not begin to describe what has been done to her face, the very structure of which has been taken apart by violence'.[49] With its close crop and flat lighting the photograph resembles a mugshot, yet it is of the victim of violence, not its perpetrator. As Uzwick notes, such images are usually part of a juridical apparatus that requires visual proof. However, in the documents of violence collected by the police or medical experts, 'we see the wounds but not what makes them possible'.[50] One of the effects of Strauss's image is to make visible a private act of violence. However, it goes beyond an individual act of testimony; by presenting it within a body of work Strauss locates this image in a larger narrative that includes not only other violences but also 'moments of survival, love, and resilience'.[51] Such an approach allows us to read the violence depicted in Monique's black eye as both individual and social.

Dean has argued that we should not limit our use of intimacy to that which 'takes place (or fails to occur) between the photographer and her or his subject' and argues that 'some of the most interesting and politically effective modes of photographic intimacy take place between viewers, or subjects, and photographs'.[52] The challenge of Strauss's work is that the viewers are asked to engage with uncomfortable proximity of the intimate to the public. We are asked to reflect upon the ever-widening social disparities of neoliberalism in everyday life – how it impacts on individual lives in a multitude of acts and moments. In this way, Strauss's work asks us to recognize the political potential of the intimate address of the photographic portrait.

3

The portrait and the contemporary self

The contemporary self is characterized by its visibility. *Facebook, tumblr, Instagram,* blogs, vlogs, product reviews and citizen journalism are just some of the new platforms through which we are made present and visible to others. We opt into these platforms for the social visibility they afford us, or the fear of the social invisibility if we do not. The ideal self is 'linked-in': checking in is demanded of us not just as a social being but as a consumer, an employee and a subject of the state. As such, the visibility that characterizes the contemporary self must be considered in relation to not only technology but also neoliberalism and increased state surveillance. As Catherine Zimmer notes, 'The production of the body as visible, measurable, and categorizable is without question one of the defining facets of both surveillance practice and modern subjectification.'[1] That visibility is now a demand rather than a privilege requires that we reconsider the meaning and function of the portrait. The subject who is visible to facial recognition technology, social media and the database demands a different understanding of identity than that explored in earlier chapters. Indeed, contemporary identity is not always located on the body; it is also produced through data and algorithms. The artists considered in this chapter use the portrait as a space for contesting these new demands for the self to be visible, transparent and legible.

Sophie Calle: *Cash Machine*

What is perhaps often overlooked in popular accounts of surveillance is the way in which its inclusion in our everyday lives is naturalized. Indeed, demands for visibility are often produced by rather mundane instruments. As David Lyon reminds us, 'It is in the mundane routines of everyday life that the effects, the dangers, of surveillance appear.'[2]

The portraits that make up Sophie Calle's project *Cash Machine* (1991–2003) draw on the everyday form of surveillance that occurs through the corporate security camera. While using an ATM might seem to be a matter of individual convenience, this simple, everyday interface is emblematic of a transformed relationship between individual subjects, a company and the technologies that mediate between them. It is an example of what David Lyon calls the 'technosocial'[3] relationship, the term he uses to describe the way in which social relations and personal identity are increasingly permeated by technology.

ATMs were introduced to the public in the late 1960s and replaced the face-to-face encounter for a number of routine banking transactions such as checking your account balance and withdrawing cash. While many of us would think of our use of the ATM only in terms of our interaction with a screen, there are also two cameras involved in the architecture of the ATM: the first is located in the interface to observe who is using the machine and the second is positioned behind the user to observe the machine. As Mark Hayward's study of neoliberal optics has shown, the ATM is a very particular kind of space: a public setting in which we deluge private information under conditions of surveillance.[4]

It is significant that the private information we give is not to a person, but to a machine. Removing people – in this case the bank teller – promises greater security by removing human error; however, it also reduces the encounter to a predetermined set of outcomes, including how the subject's identity is established. The introduction of PIN numbers might seem of little consequence. However, the understanding of identity that underpins technologies of identification such as PIN numbers that distinguish it from the examples we discussed in Chapter 1, such as rogue's gallery or *carte de visite*, is that they 'introduce a new language – a binary language of ones and zeroes'.[5] The ATM wants to know your code, not see your face. As such, and despite the rhetoric of increased security that surrounds them, contemporary methods of securing identity are only able to assess if you are 'an efficient user of the system'.[6] Indeed, it could be argued that in digital identification systems, identity is established through disembodied codes that *supplant* the user. As Edward Welch has observed, 'Our identity is mediated by codes, passwords and other traces to such a degree that our physical presence or embodiment in the world is no longer a sufficient guarantee of our identity or existence. Without the correct code or password, we cease to exist: we become invisible or, in the strictest sense, invalid.'[7] Thus, in contemporary forms of security, identity reveals itself to be highly contingent.

The ATM is one of an increasing number of sites at which the body is no longer the site of personhood, and the anxiety that attends such encounters is what is captured in Calle's images. What is remarkable about the portraits in *Cash Machine* is that while the transaction in which the subjects are engaged asks only for a disembodied code, it is nonetheless shown to be a very embodied act. In this mundane transaction we are surprised to see people experiencing a range of emotions including joy, confusion and anger.[8] In this way Calle asks us to consider both the subjugating and subjectifying effects of surveillance. As Sarah Hollenberg has summarized, 'In Calle's world, paying attention to the drama of an individual life is not only an invasion of privacy; such attention has the potential to redeem that life, to rescue it from the abstractions that transform people into statistical or financial data.'[9] In these small, personal moments Calle shows those aspects of identity that cannot be assimilated into code.

Zach Blas: *Facial Weaponization Suite*

In contemporary forms of surveillance such as facial recognition technology there is an expectation that one's identity is available and easily readable from the body. As the writings of Rachel Hall have shown, this demand for transparency has transformed the body into something that is both seen and *processed*. The body is both spectacle and data.[10] Despite repeated claims of technology's neutrality, technological developments are inextricable from cultural politics. The processes of sorting and categorizing that underpin facial recognition technology are descended from the assumptions that informed nineteenth-century practices and modes of identification. In short, 'contemporary facial recognition programmes inherit the ideology of earlier modes of surveillance.'[11]

As we discussed in Chapter 1, in the nineteenth century bodily markers were used to classify different types of human beings. For example, the work of Francis Galton used composite photography in order to position 'deviant' bodies, such as the criminal, as physiognomically distinct from 'normal' bodies. What informed Galton's work was the understanding that core truths about the subject could be extracted from calculations derived from the surface of the body. This understanding persists in the very modern techniques used in contemporary surveillance practices.

As Lisa Nakamura has noted, it is important to recognize that 'surveillance is a signifying system that *produces* a social body, rather than straightforwardly reflects it'.[12] Surveillance technologies create new subjects and subject categories. In addition to the categories we have already explored, there is an emergent category created by those bodies that are not readable by contemporary technologies of identification. Biometric technology often fails to process bodies that do not conform to 'appropriate' visual formations of age, gender and race. For example, because reflections in darker corneas can interfere with the observation of the veins in the retina, the efficacy of retinal scanning is limited to light-coloured eyes. Thus, we might see that although biometrics is premised upon a stable, legible body, its use 'more often reveals the impossibility of such a subject, and the discriminatory ideologies encoded in acts of recognition'.[13]

The contemporary demand for legibility means that the understanding, central to many campaigns by feminist, civil rights and gay activists, that visibility brings social acceptance to marginalized bodies and experiences is challenged. Gaining visibility might offer a route to recognition; however, it can also mean being subject to surveillance. These issues are central to Zach Blas's work *Facial Weaponization Suite* (2011–14).[14] Concerned with the way in which 'invisibility is often an unequally distributed privilege',[15] Blas's work is a series of 'collective masks' produced in community-based workshops. Each mask is made by aggregating the biometric facial data of all of the workshop participants to produce a collective mask that allows each to 'simultaneously wear the faces of many'.[16] The masks, which reference the use of masks in protest and social movements, are intended for public interventions and performances.

Our example, 'Fag Face Mask' (Figure 3.1) is a response to scientific studies that propose that sexual orientation can be determined through facial features.[17] As Blas has stated, 'I wanted to develop an artwork that articulated what a queer politics might look like within newly emerging digital identification technologies, like biometrics, which not only employ reductive global standards to identify people but are also used by various governing bodies to police and criminalize minority groups.'[18] Blas adopts a strategy that is repeated across the artists we will consider in this

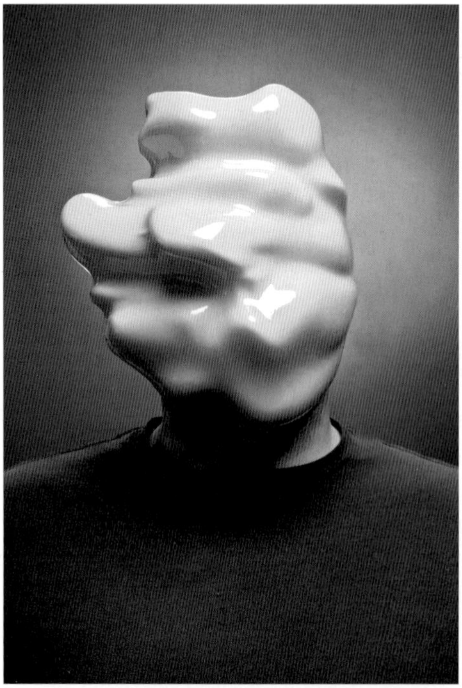

Figure 3.1 Zach Blas, *Facial Weaponization Suite*: Fag Face Mask – 20 October 2012, Los Angeles, CA. Photo by Christopher O'Leary. Courtesy of the artist.

chapter: he over-engages with technology, pushing it to the point where its functioning becomes visible. Because the information Blas collects is not averaged, the result is unreadable; instead of a composite that produces an – assumed – archetypal physiognomy, Blas's masks produce an 'uncategorizable alterity that no biometric can parse'.[19] As such, Blas's works challenge the notion that identity can be read from the body by humans *or* technology.[20]

Dataveillance and algorithmic identity

Despite the centrality of looking to many artistic responses to surveillance, the majority of contemporary surveillance does not take place through visual observation, but through dataveillance. Dataveillance is the collection of data about our online activities such as emails, purchasing history and browsing habits as well as those actions that we might not consider to offer any significant information such as login times, duration and location. Unlike traditional forms of surveillance, this data is collected and used with no interest in particular subjects. Once collected it can be acted on and organized in a number of ways.

John Cheney-Lippold's writings on 'algorithmic identity' are useful in understanding the connections between dataveillance and subjectivity. Cheney-Lippold uses the term 'algorithmic identity' to describe this new type of 'identity formation that works through mathematical algorithms to infer categories of identity on otherwise anonymous beings'.[21] This emergent form of identity is not something that individuals can declare or even know about themselves; it is a particular configuration of subjectivity produced by the use of algorithms to organize data sourced from the internet.

Data, like the camera, is frequently credited with inherently 'objective' qualities, and the promise that underlies the collection of 'Big Data'[22] that drives dataveillance is that the mass aggregation of data will produce more accurate, more objective knowledge. However, this ignores the way in which data must be 'cleaned' and ranked, and that the same data can be modelled, visualized and interpreted differently depending on its intended purpose. In short, 'Data are what they are only in practices of data creation and use.'[23]

Tyler Reigeluth has suggested that it is useful to understand the algorithms that make data meaningful as 'a cooking recipe or an itinerary involving a series of steps and directions which must be taken in order to achieve a certain output'.[24] Social biases persist in the directions given for how data is to be collected, modelled and put to use.[25] In short, code is cultural, and practices of surveillance remain disproportionately directed at disenfranchised groups. It is therefore important to move away from the popular understanding of data as objective.

While recognizing that the contemporary use of algorithms to determine categories of identity remains underpinned by a drive to organize individuals in line with a set of social objectives, there are also significant differences from the social stereotyping we discussed in Chapter 1. In contemporary practices, categories of identity continually shift. Cheney-Lippold proposes the terms 'statistical stereotyping' and 'cybernetic categorization'[26] to describe these new practices.

If we take gender as an example; the use of algorithms to define gender in terms of a variable might appear to be progressive in that it 'de-essentializes gender from its corporeal and societal forms and determinations'.[27] However, the statistical coordinates of gender are nonetheless still subject to regulation. As Cheney-Lippold explains, instead of 'masculinity' being determined through recourse to social codes that steer an individual's behaviour in particular ways, one's assumed digital gender is determined through the uptake of ad click-through rates, purchases and page views. As such, gender as a category 'becomes wholly embedded within the logic of consumption'.[28] Gender here becomes a category that is meaningful as a means of organizing predictable consumer behaviour. Through cybernetic categorization, users are persuaded to adopt particular choices: 'If a certain set of categories ceases to effectively regulate, another set can quickly be reassigned to a user, providing a seemingly seamless experience online that still exerts a force over who that user is. This force is not entirely benign but is instead something that tells us who we are, what we want, and who we should be'.[29] As such, it is important to be attentive to the new ways in which contemporary identity is defined, shaped and monitored.

Erica Scourti: *Life in AdWords*

Erica Scourti works across performance, film, photography and writing as a way of locating and commenting upon the infrastructure of the internet and its subject-effects. As George Vasey has summarized, 'Ultimately, all of Scourti's work asks a series of fundamental questions. How do institutions seek to define forms of representation? How has technology, and specifically social media, affected our understanding of identity and subjectivity? Where does our agency reside in an online environment where our data is tracked and our behaviour is persistently manipulated?'[30]

Life in AdWords (2012–13) was a project lasting nearly a year during which Scourti would write a daily diary and email it to her Gmail account. Scourti would then use her webcam to record herself reading the list of suggested keywords generated by Google-patented algorithms that had selected words and phrases from her diary entries. Scourti's deadpan delivery can be seen as a comedic response to Google's oft-repeated response to concerns about its data-mining practices that 'no humans read your email'. More complexly, we might see Scourti as trying to articulate the

with photography, and to develop different photographic forms and devices suitable to the varied contexts in which the photograph is placed and used'.[52] Photography can be used in ways that sustain hierarchies but also to create new understandings of ourselves. All of the photographers considered in this first section have engaged with the photograph as a site of challenge and resistance and sought to forge new meanings for the photographic portrait.

Part Two

Photography, landscape and place

The 'naturalness' of landscape 'would seem to preclude any meanings other than nature's own leafy-green facts',[1] but as William Marshall noted in 1785, 'nature scarcely knows the thing mankind call a *landscape*'.[2] Landscape might be best understood as a discourse that includes literature, painting, photography and economics through which we assign meaning and significance to land. The following anecdote by the art historian Joseph L Koerner is useful here:

> My father was a painter and he used to drag us around to views he wanted to paint. … I would always try to find a spot in whatever he was painting so that I could paint it myself. But one time I rebelled and decided to turn away from his view and look some place else. All of a sudden, the world looked completely without organization and interest.[3]

Koerner's description shows us that – although the elements that are privileged may change over time – what is common to aesthetic, philosophical and historical interpretations of landscape is that they offer a way of organizing the world around us in a meaningful way. In the landscape photograph it is 'the point of view of the camera … [that] organizes what is there into a cultural artefact: a landscape view'.[4] In this section we will be following W. J. T. Mitchell and asking 'not just what landscape "is" or "means" but what it *does,* how it works as a cultural practice'.[5] How artists have chosen to photograph land reflects different historical, cultural and social values, hopes and fears. What links all of the examples we will be considering in this section is the understanding that 'landscape is already artifice in the moment of its beholding, long before it becomes the subject of pictorial representation'.[6] In short, landscape is a way of seeing that 'naturalizes a cultural and social construction, representing an artificial world as if it were simply given and inevitable'.[7]

In Chapter 4 we will consider two approaches to photographing the landscape: the picturesque and the sublime. Although they have their roots in historical genres of painting, the picturesque and the sublime continue to be important terms of reference as they are 'latent categories'[8] in contemporary fine art practice. Chapter 5 will look at how photographers have developed new approaches to document emerging categories of place brought about by neoliberalism. To conclude, Chapter 6 will look at the ruin and address how the idea of the Anthropocene is being mobilized by a number of artists in order to ask questions about our current understandings of land and place.

4

The politics of place

In this chapter we will be addressing the 'picturesque' and the 'sublime'. These terms do not relate to different kinds of spaces or objects – the same elements can be used to signify *either* picturesque or sublime, but to their organization. As David Bate has summarized, 'The picturesque and the sublime scenes offer a space for the identification of two different types of feeling and emotion in the viewer located in a pictorial space.'[1]

The picturesque

The picturesque first emerged as a literary and artistic aesthetic during the second half of the eighteenth century. The paintings of Claude Lorrain and Nicholas Poussin and the Reverend William Gilpin's writings and drawings all played an influential part in defining the movement. In his early writings on the subject, Gilpin described the picturesque as 'expressive of that peculiar kind of beauty which *is agreeable in a picture*'.[2] This understanding of the picturesque as that which is suitable for painting continues to inform the popular understanding of the term. However, to understand the picturesque only as a style of painting does not encompass the complexity of this once much debated term.[3] Indeed, even Gilpin modified his early description of the picturesque to argue that it was 'an effect on the mind'.[4]

In *An Analytical Inquiry into the Principles of Taste* (1805), Richard Payne Knight also defines the picturesque as a mode of viewing and criticizes those theorists of the picturesque who seek 'distinctions in external objects, which only exist in the modes and habits of viewing and considering them'.[5] It is notable that in Knight's account the picturesque is a mode of viewing that is not available to all: only 'a mind richly stored'[6] will be able to discern the picturesque. To the beholder of a scene who is not equipped with the necessary associations, the picturesque will be virtually invisible.[7]

As John Tagg reminds us, seeing is 'a site of work, an active process of making sense, dependent on social practice and codes of recognition, and imbricated in structures of address through which viewers, or readers, are invested or denied as subjects.'[8] In both Payne and Knight's accounts we might find an exposition on the merits of a particular kind of subject who was seen to possess a rarefied relationship to land. Through the picturesque, those who understood the land in aesthetic and philosophical terms asserted their superiority over those who worked on it. Here 'the rhetorical freedoms of the liberal bourgeois subject are advanced through images consistently downplaying figuration and labor'.[9] Thus, we can see that the picturesque, far from an intuitive appreciation of the beauty of the natural world, was a site for the production of social and cultural divisions.

The writings, drawings and paintings that provided detailed descriptions of how to appreciate particular sites do, however, evidence that seeing with a picturesque eye often required assistance. In addition to these texts, those privileged subjects who still struggled to see the picturesque were able to use a Claude glass. The Claude glass was a small convex mirror, about 4 inches in diameter, that could be obtained in various tints that would impart different tones to the view in a way that increased its resemblance to a painting, in particular, those of Claude Lorrain. It is notable that using the glass actually required the user to turn their back to the view. As Samuel Monk wryly observed of the time,

> Throughout the picturesque phase nature was frequently scarcely seen at all, for the lover of the picturesque was bent upon discovering not the world as it is, but the world as it might have been had the Creator been an Italian artist of the seventeenth century. Shut up in the Palace of Art, he could look out only through stained-glass windows which falsely colored the natural world.[10]

In relation to contemporary photographic practice, the picturesque is often quoted in order to subvert its unifying function and thus to articulate a tension between landscape as a view and land as socially, politically and historically contested.

Mohini Chandra and Christopher Stewart: *Dark Pacific Sun*

Mohini Chandra and Christopher Stewart's multimedia project *Dark Pacific Sun* (2014) is made up of landscapes, seascapes and still lives of the Asia-Pacific region (Figure 4.1a,b). The work draws on a range of forms including wildlife photography, anthropological study and the tourist image in order to critically engage with photography's ongoing role in construction of the Pacific as an Edenic paradise.

As Mitchell reminds us, 'The representation of landscape is not only a matter of internal politics and national or class ideology but also an international, global phenomenon, intimately bound up with the discourses of imperialism.'[11] Photography

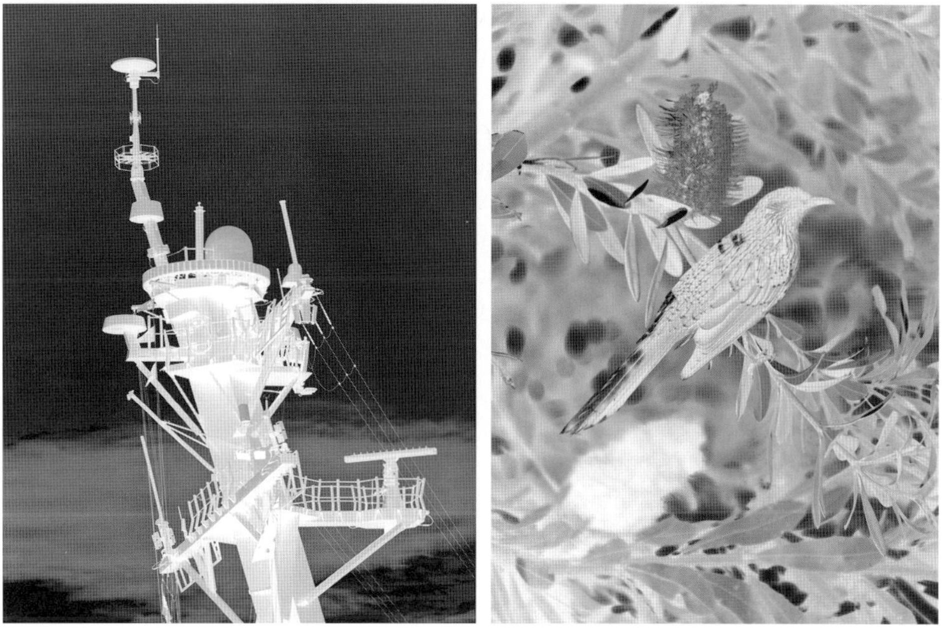

Figure 4.1a,b Mohini Chandra and Christopher Stewart, Untitled from the series *Dark Pacific Sun*, 2014. © Mohini Chandra and Christopher Stewart. Courtesy of the artists.

functioned as a cultural and political medium intricately tied to the establishment and support of colonial power. Through photography and the aesthetic of the picturesque, the appropriation of land for a range of purposes including military testing, resources, labour and culture was transformed into something visually pleasing. As Clarke notes, 'The photograph allowed the land to be controlled, visually at least to be scaled and ordered, in the way that white colonial settlement attempted politically.'[12]

Jeffrey Auerbach's writings on the 'colonial picturesque'[13] are useful here. Auerbach has traced how the use of the picturesque to record the British empire evolved. In the late eighteenth century the picturesque was used in its Edenic aspect to stimulate overseas exploration. However, by the mid-nineteenth century, as settlement became paramount, the picturesque encouraged emigration by presenting these regions as domesticated and cultured, a 'home away from home'. Not only were colonial lands named after important figures, events and sites in Britain, but the representation of these lands – in spite of their vast geographic and cultural differences – followed the aesthetic dictates of the picturesque. Here the picturesque played a role in enabling Britons to conceive of and represent their empire. Through the picturesque, regions as diverse as South Africa, India, Australia and the Pacific Islands were unified and made familiar. As Simon Pugh has famously expressed it, 'Empire was the countryside writ large.'[14] Although the picturesque is popularly conceived as an aesthetic belonging to the late eighteenth and mid-nineteenth centuries, it has a continued presence and can readily be seen in contemporary travel photography and advertisements.[15] It is the history and legacy of the colonial picturesque that is the subject of *Dark Pacific Sun*.

As Mitchell has observed, historically, the South Pacific provided 'a kind of tabula rasa for the fantasies of European imperialism, a place where European landscape conventions could work themselves out virtually unimpeded by "native" resistance, where the "naturalness" of those conventions could find itself confirmed by a real place understood to be in a state of nature'.[16] For the multiple colonial powers that have sought jurisdiction over the islands, the picturesque was a flexible mode of representation that served a range of strategic purposes including naturalizing the position of the colonial settler and managing 'the experiential contradictions of exile and domestication, exoticism and familiarity.'[17]

In *Dark Pacific Sun*, Chandra and Stewart use a range of mediums: black-and-white and colour photography and video, all of which have been inverted into negative form. Film and photography are used side-by-side to produce an extended range of images including wildlife, seascapes, flora and fauna, demonstrating the way in which the visual discourse of the Pacific has been shaped not only by colonial vision but by anthropological, tourist and military gazes. As such, this work asks us to recognize imperialism as 'a complicated process of exchange, mutual transformation, and ambivalence'.[18]

The reversal of the images does metaphorical and ideological work. In particular, it makes us aware that we are looking at a construction. By employing a different optic, the work of Chandra and Stewart destabilizes our viewing practices. We could say that it 'undoes' the effect of the Claude glass. In our examples, the narrative of the islands as tourist paradise is juxtaposed with the dormant knowledge of their use as an atomic testing ground and site of ongoing military activity. The reversed image presents the military vessel as both a stark interruption and a spectral manifestation, while, rather than offering a vibrant spectacle, the native plants and wildlife become abstractions. Here the Pacific appears not as a tourist idyll but as an uncertain space that resists our visual mastery. There is a deliberate tension in the work; while its subject might be colonial vision, it does not seek to replace this with a 'correct' view. It creates a visual disturbance which, rather than naturalizing the landscape, defamiliarizes it: the inversion produces strange and fascinating images that ask us to reflect upon the Pacific as a site of 'ominous contradictions'.[19]

Sally Mann: *Deep South*

Deep South[20] is an exploration of the American South through the genre of landscape photography. Many of the photographs in this work were made using the wet collodion process. This early photographic process requires the use of a portable darkroom as the entire process, coating, exposing and developing the glass plates, must be completed in approximately fifteen minutes. When it was first invented in 1851, the collodion process was prized for the finely detailed negatives it can produce. However, the skill required in coating the glass plates means it can equally produce blurred negatives with uneven areas of chemical development. Mann fully embraces the vagaries of the process and the inconsistencies of the technology she uses. For example, she deliberately uses ill-fitting lenses and long exposure times to introduce 'errors' such as blurred edges and camera shake. As Vicki Goldberg has noted, Mann encourages 'mistakes that would have horrified earlier photographers'.[21]

In her article, 'Sally Mann's American Vision of the Land', Ayelet Carmi reads Mann's landscapes in relation to both cultural representations of the South and the history of photography to argue that Mann's work questions 'landscape photography as an open field of ideological neutrality [as a means of] revealing its historical construction'.[22] Carmi's writing traces the way in which, since the late nineteenth century, the tourism industry has promoted the South as simultaneously an exotic and nostalgic region. The invocation of an antebellum land was central to the discourse of tourism industry. This myth has also been mobilized by Mann in earlier works such as *Immediate Family*,[23] in which an 'exquisite and often discomfiting pastoral drama'[24] is played out against the backdrop of 'an enigmatic American Eden'.[25] However, as Carmi notes, the visual construction of the South is one of dichotomies: the pastoral 'Eden' is tempered by the presentation of the South as a violent and backward region. Photographs of the Civil War, the first photographs to depict the South, established a landscape iconography defined by violence and loss. The Great Depression reinforced the association of the Southern landscape with violence and overlaid it with economic ruination. However, it is racial violence that is perhaps the prominent association that many have with the South. It is this legacy that Mann addresses in *Untitled (Emmett Till River Bank)*, 1998 (Figure 4.2).

Mann's image of this site departs from picturesque conventions for photographing the landscape in a number of ways. First, it is not framed as a traditional view: Mann's composition is directed across the river, and her decision to focus on the immediate foreground has the effect of 'shortening' the space of the work. This disrupts our accustomed immersion in the landscape as a view. In addition, the limited depth of field draws attention to the particularly photographic vision of the scene. Both of these devices serve to make the viewer aware of the constructed nature of what they see. That is to say, it shows landscape – to reprise Mitchell's words – 'as a cultural practice'.[26]

This haunting photograph of the site at which Till's body was discovered includes no signs of the violence that took place. Indeed, Mann herself has stated, 'How could a place so fraught with historical pain appear to be so ordinary?'[27] Although there is no trace of the events which took place, nor their attendant impact upon the social

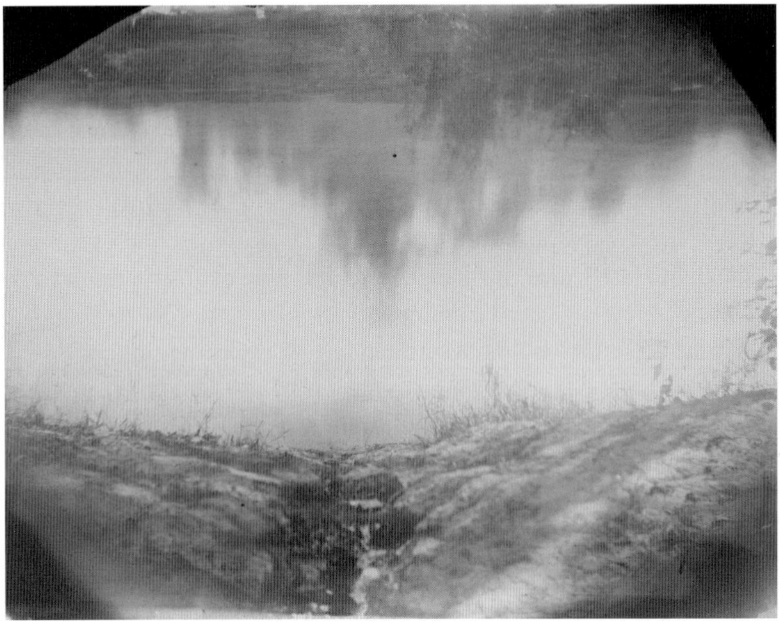

Figure 4.2 Sally Mann, *Deep South, Untitled (Emmett Till River Bank),* 1998. Gelatin silver print, 40 × 50 inches (101.6 × 127 cm). © Sally Mann. Courtesy of Gagosian.

landscape of America, Alison R. Hafera has claimed that Mann's photograph 'becomes the truest posthumous portrait of Emmett Till, capturing the painful essence of the culture that killed him'.[28] In such an understanding, the disturbances of Mann's work, its departure from traditional landscape compositions, the evocative and disturbing singularities produced by the technology she uses and the disquieting unexceptional nature of this site, direct us to reflect upon the complex relationship between land, history and culture. In the space created by this work we might, for example, reflect upon how the convention of representing the South as a site of past acts of racial violence displaces both the pervasiveness and the *present*-ness of issues of race and violence, for young black men are still being murdered today on sites that look similarly unexceptional.[29]

By contrast, Claire Raymond questions whether Mann's work has the potential to agitate for cultural change or social awareness in the present. As she states of the series as a whole, 'One is forced to ask exactly how, by precisely what visual marks, Mann's photographs ... critique the region's history of slavery and Jim Crow.'[30] Raymond thus concludes that 'Mann's work may not go far enough in revealing its own origins in the violent privilege of whiteness'.[31] Similarly, Laura Elizabeth Shea has argued that 'Mann's desire to find death in the land through her travels South is always from a position of power, behind the camera, that does not have to contend with ever-present threats of moving through spaces and situations still dangerous for many'.[32]

These debates are central to the work. As Carmi summarizes, 'Mann's photograph, like the national memory of the murder, demands recurrent decoding of meanings and context. The American landscape, the photograph shows us, is never a neutral space. It is always historically constructed, politically used and emotionally complex.'[33]

The sublime

The 'picturesque' and the 'sublime' are often conceptualized as opposing terms. This opposition is described in a number of ways. For example, Miles Orvell contrasts these terms in relation to the position of the viewer: 'Where the picturesque featured trees and rivers, a scene one might walk into, the sublime invited the viewer to gape in awe at the vista, often seen from above, looking into a vast valley.'[34] Alternatively, David Bate has contrasted them in terms of the picturesque 'beauty spot' or a sublime 'black spot'.[35]

Edmund Burke's *A Philosophical Enquiry into the Origin of Our Ideas of the Sublime and Beautiful* is the starting point for many discussions of the sublime. Written in 1757, this text represents one of the earliest attempts to draw a critical distinction between the beautiful and the sublime. For Burke, the beautiful produces pleasure; it is that which confirms our understanding of the world. The beautiful comforts, settles and reassures. By contrast, the sublime is associated with pain and danger, with 'whatever is in any sort terrible'.[36] Key to Burke's theory of the sublime is that this danger is least one step removed from personal experience: 'When danger or pain press to nearly, they are incapable of giving any delight, and are simply terrible; but at certain distances, and with certain modifications, they may be, and they are delightful, as we every day experience.'[37] The sublime experience in Kant follows a particular trajectory: an overwhelming sensation – variously described as pain, shock, awe – directs the viewer towards an enlarged experience of 'something more'. As Philip Shaw has summarized: 'Sublimity, then, refers to the moment when the ability to apprehend, to know, and to express a thought or sensation is defeated. Yet through this very defeat, the mind gets a feeling for that which lies beyond thought and language.'[38]

The literature on the sublime is vast, and there is not adequate space in this text to give an account of the many ways in which this concept has been utilized by scholars. However, as with the picturesque it is important to move away from asking what sublime 'is' to understanding what it 'does', how it works as a cultural practice. As David Nye has stated, 'The history of the sublime from antiquity shows, if nothing else, that, although it refers to an immutable capacity of human psychology for astonishment, both the objects that arouse this feeling and their interpretations are socially constructed.'[39] Hence, we might see that 'despite all the vexations about what the sublime *is* – its conceptual definition – the sublime has played a remarkably similar *role* across its various iterations; it dramatises the limits of one order by declaring the presence of some greater order or totality beyond articulation, imagination, and relative (in)determination.'[40]

Ned O'Gorman argues that we should understand the sublime neither as a thing nor as a particular experience, but as a rhetorical construction. As such, 'Discerning the sublime becomes neither a strictly matter of terminology (e.g. finding words like "sublime" or "ineffable"), nor subjectivity (e.g. ecstasy and terror), nor of aesthetic form per se (e.g. magnitude and movement), but of identifying rhetorical manoeuvres which declare the limits of one order through the vigorous assertion of another "greater" order.'[41] Nathan Stormer has also proposed that it is necessary to focus on the rhetorical space opened by the act of looking at sublime scenes in order to appreciate that 'such visualizations successfully constitute the subjects they address as commonplaces within discourse'.[42]

What is consistent across the discourse of the sublime is that it entails both an experience of loss and the compensation for this loss. Through a moment of subjective loss, the subject is offered a place within the larger category of humanity. In this way, we can see how 'particular visions of humanity are enacted by sublime aesthetics'.[43] Like the picturesque, those who describe a landscape in relation to an experience of the sublime are laying claim to a particular subject position. We must therefore be attentive to the ideological work of the sublime. The visions of humanity marked out by the sublime are not by any means universal,[44] and have been used in the service of local, national and corporate interests.

Justin James King: *And Still We Gather with Infinite Momentum*

And Still We Gather With Infinite Momentum (2009) by Justin James King depicts sightseers gazing at a black void (Figure 4.3).[45] While the subject of King's series is the sublime, the effect of his photographs is not. This is not to say that they are unsuccessful, but rather that King's work seeks to draw attention to the operations of the sublime. As 'something beyond words', the affective weight of the sublime often conceals its workings. However, by removing the sublime scene, King asks us to adopt a different mode of viewing and thus directs us to the way in which the discourse of the sublime organizes affective responses to land.

The tourist viewpoint is a key location at which we are asked to publicly rehearse particular responses to land, and the crowds in King's work direct us to an overlooked aspect of the sublime: that it is a shared phenomenon. What is pictured in King's

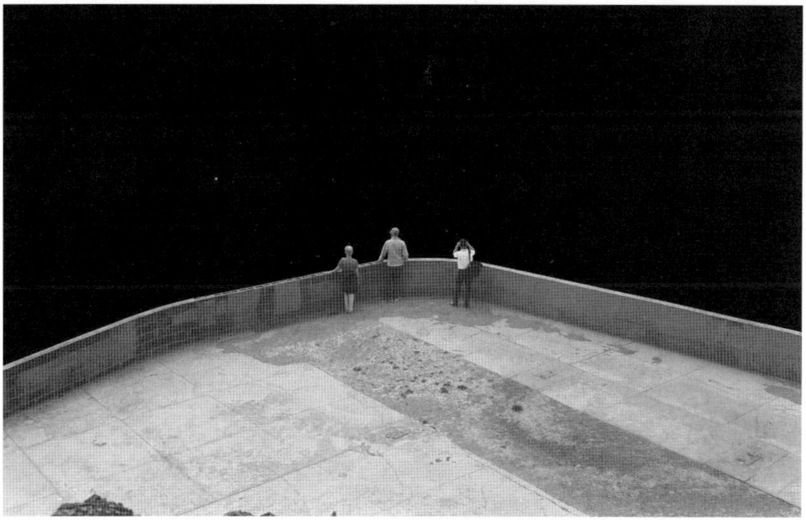

Figure 4.3 Justin James King, Untitled from *And Still We Gather With Infinite Momentum*, 2009. © Justin James King. Courtesy of the artist.

work is the way in which we enter into a shared identification with strangers at sites designated as sublime. In collectively gazing upon a sublime landscape 'we experience the rather peculiar moment of visually rehearsing for one another precisely where words *should* fail us'.[46] Thus, King's work foregrounds the sublime as a mode of civic engagement: the way in which we visit sites designated as sublime as a means of consolidating ourselves particular kinds of subjects.

We learn to look upon certain locations as sublime objects as a way of affirming our relationship to a set of ideals. The sublime might therefore be seen as a normalizing discourse. As we explored in Part One, we are normalized as subjects by how we are looked at. However, we are also normalized as subjects by how we look. The absence of the landscape in King's work allows us to reflect on what the sublime directs us away from at tourist sites, in particular those things that do not fit with the national narrative such as industrial devastation, toxic contamination and the destruction of indigenous inhabitants. In short, it directs us to recognizing that the production of sublime spectatorship is an ideological exercise.

Thomas Albdorf: *General View*

The repetitious reproduction of particular ways of looking at the American landscape is explored with a different inflection in Thomas Albdorf's work *General View* (2017).[47] *General View* is a fictitious narrative involving a trip to Yosemite National

Park. Albdorf used Google Street View, image searches, promotional materials, his studio and a local park to recreate the experience of visiting this intensely photographed site. As Albdorf has posed, 'If countless images of a specific place are readily available, has one been there already?'[48] Although he does not use traditional techniques, Darren Campion proposes that Albdorf is a landscape photographer 'in so far as "landscape" is essentially a set of pictorial conventions he [Albdorf] can enter into and wilfully deconstruct'.[49] Campion argues that 'by making use of the prevailing ideas about how it is pictured he [Albdorf] could, essentially remake the kinds of view those ideas produce. These pictures look like other pictures because of how they reproduced (as visual codes) the cultural assumptions that surround certain kinds of landscapes.'[50]

Although Yosemite has been subject to many representations it is notable that the title of Albdorf's work recalls a particular photograph, 'The Yosemite Valley from the "Best General View"' (1866), by Carleton E. Watkins. The work of Watkins is perhaps best known for the role that his photographs played in helping to convince Congress to set aside Yosemite as a federally protected area. Although the National Parks are now understood as natural sites in need of protection, that cultural perception had to be learned. Wilderness is not a natural fact, but a political achievement. One that was aided by Watkins's presentation of Yosemite as a sublime, unspoilt site.[51]

The meaning of wilderness has been further transformed through contemporary technology. As James Stinson expresses it, 'Camping on Twitter, hiking in Google Street View, mountaineering on Snapchat. Wilderness is dead. Long live Wilderness 2.0.'[52] The emergence of a new digitally mediated experience of nature has given rise to new kinds of subjects. As Stinson writes, the 'cyborg-subjects of Wilderness 2.0 are not just characterized by the technology they use, but by the way they see and engage with wilderness.'[53] For Stinson, one of the defining features of Wilderness 2.0 is 'a move away from an ethic of visual consumption … toward an ethic of digital sharing and prosumption'.[54] In Wilderness 2.0, nature becomes a resource for 'share-worthy' content for social media. Thus, Stinson argues that 'Wilderness 2.0 represents the re-creation of wilderness as a site of economic production (rather than simply visual consumption) and a landscape of virtual labour'.[55]

Although these changes are significant, Albdorf's work directs us to the way in which technologies such as Google Street View also help to produce spaces in a way that is consonant with previous regimes of representation and their attendant understandings of land. As Campion notes, by using his own photographs alongside imagery from Google Street View Albdorf is able to bring to light 'an unexpected continuity between these different ways of making the landscape visible, of framing a view, where we might otherwise imagine there has been a fundamental break'.[56]

While we might regard the view we are offered by Google Street View as 'neutral', it is important to be aware of the way in which new technologies associated with the picturing of the land remain wedded to a colonial perspective. Lukasz Zaremba is one of the many writers who have drawn attention to the colonial optic that underpins the totality of Google's enterprise. Zaremba argues that the ideological and imperial strategies of Google are explicit in their slogan, 'To organize the world's information and make it universally accessible'. For Zaremba this demonstrates 'not only a simple appropriation of the world, a pictorial colonization, but also its standardization and subordination to (post-Enlightenment) systems of value'.[57] Google Street View continues the historical role of photography in the colonial, scientific and bureaucratic mapping, classification and registration of the world.

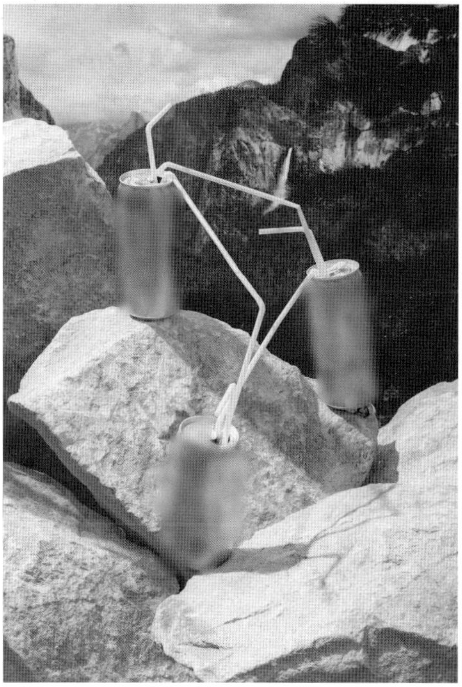

Figure 4.4 Thomas Albdorf, 'Dad and Me made Some "Art Installation" LOL while Taking a Break from Hiking (Nice View Tho)' from the series *General View*, 2017. © Thomas Albdorf and Webber. Courtesy of the artist.

In her writings on mapping technologies, Laura Kurgan has proposed that 'we do not stand at a distance' from these technologies, rather we are both 'addressed by and embedded within them'.[58] Kurgan argues that, despite their politicized history and use, these technologies can be used tactically and the images they produce be read subversively. Indeed, for Kurgan 'only through a certain intimacy with these technologies – an encounter with their opacities, their assumptions, their intended aims – can we begin to assess their full ethical and political stakes'.[59] Jason Farman also sees a political potential in the new ways of looking at land that might be opened up by alternative uses and organizations of visual mapping technologies. Farman argues that by integrating a social network with GIS technology, platforms such as Google Street View offer us a means to reconfigure the visualization of land: here maps are no longer simply a set of 'static visual facts to be received, but instead flexible signs that can be engaged in free play'.[60]

An interesting example to consider in light of these arguments is the image that opens Albdorf's book: a montage in which a sculpture of *Coke* cans that have been blurred in post-production stand in front of what appears to be a painted backdrop of the Yosemite Valley (Figure 4.4). In Albdorf's image we see a layering of past and present activities in the landscape which includes painting, leisure and commerce. The priority of these in organizing our vision of land is encapsulated by Albdorf's text:

> Dad and Me made Some
> 'Art Installation' LOL while
> Taking a Break from Hiking
> (Nice View Tho)

General View is filled with many of these strange and playful textual, visual, material and digital interventions into the landscape. As Chandra and Stewart, Mann, King and Albdorf all show, by intervening the materiality of the photograph, new renderings of traditional genres that might afford us the opportunity to see land in different ways can emerge.

Non-place and new topologies

This chapter will consider contemporary organizations of space that are particular to neoliberalism. To begin we will look at the *New Topographics* exhibition. This exhibition and the work of photographers such as Lewis Baltz, Bernd and Hilla Becher and Robert Adams have been incredibly influential in establishing a topographic aesthetic as the authoritative model for a photography that seeks to critically evaluate place. In the second part of the chapter we will consider Marc Augé's writings on non-place as a way of thinking about the complexity of the contemporary spaces produced by neoliberalism and globalization. As an example, we will look at Roger Eberhart's *Standard*. Recent writings on non-place have sought to extend Augé's work to critically engage with the ways in which non-place is inflected by different mobilities. To explore some of these writings we will consider Andreas Gefeller's surreal and dystopia vision of non-place in his work *Soma*. To conclude the chapter, we will be looking at how the work of Trevor Paglen intersects with new writings which engage with space topologically rather than topographically. What unites all of the photographic artists discussed in this chapter is a concern with how land is mapped; they each seek – in different ways – to make visible the power relations that give land meaning and form.

New Topographics

In any discussion of contemporary landscape photography, the exhibition *New Topographics: Photographs of a Man-Altered Landscape* is seen to be a key moment. Held at the George Eastman House in Rochester, New York, in 1975 and curated by William Jenkins, the exhibition is widely credited with producing a radical shift in the tradition of the American landscape photography. The exhibition was re-staged in 2009, and the place of *New Topographics* in the canon of landscape photography is further secured by the number of artists working today who continue to make reference to and produce work that bears its influences.

While there are important differences between photographers such as Stephen Shore, Lewis Baltz, Robert Adams and Bernd and Hilla Becher, they all share a topographic approach to photographing land. Associated with an objective survey of the features of a place often for the purposes of development, the role of the topographic photograph is to provide an accurate record. When utilized by these artists, the use of a topographical aesthetic, often sustained across an extended series, serves to produce a critical commentary upon the meanings and uses of land. The work of the New Topographic photographers marked a change not just in the aesthetic but also in the subject matter of landscape photography. As Wendy Cheng notes, these artists 'rejected the picturesque, romanticizing, and purportedly human-free landscapes of their immediate forebears' to photograph the common and the banal: 'Everything that had previously been cropped out of American landscape photographs: the "spaces in between," such as parking lots, industrial buildings, grain elevators, tract developments, shopping malls, freeway underpasses, and the like.'[1]

These choices were in service of critiquing the transformation of the landscape by industrial and urban development. As John Beck writes,

> The same Western landscapes made iconic by Ansel Adams and Weston are revisited but this time the vernacular architecture of urban sprawl and commercial exploitation fills the frame. This is 'straight' photography put through the wringer of historical self-reflexivity, whereby technical excellence is deployed to craft hard images of engineered entropy and where the abstracting tendency of deep focus reproduces the serial forms of manufactured homogeneity.[2]

Despite its now canonical status, the exhibition was poorly received at the time. As Wendy Cheng notes, 'The simple presentation – combined with the photographers' deliberately evenhanded treatment of their apparently mundane subject matter – was so unassuming as to be confounding and even offensive to some of the show's first visitors in the 1970s.'[3] 'Look at this picture, I just … why? What is he trying to show?' one visitor complained before describing the pictures as 'dull and flat' and concluding, 'I just don't like this at all.'[4] The strength of these initial responses perhaps gives a sense of the extent to which the work of the New Topographic photographers asked viewers to engage in a conceptual revaluation of what place means. Just as people originally struggled to 'see' the picturesque, the way in which land is given form and meaning through a critical topographic approach requires a new way of looking. As such, rather than neutral or objective Cheng has argued that we should describe these works as 'opaque'. For Cheng, opaque is a way of signalling the way in which these works 'push their viewers to reinvent their own notions of landscape and, if one looks closely, to accept the implicit challenge to engage the visual as a tool for critical inquiry'.[5]

Although a topographic approach is still widely embraced as a model for a critical practice of landscape photography, the *New Topographics* exhibition – opening between the resignation of Richard Nixon, the end of the Vietnam War and the ascent of neoliberalism – should be understood as offering a critique suitable to a particular historical moment. New ways of theorizing and visualizing the relationship between land, power and subjectivity are required by the contemporary era.

Non-places

The writings of the anthropologist Marc Augé have made a significant contribution to theorizing the new spaces that have emerged with neoliberalism. Augé's concept of non-place shows how current political, social and economic era has given rise to new organizations of place. In his book *Non-Places: An Introduction to Supermodernity*[6] Augé seeks to describe a particular type of place that has emerged with what he terms 'supermodernity'. In contrast to 'anthroplogical place' which is associated with sense of social, cultural and historical meaning, non-places are generic spaces produced by economic and commercial activity. As Augé states, 'If place can be defined as relational, historical, or concerned with identity, then a space which cannot be defined as relational, or historical, or concerned with identity will be a non-place.'[7] Some of the examples of non-place given by Augé are airports, motorways, hotels and shopping malls. Such places are distinguished by being organized around particular purposes, most commonly, transport, leisure or commerce. As a nodal point in the circulation of people, capital and goods, the non-place is a place of transience characterized by movement.

Roger Eberhard: *Standard*

Inspired by Conrad Hilton's statement that every Hilton should be 'a little America',[8] Roger Eberhard visited thirty-two cities across five continents and photographed the standard double room at the Hilton hotel (Figure 5.1b). In the aesthetic gentrification of the Hilton Hotel's 'standard room' we are presented with a strangely dull, yet engaging repetition of particular attributes of space. As Augé has noted, the feeling of familiarity produced by the non-place can temporarily be 'felt as liberation';[9] indeed, the traveller can find comfort, even 'feel at home', in 'the anonymity of motorways, service stations, big stores or hotel chains'.[10] However, because the non-place cannot support individual identity or personal relations, it is predominantly a place of 'solitude and similitude'[11] where 'he becomes no more than what he does or experiences in the role of passenger, customer or driver'.[12] Or as Benedict Wells, writing on Eberhard's project, expresses it, 'A hotel room radiates that we do not

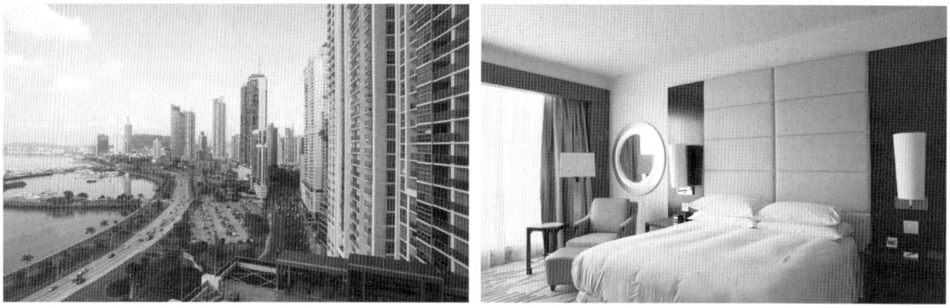

Figure 5.1a,b Roger Eberhard, 'Panama City, Room 1704', from *Standard*, 2015. © Roger Eberhard. Courtesy of the artist.

mean anything to it, we are one of many exchangeable goods. I am not going to leave anything behind, or change anything. ... I ... am an insignificant one-night-stand for the room in which I sleep'.[13]

The hotel room is only part of Eberhard's project. *Standard* is a double typology: as well as a photograph of the room's interior, Eberhard also photographed the view from its window (Figure 5.1a).[14] As Franziska Solte notes, Hilton Hotels were often among the first high-rise buildings in the city centres, here the 'foreignness of the immediate surroundings could be observed from inside through the broad glass fronts, from a safe, elevated perspective'.[15] Although these two spaces can be opposed as inside/outside, they both show the effects of globalization. Here 'a desire for homogenization – whether of space, goods or behaviours – which seems to be characteristic of neo-liberalism (and in ironic contradistinction to the discursive construction of the "free market" as guarantor of competition, diversity and "consumer choice")'[16] has produced a standardization of both the hotel and urban space.

Kyle Chayka has coined the term 'AirSpace' to describe the way in which digital technology is changing both the appearance and our experience of place. Giving examples such as the traffic app *Waze* rerouting traffic through previously quiet neighbourhoods, *Airbnb* producing an influx of tourists into residential communities or *Foursquare* 'sending traveling businessmen to the same cafe over and over again',[17] Chayka argues that as this 'affluent, self-selecting group of people move through spaces linked by technology, particular sensibilities spread, and these small pockets of geography grow to resemble one another'.[18] The homogeneity of these spaces means that travelling between them is frictionless. However, this does not mean that these spaces are politically neutral. Chayka cites the example of Quirtina Crittenden who started the hashtag #AirbnbWhileBlack to highlight experiences of discrimination on the platform. These included hosts refusing reservations from an account with a dark-skinned avatar or being turned away when they arrived. The recognition that we must be attentive to the economic, political and social forces at play in non-place has led a number of critics to revisit Augé's work.

Non-places revisited

As Jana Costas has noted, the concept of non-place is 'not absolute but relative, depending on the individual and his/her lived experience'.[19] If we take the airport as an example, first-time flyers, first-class passengers, cabin crew staff and air traffic controllers will all have very different experiences of the same space. While some may pass through without creating any social bonds or ascribing history or meaning to the airport, for others it will operate as a place. As such we can see the way in which 'place and non-place are always relational, contingent and continually folded into one another'.[20]

The airport also offers a way of considering the politics of mobility in the non-place. As Tim Cresswell has noted, 'There is no system on Earth that quite so explicitly makes the existence of a kinetic hierarchy so clear.'[21] For the kinetic elite – the upper class, connoisseur or elite ticket holder – the journey will involve a seamless transition from their front door to the airport lounge facilitated by a complimentary chauffeur-driven limousine and a fast-track lane at immigration. However, this idealized journey, foremost in many accounts of the non-place, belongs only to a privileged group and fails to be attentive to the nature of the airport as an exclusive space replete with increasingly invasive surveillance technologies. Thus, Creswell argues that 'while airports are often mobilized as symbols of globalization and transnational identity, they also illustrate the politics of mobility at the scale of the body'.[22] In short, while mobility is often presented as an abstract, ahistorical attribute that characterizes the function of the non-place, it is an attribute of particular bodies. Indeed, a rigorous social sorting takes place in non-place. As Sarah Sharma has noted, 'Non-places are replete with the most up to date surveillance technologies to "find" and sort the population into various categories – consumer, citizen, terrorist, and frequent flyer to name a few.'[23] Far from a politically or historically neutral space, in the airport 'unsuspected travellers are quite often unwittingly treated to a conjectural theater of the geopolitical tensions of the day':[24]

> Who is getting detained? Who is taking so long in the line-up? Who is being escorted off of the plane? Who have the risky and questionable bodies these days? As a site where the differential flows of immaterial and material traffic (of bodies, monies, and information) mix, mingle, and sometimes clash, the non-place must be contended with as a critical space within the political architecture of contemporaneity.[25]

Indeed, Edward Welch has argued, if the non-place is the organization of space that emerges in response to the need for the efficient circulation and management of commodities, capital and labour, then we must recognize that airports, hotels and also detention centres are 'variants of the same phenomenon or outcomes of the same fundamental processes'.[26]

One of the criticisms of the way in which the concept of the non-place is used is that it is not always sufficiently attentive to differential relations of power that traverse

topography usefully describes a style of landscape photography which adopts a neutral aesthetic and often works across an extended series as a means of mapping an area, exploring the critical significance of contemporary works calls for an expanded theorization of place. Addressing place in terms of topology offers a way of recognizing that place is produced through particular power relations that privilege certain things happening in particular places at specific times. The work of Trevor Paglen is a useful example to consider here.

Paglen is an artist, geographer and author who describes his practice as an 'experimental geography'. For Paglen, experimental geography means 'practices that take on the production of space in a self-reflexive way, practices that recognize that cultural production and the production of space cannot be separated from each another, and that cultural and intellectual production is a spatial practice'.[37] As Jill Dawsey notes, Paglen's photographs testify to the way in which 'space is in fact a socially constructed system, a system produced by human beings through our social and economic relations'.[38]

Paglen argues that the task of experimental geography is to move beyond critical reflection or critique alone. Thus, Paglen is concerned not only with showing that space is produced through power but also with experimenting with the production of space as part of his practice. In Paglen's words, 'If human activities are inextricably spatial, then new forms of freedom and democracy can only emerge in dialectical relation to the production of new spaces.'[39] He does, however, recognize that 'the production of new spaces isn't easy'.[40]

The focus of Paglen's work is secret military and state practices; although this might not immediately seem to concern geography, Paglen proposes that geography offers an important way of thinking through the contemporary politics of the secret. As Paglen summarizes, since all 'human undertakings are spatial … even though classified programs are organized in such a way as to maximize their invisibility, they have to happen somewhere'.[41]

Paglen gives the stealth fighter as an example of how the production of a secret weapon produced particular kinds of spaces. As Paglen explains, 'Secret relations, programs, sites, and events have to be made out of the same "stuff" that everything else (i.e. the nonsecret world) is made of. Because there are no such things as invisible factories, airplanes made out of unearthly ghost-matter, or workers who "don't exist," logics of secrecy are contradicted by their material implementations.'[42] Thus, the creation of the stealth fighter did more that create an 'invisible' weapon; it created a 'space of stealth'.[43] This space of stealth extended beyond the location of the stealth fighter: as 'the Air Force sought to manage the contradictions created when the space of stealth intersected other spaces around it, those spaces, in turn, were transformed. They, too, became "stealthy"'.[44] This is why Paglen proposes that it is important to incorporate a critical geography into ways of thinking about power.

Paglen has explored the contemporary politics of visibility through a number of works. Our example is taken from *Limit Telephotography*, a collection of photographs of classified military bases in the United States. Access to these sites is difficult – aside from military security on the bases, they are surrounded by a vast amount of open land, up to 4,600 square miles in some cases. Paglen describes these locations as 'blank spots'.[45] In relation to ideas discussed in Chapter 4, we might say that while the picturesque calls into being a particular type of person by asking them to respond to a specific organization of land as picturesque, contemporary politics calls into being a particular type of person by asking them to see nothing at these sites. Blank spots, like spaces of stealth, are contradictory; they exist as specific locations, yet they are absent from official forms of documentation such as maps and allowed to surface in public discourse only in the form of conspiracy theories.

Paglen's photographs do not allow us to see these sites clearly. Indeed, 'Open Hangar, Cactus Flats' (Figure 5.3) resembles an abstract painting more than a photograph. The frame is filled by three vertical bands of colour: blue, white and green. There is a small amount of detail in the top two bands, and, with the aid of the title, the viewer might adjust their eyes to make out some clouds, a building and a plane. Clare Birchall offers a useful description of the effect of encountering Paglen's photographs: 'They appear less like fixed images and more like processes; the interference of dust and heat makes them seem as though they are coming in or out of focus and leave the onlooker in a suspended state of curiosity and expectation teetering on the edge of fear, disappointment or frustration.'[46]

Paglen's hazy, distorted photographs – a consequence of the enormous distance from which the photos were shot and the long exposure times necessary to shoot them – may initially appear to be 'failed' images as there is insufficient detail to make

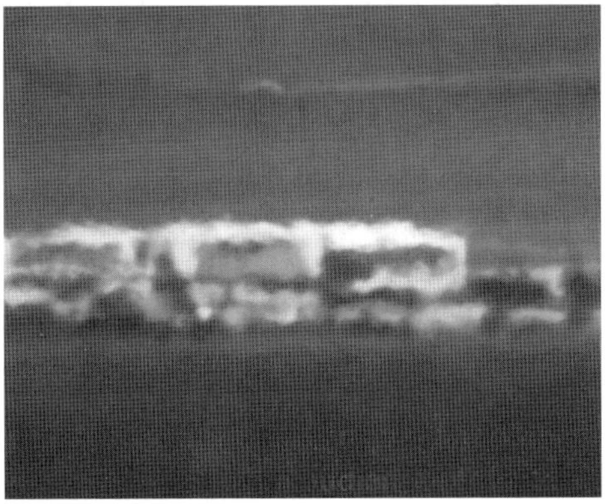

Figure 5.3 Trevor Paglen, 'Open Hangar, Cactus Flats, NV, Distance ~ 18 miles, 10:04 a.m', 2007. C-Print 30 × 36 inches, 76.2 × 91.4 cm. © Trevor Paglen. Courtesy of the artist and Metro Pictures, New York.

out any 'useful', let alone 'secret' information. As Gary Kafer succinctly notes, 'More often than not, there is nothing to see in Trevor Paglen's *Limit Telephotography* series.'[47] However, critics argue that these 'failures' are key to the meaning of the images. For example, Brian Wallis has proposed that the true subject of Paglen's project is 'the limits of seeing – and of photography itself'.[48] For others, Paglen's work is best understood as a visual response to the post-truth era and the way in which the workings of power escape the traditional means of visual representation. Jack Bratich's notion of spectacular secrecy is useful here. Bratich argues that the traditional understanding of secrecy, which might be visualized as a box or envelope with hidden contents, is one that gives rise to calls for transparency and openness normally expressed as the 'public right to know'. The understanding advanced here is that 'exposure destroys the secret'.[49] However, Bratich argues that the dominant mode of contemporary politics is that of the spectacular secret. Here secrets are still revealed but in a way that increases, rather than puts an end to secrecy. Spectacular secrecy 'orbits around revelation-management'[50] where it is the spectacle of revelation that is central. In terms of advancing a critique, what is key is understanding that calls for 'transparency' actually sustain this mode of power. This is because public campaigns that advocate transparency entrench the spectacle of the secret at the centre of our vision of democracy in a way that leaves power relations intact. As Thomas Keenan expresses it, 'Faced with something obscure – something essentially dark – it is radically insufficient merely to shine the light of publicity. It misses the point: to turn on the lights tells us nothing about the dark itself.'[51] Learning to 'look beyond' the secret becomes increasingly pressing under the Trump administration which has seen spectacular distraction from the workings of power reach new heights.

Here lies the significance of *Limit Telephotography*; as Jayne Wilkinson notes, 'There is no dramatic disclosure here, no unmasking of the war apparatus, no shocking military secret uncovered. … Instead his work offers the viewer a means of inquiry through the process that makes visible the structures of power that seek to operate through invisibility.'[52] Rather than showing us what a classified landscape looks like, Paglen uses the landscape photograph to organize our vision – and therefore our attention – differently. As Thomas Keenan notes, Paglen's work challenges our habits of looking: 'the announcement that the image makes, before any reading starts, is that the reading will be difficult, somehow beyond our control – but still we have to do it'.[53]

6

Ruins and the Anthropocene

As Deborah Bright reminds us 'whatever its aesthetic merits, every representation of landscape is also a record of human values and actions imposed on the land over time'.[1] As we have seen in the previous chapters of this section, landscape is a discourse that shapes land in accordance with social and cultural values. The dominant way in which landscape is mobilized is to present a certain way of looking at land and the organization of space as natural and ahistorical. What then can we make of the emergence of ruined and apocalyptic landscapes in contemporary practice? Rather than giving form to a particular set of values, these landscapes seem to show their destruction.

The ruin, of course, is not a contemporary form and has a long history. In the modern era, ruins were celebrated and even artificially constructed to offer a philosophical space in which to engage in a contemplative nostalgia. This was a practice that sought to secure the legitimacy of the present and its orientation towards a 'better' future. However, as the twentieth century progressed the ruin acquired a different inflection, speaking instead of the human capacity for destruction through war, industry and economic collapse. As Magali Arriola notes,

> While there was confidence in the linear and progressive construction of history, traditional ruins promised redemption, inasmuch as they secured an understanding of continuity. Having experienced the disruptions and disasters that resulted from the myths of social progress and mass utopia that shaped the history of the 20th Century, it now seems that there is no possibility of redemption, only a longing for an interrupted future of gloomy reassurance that one has survived its ruin.[2]

In its contemporary use, the ruin is an ambivalent, conflicted object. On the one hand, the spectacular pathos associated with a number of photographic representations of ruination has attracted charges of 'ruin porn'. On the other hand, the same images of ruins have been read as a way of subverting the dominant narrative that consigns particular places – and people – to the past.[3] As such, we might follow David Lloyd who has proposed that 'in itself, the ruin is neither symbol nor allegory but the object of contestations over meanings, memories, histories, and the form in which meaning is presented.'[4] In this way, rather than understanding the ruin as particular object or scene, we can be attentive to the way in which 'ruins merrily transgress and collapse a whole set of binaries: transience/persistence, nature/culture, attraction/repulsion, power/vulnerability, potential/purposelessness, abandonment/appropriation, presence/absence, aestheticization/abjection.'[5]

Although the ambivalence of the ruin means that the political potential of ruination is open to appropriation, the examples considered in this chapter share a commitment to using photography and the ruin as means to advance a critical reading of land. To begin we will consider Joel Meyerowitz's project *Aftermath* alongside a number of writings that are concerned with exploring the meaning of the ruin of the Twin Towers. In the second part of this chapter we will consider works by Tong Lam, Joanna Zylinska and Matthew Buckingham which engage with the idea of the Anthropocene and the politics of what it means to visualize a landscape 'after the human'.

Joel Meyerowitz: *Aftermath: World Trade Centre Archive*

In his work *Aftermath: World Trade Centre Archive*,[6] Joel Meyerowitz documents the process of clearing the sixteen-acre site where the Twin Towers once stood. Using a 10 × 8 view camera and a 35 mm Leica, Meyerowitz took over 8,000 images. In this extensive project, we see vast images of destruction alongside a documentation of the daily lives of people involved in clearing the site. Meyerowitz's aesthetic and rhetorical frame for the project draws explicitly on the sublime. As László Munteán notes, images with captions such as 'Firemen and Cloud', 'Twilight' and 'Smoke Rising Through Sunlight' 'are just some of the examples in which documentary detail is … filtered through an aura of the sublime.'[7] Noting that it acknowledges 'beauty in the scenes' and flirts 'with the elegiac elements inherent in photography',[8] Liam Kennedy also situates Meyerowitz's work in relation to the sublime. Although Kennedy acknowledges that Meyerowitz's work is nuanced, he argues that the propagandistic framework of the exhibition *After September 11: Images from Ground Zero* in which many of the photographs were first shown to the public compromises the work. For Kennedy, the seeping of meaning characteristic of photography means that, in this context, Meyeorwitz's images come to 'crudely animate'[9] a politically motivated narrative of heroic redemption.

As we discussed in Chapter 4, the sublime has often been mobilized in the service of conservative political purposes. As Ned O'Gorman expresses it, the sublime usually serves to 'reify rather than challenge dominant power'.[10] O'Gorman has traced the way in which the sublime has appeared in political rhetoric in the United States from 'manifest destiny' in nineteenth-century America to the strategy of 'Shock and Awe' offered by the Pentagon in the Gulf War.[11] For O'Gorman the sublime is a key means through which democratic political practices are marginalized: via the sublime, democratic principles and ideals are dwarfed by 'the absolute unmodified largeness of America'.[12] In the case of *Aftermath*, Kennedy argues that the political framing of Meyerowitz's work is one in which the sublime is mobilized to obstruct an engagement with the specifics of foreign policy in order to assert narrative of unspeakable loss that forms the justification for war.

However, a number of critics have argued that there is a critical potential in Meyerowitz's work that should not be ignored. For example, Weena Perry maintains that 'these rather ham-fisted political uses of Meyerowitz's photographs should not be confused with the photographer's intentions or the emotional connection that the public and professionals alike have expressed after looking at the images. ... The political interest expressed in Meyerowitz's photographs represents an intriguing attempt to recuperate the inherent ambivalence of the contemporary ruin'.[13] Chris Vanderwees has similarly argued that, although Meyerowitz's photographs of Ground Zero have been used – and may continue to function – as a form of propaganda that serves the dominant discourse of American exceptionalism, the publication of *Aftermath* in book form presents the opportunity to view these photographs in a new context. For Vanderwees, Meyerowitz's use of the sublime produces 'imagery that uncannily communicates political anxieties, which both serve *and counter* the intense memorialization and the nationalist narrativization of Ground Zero'.[14] In short, while a sublime perspective is certainly fostered by the images, seeing the work only from the point of view organized by American political rhetoric limits what we see.

One of the ways in which *Aftermath* advances an alternative use of the sublime and the ruin is through the inclusion of personal narratives and observations. This introduces a shift in perspective which allows us to reflect upon how much the sublime privileges a certain type of – distanced – viewer. For those at Ground Zero, the experience is not one of the sublime. Indeed, that a shift in perspective might allow for the possibility of alternative visual engagements is noted in Kennedy's writing on Meyerowitz's work. Here the scale and detail offered by the photographs does not serve to immobilize us in front of a sublime spectacle, but activates an intense kind of looking that raises ethical questions: 'Our eyes move across the images, searching – for what we may not be sure, but mimicking the search going on in the photographs by the firefighters, police officers and others at the scene. As every spot of colour emanating from the masses of twisted steel and debris catches our eye – we sense the moral ambiguity of looking'.[15] Such devices might allow us to engage with the complexity of the ruin of the Twin Towers. As Perry notes, 'The aesthetic appeal of the ruins poses a moral dilemma for photographer and viewer alike because this imagery emerges from mass murder.'[16] Or as Magali Arriola has posed, 'What is it that encourages us to perceive debris as waste in one place and as ruins, or even monuments, in another?'[17]

Here it is important to note that the ruins pictured in *Aftermath* are not the neglected and decaying structures of America's inner cities, rather they show the destruction of well-known corporate buildings. Vanderwees thus argues that the ruins pictured in Meyerowitz's work might 'uncannily manifest as a fulfilment of utopian fantasies of a post-capitalist future'.[18] In his discussion Vanderwees cites Frederic Jameson's famous statement, 'That it is easier to imagine the end of the world than to imagine the end of capitalism.'[19]

The writings of Claire Colebrook offer a way of exploring this aspect further. As Colebrook notes the popular understanding of capitalism is as follows: 'Capitalism is insistently linear, ever-expanding, intent on "progress" (defined as increasing production, consumption and market reach) *and* presents this forward movement as inevitable, natural, proper and post-ideological.'[20] However, Colebrook proposes that 'it is easy to imagine the end of capitalism because capitalism – at least in its manifest mode of a free market, even a free market operating by way of ruthless competition – has ceased to exist, and never existed'.[21] Indeed, Colebrook proposes that what traditional post-apocalyptic landscapes picture is not the future, but an unacknowledged *now*. These 'worlds without order, abundance, personhood or leisure – are accurate depictions of what life already is, and has necessarily been, outside the luxuries of first-world anxieties about the future of "humanity"'.[22] What is presented in viewing mainstream representations of 'the ruins of capitalism' such as those offered by Hollywood disaster movies is the opportunity for engaging with a world 'after capitalism' at the safe distance of 'the future'. However, a shift in perspective – such as that advocated by Colebrook – might bring with it the recognition that 'precarity, or life in the ruins, is no longer something that only happens to a select few'.[23]

Here it is relevant to note that it is the clearing of the site that is the subject of Meyerowitz work. That is to say, it is concerned with the *removal* of the ruin. This includes the remarkable, yet rarely remarked upon, selling of the materials from the site for scrap. As Munteán notes, the 'various forms of dissemination of the ruins – the handing out of urns to family members of the dead, parts of the wreckage's incorporation into the USS New York, and as scrap metal sold in Asia – constitute a palimpsest which complicates the relation between ruin and progress'.[24]

It is not just the contemporary resonances that are important in exploring how the ruin might offer a way of puncturing the discourse of the sublime. As Martia Sturken has noted, 'Ground Zero is a name pulled from history.'[25] A number of writers have commented on the connections between the ruin at Ground Zero and the ruins of the Second World War, in particular the bombings of Dresden and Berlin. However, despite the term 'ground zero' being consistent with the vocabulary of atomic warfare, very few comparisons to Hiroshima or Nagasaki were drawn in the media. The bombing of Hiroshima and Nagasaki by the United States expands the framework through which we might read *Aftermath* and further complicates the relation between the ruin and a narrative of progress.[26] As Brian Dillon has written, 'The ruin casts us forward in time; it predicts a future in which our present will slump into similar disrepair or fall victim to some unforeseeable calamity.'[27] This temporality is key to the ethical possibilities of the ruin. In short, the ruin might offer a means of imaging an alternative future rather than confirming the politics of the present. This is central to Vanderwees' re-reading in which he argues that 'the affective encounter with Meyerowitz's photographs might uncannily refer to other tragedies and atrocities, generating fragmentary traces that trouble narratives of exceptionalism'.[28]

While the affective encounter with the sublime ruin in *Aftermath* has been used to advance a particular set of political concerns, returning to the work through the writings of Vanderwees, Colebrook and others allows us to see the critical potential of work that engages with the sublime and the ruin. Here the potential of the ruin is that its temporal ambivalence serves to destabilize and unsettle hegemonic discourses such that a politics of critique and questioning is opened up to us.

The Anthropocene landscape

Coined by ecologist Eugene Stoermer in the 1980s, and later popularized by the work of Paul Crutzen, the term 'Anthropocene' designates a planetary shift so significant that the earth is understood to be undergoing a sixth extinction. The concept of the Anthropocene confronts us with the humbling thought that humankind's existence will have only constituted a brief moment in the earth's history. The idea of the Anthropocene quickly found a place in arts and humanities in the writings of theorists such as Bruno Latour and Donna Haraway and as theme for a number of exhibitions and publications. In this section we will be looking at how the aesthetics of the Anthropocene might offer an opportunity to rethink the sublime. In short, if the sublime is centred upon the limits of the human subject, can there be a sublime *after* the human?

The philosophical challenges posed by the Anthropocene are foremost in the writings of a number of critics. In her book *Minimal Ethics for the Anthropocene*, Joanna Zylinska calls the Anthropocene a 'crisis of critical thinking'.[29] While for Kathryn Yusoff, the Anthropocene represents a new epoch of thought, one that calls for new philosophies and forms of representation.[30] For these and other thinkers, adapting to a changing climate means reimagining how we organize ourselves politically, socially and economically. In thinking about how to do this, a number of thinkers see the visual as playing a key role. For example, Nicholas Mirzoeff argues that the challenge presented by the Anthropocene is one that requires us to 'create a mental space for action that can link the visible and the sayable',[31] while Zylinska argues that we need to adopt radically new practices of seeing:

> In liberating vision from the constraints of the embodied human eye, with its established set of visual relations and the limited directionality of its outlook, a possibility arises of glimpsing another setup, or rather, of glimpsing it differently. This seemingly minimal intervention (when compared, say, with direct action or political engagement) can actually have earth-shattering consequences, because it plants in our human minds a radically different set of images and imaging practices, one that transcends the subjectivism of the human eye. Un-seeing ourselves and what we are calling 'the world' in this way, abstract as it may sound, must be a first step in any kind of concrete and responsible reconfiguration of our here and now.[32]

Central to both Zylinska's and Mirzoeff's understanding of a critical aesthetics of the Anthropocene is the need to challenge the trope of the Anthropocene as a romanticized ruin and to counter what Jodi Dean has termed 'anthropocenic enjoyment'.[33] Dean argues that the dominant tropes for visualizing the Anthropocene, for example, images of ice caps melting or vast polluted landscapes, often leave us 'incapacitated by magnitude, boggled by scale'.[34] Here there is a danger that we only see 'the end of the world' and therefore fail to see the uneven and unequal consequences of planetary changes. In such images, the sublime is mobilized to universalize that which does not have equal effects, in particular, the disproportionate impact of pollution and climate change on areas and populations that have already been left devastated by capitalism, colonialism and militarism. Further, as T. J. Demos has noted, the 'activities' that are shown in the imagery that commonly depicts the Anthropocene 'are hardly "human," at least in that generalizing, species-being sense, but are in fact mostly the "activities" of corporate industry, an area generally occluded in Anthropocene discourse'.[35] For Demos, this raises the question of what ideological function the Anthropocene might serve.[36]

What role can the photographic medium play in meeting the ethico-political challenges of the Anthropocene? The future-oriented perspective invoked in addressing the fate of the planet after our own extinction poses a number of challenges to photography's relation to time. Yet, perhaps the Anthropocene might offer the opportunity to rethink both the human *and* photography.

In his article 'Contemporary Photography and the Technological Sublime, or, Can There Be a Science Fiction Photography?' Roger Luckhurst proposes that 'the tension of the sublime between terror and pleasure and between adequate and inadequate or possible and impossible representation is also a temporal tension: the sublime opens on to the future, or hints at different temporalities within the unified space and singular time of the photograph'.[37] While Joanna Zylinska has proposed that there are some recent examples in which the photography of ruins might offer a way to 're-imagine our relation to the world … in the little time we have left'.[38] One of the examples considered by Zylinska is Tong Lam's *Abandoned Futures* (Figure 6.1).

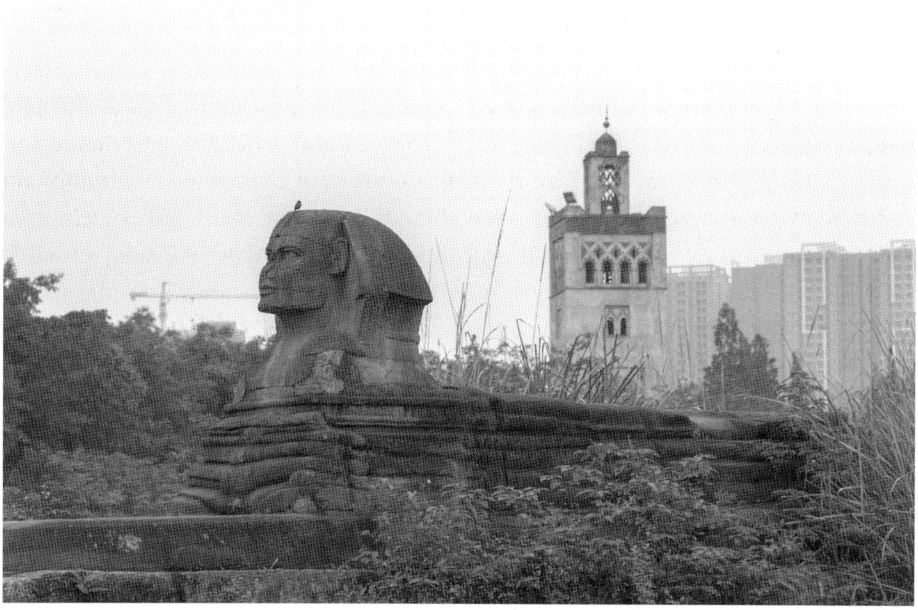

Figure 6.1 Tong Lam, 'An outdated and abandoned theme park in Chengdu, Sichuan Province', 2013. © Tong Lam. Courtesy of the artist.

For Lam the purpose of engaging with sites of ruination through photography is to critique the linear model of time that underpins both capitalism and Chinese state narratives of development as progress. As he has stated, 'Ultimately, I hope [the] debris of modernization ... can be used to construct an alternative set of symbolic repertories. Only then may we be able to begin to reimagine history not as linear progress but as fragments, disintegration, and destruction.'[39] Lam's critical approach is one that asks viewers to 'resist the temptation to view these devastations merely as the inevitable cost of modernization in a way that would further valorize the narrative of progress'.[40] What is key for a number of critics who have responded to Lam's work is the way in which his photographs allow the viewer to adopt what Jason McGrath calls a 'deanthropomorphized gaze' in which 'we cannot help but imagine these scenes as eventually having no human observer at all'.[41] For McGrath the deanthropomorphized gaze at ruins 'reminds us that, no matter how many new objects we produce, consume, and discard, those objects will in many cases far outlive us and the purposes to which we put them. The fake sphinx may go unappreciated by any human observer, but its head will continue to make a fine perch for a bird.'[42] While Zylinska proposes that adopting a deanthropomorphized or post-human gaze offers a way of introducing 'a certain humility into our political frameworks, from which a new image of the world, and of ourselves in this world, can hopefully emerge – although, of course, there are no guarantees'.[43]

Joanna Zylinska: *iEarth*

iEarth (2013) by Joanna Zylinska is a gif animation of four landscapes constructed using a child's diorama kit (Figure 6.2). The cultural practices of shaping and viewing land are foregrounded by the use of everyday consumer technology and the limited options presented by the prefabricated kit that offers only bright green grass and trees from which to build a landscape. These modest everyday processes and practices are used by Zylinksa in order to destabilize our conventional ways of viewing photography and land. As Zylinksa states, the work is a reminder that 'a photographic representation, be it analogue or digital, is always already technological, and that what we think of as "landscape" or "nature" comes to us via the physical and technological effort of capturing, carving, moulding and freezing, by means of a whole sequence of technological tools such as ploughs, tractors, excavators, secateurs, easels, paintbrushes and cameras'.[44]

The central concern of the work is with physically and politically destabilizing our viewing position. As Zylinska has explained, 'The homonymy between the "I" and the "eye" in *iEarth* is not only a commentary on our practices of looking at the world but also on our narcissism when engaging with it'.[45] While the aerial view might mimic a God's eye view, any sense of mastery is undercut by the gif animation which forces us to view the images at a dizzying speed: unable to sustain our gaze, we must either look through squinted eyes or turn away.

We might see Zylinska's work as an example of what T. J. Demos calls 'decolonizing nature'. Demos argues that our concepts of nature and ecology are intricately linked to the history of European colonialism, and the dominant imagery of the

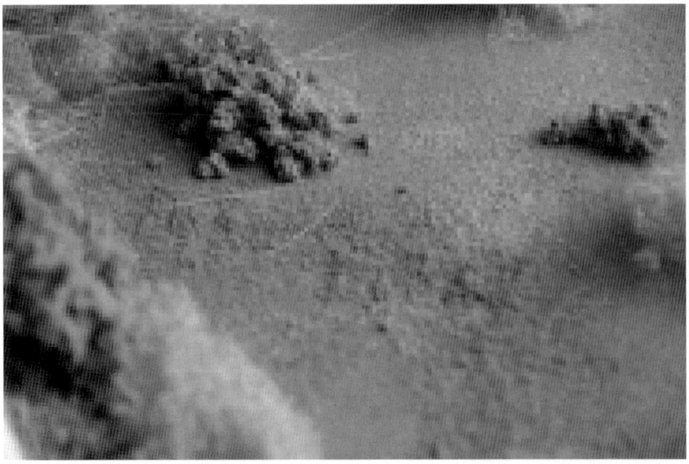

Figure 6.2 Joanna Zylinska, still from *iEarth*, 2013. © Joanna Zylinska. Courtesy of the artist.

Anthropocene reinforces the colonial position that 'we' have indeed mastered nature. Demos thus calls for a new relationship between humankind and earth that is 'based on postcolonial equality between human and nonhuman life'.[46] However, Demos stresses that we must decolonize 'our conceptualization of nature in properly political ways',[47] and this is where art can come into play. For Demos, art holds the promise of initiating the creative perceptional and philosophical shifts necessary in order to comprehend 'ourselves and our relation to the world differently than the destructive traditions of colonizing nature'.[48]

Matthew Buckingham: *The Six Grandfathers, Paha Sapa, in the Year 502,002 C.E.*

Matthew Buckingham's *The Six Grandfathers, Paha Sapa, in the Year 502,002 C.E.* is a digital imagining of Mount Rushmore at a time when the portraits of the four US presidents carved on the mountains will have eroded and become unrecognizable. The photograph is installed alongside a timeline which bookends with work with the dates 66,000,000 BCE and 502,002 CE (Figure 6.3a,b).

Buckingham's work offers a trenchant critique of the meaning of Mount Rushmore often described as 'the shrine of Democracy'. As Mark Godfrey notes, picturing the

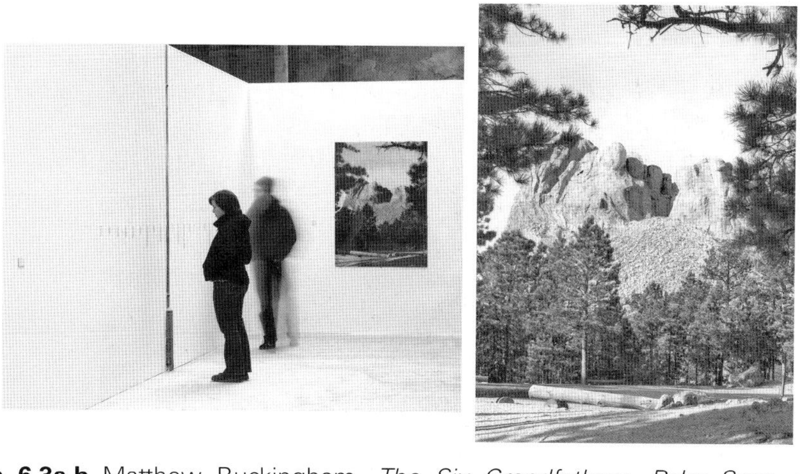

Figure 6.3a,b Matthew Buckingham, *The Six Grandfathers, Paha Sapa, in the Year 502,002 C.E.*, 2002, black and white digital c-print, 31.7 × 23 cm | 12½ × 9 in, Edition 7. *The Six Grandfathers, Paha Sapa, in the Year 502,002 C.E.*, 2002, black and white digital c-print, wall text, 152.5 × 110.75 cm | 60 × 43 2/3 in, Edition 5. Courtesy of the artist and Daniel Marzona, Berlin.

erosion of the sculptures of the presidents George Washington, Thomas Jefferson, Abraham Lincoln and Theodore Roosevelt chosen, respectively, to represent the birth, growth, development and preservation of the United States renders futile efforts 'to inscribe the presidential forms in stone for eternity'.[49] Further, through the device of the timeline Buckingham exchanges the history memorialized at this site with 'a tale of exploitation and commerce'.[50] The timeline, which stretches for thirteen feet, describes how the Sioux were violently removed from the Black Hills (the area they called Paha Sapa) in order to make way for gold mining and other forms of Western expansion. We also learn that Gutzon Borglum, who was employed to carve the presidential portraits, was an active member of the Ku Klux Klan. The timeline continues to detail key moments in the struggles between the Sioux and the US government over the land as well as the tourism boom around Mount Rushmore, before concluding with the projected future return of the mountain to 'nature'.

Buckingham's work goes beyond presenting us with a revisionist history; the extended timeline mobilizes a past and future beyond human time or history, disrupting their authority over this site. To attempt to think of the year 502,002 CE, the viewer must project themselves into a world in which the human may no longer exist and concepts such as history, nation, nature and landscape cease to have any meaning. The scenic foreground of the image with its long shadows and felled tree seems to offer us a seat from which to contemplate our insignificance. However, unlike traditional uses of the picturesque, the place for the human viewer is empty, and the land we see at a distance in the background – the land that we once fought over, claimed mastery over and assigned meaning to – exists apart from us, indifferent to our presence.

As Marija Grech has observed, our attempts to visualize a post-Anthropocene world often fail because we remain 'unable to conceive of a future in which the earth's geological past and the human legacy recorded within it are not read, interpreted and mourned'.[51] Thus, 'In an anthropomorphic sleight-of-hand, the anthropocene restores and revives the notion of the human at the very moment that it appears to annul it.'[52] However, Buckingham's re-visioning does a different kind of work; rather than picture a world without the human, it allows us to 'glimpse the possibility of a world and a future that do not and cannot be made to belong to the human'.[53]

Part Three

Photography, performance and the politics of representation

In this section we will be considering photographers who use performance as a way of drawing attention to how identity is structured though discursive norms that include photographic representations. We will be addressing the politics of representation in relation to gender, race and disability. Across the three chapters we will consider a range of strategies that contemporary photographers have used to challenge traditional codes of representation. In particular, we will be looking at the way in which artists have used self-portraiture and performance as a means of drawing attention to how categories such as gender, race and disability are historically specific cultural constructions. Performance is mobilized by these artists as a way of showing the way in which what we think of as attributes of particular bodies rely on the repeated citation of norms which obscure their construction. While this has been explored in pioneering work of a previous generation of artists, contemporary artists face new challenges in their efforts to interrupt the 'post-ing' of issues of gender, race and disability by neoliberalism.

7
Gender and the selfie

On 19 April 2014 Amalia Ulman uploaded an image to her *Instagram* account. It simply said, 'Part One'. Over the next five months Ulman posted 175 photos including self-portraits and still lives as well as videos documenting a privileged, but not always happy, life of yoga, shopping, cosmetic surgery and boyfriends. What makes this work of art? It does not use skilled photographic techniques above those available to consumer. It appears in an everyday setting and not a gallery. It does not have any indicators of strategic intervention such as the combining of genres that we have seen in previous chapters in relation to portrait and landscape photography. Indeed, it does not seem to be markedly different from the vernacular form it copies. However, the work has since appeared in galleries,[1] is spoken of as art and has even been hailed as 'one of the most original and outstanding artworks of the digital era'.[2] What allows it to do this? Performance is a key way of understanding Ulman's work (Figure 7.1).

In a very simple way Ulman is performing for the camera. This is not a new practice, as Chris Dercon notes: 'Since the invention of the photographic medium in the mid-nineteenth century, the camera has not only been used to document both theatrical and artistic actions, but also to create images that question dominant modes of representation, and the nature of identity'.[3] In order to understand how Ulman's performances for the camera might function as critical dialogue on identity and representation the writings of Judith Butler are key.

Gender trouble

The popular understanding of gender is that it is biological and fixed. However, in her influential book *Gender Trouble: Feminism and the Subversion of Identity*, Judith Butler argues that gender is produced through a series of 'acts' that we repetitively perform over time and that it is through the act of performing gender that it is constituted. Butler uses J. L. Austin's concept of the performative alongside writings by a number of feminist and poststructuralist thinkers to argue that gender is *performative*.

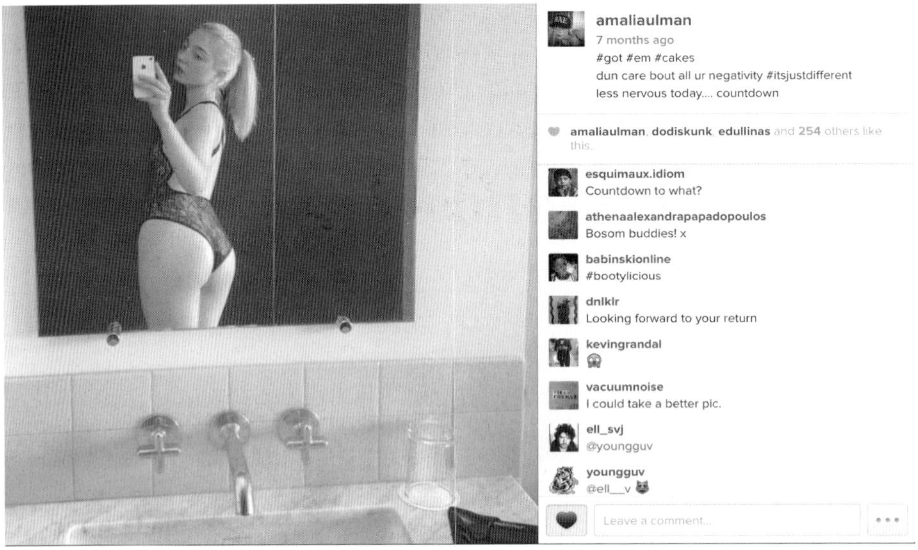

Figure 7.1 Amalia Ulman, *Excellences & Perfections* (Instagram Update, 8 July 2014) (#itsjustdifferent), 2015. Image Courtesy of the artist and Arcadia Missa.

As Butler states in her characteristically complex prose, 'within the inherited discourse of the metaphysics of substance, gender proves to be performative – that is, constituting the identity it is purported to be.'[4]

The distinction between performance and performative is vital to understanding the complexity of Butler's argument. Gender is not performed by subjects in the same way that characters are performed by actors. Gender is not something we can chose to do, or not do, with our biologically distinct bodies. As Alan McKinlay expresses it, 'The individual is not free to choose an identity in the way they might select an outfit. Equally, the individual is not condemned to simply act out a structurally determined identity.'[5] To say that gender is performative means that the subject does not pre-exist the 'doing' that is gender, but is produced through its repetitions. As McKinlay summarizes, 'Performance hinges on the authority of the actor; performativity turns on the reiteration of authoritative constructs.'[6] Or, in Butler's words: 'There is no "one" who takes on a gender norm. On the contrary, this citation of the gender norm is necessary in order to qualify as a "one," to become viable as a "one".'[7]

Although they are distinct, performance has an important role to play in making visible the performativity of gender. The example famously given by Butler is of drag. In drag performances Butler argues that 'we see sex and gender denaturalized by means of a performance which avows their distinctness and dramatizes the cultural mechanism of their fabricated unity'.[8] Elin Diamond's writings are also useful here. In *Performance and Cultural Politics*, Diamond draws on Butler's writings to distinguish between performativity as the reiterative process of 'doing' gender and performance as the individual acts that are the materialization of this process. The importance of performance for Diamond is that 'when performativity materializes as performance in that risky and dangerous negotiation between a doing (a reiteration of norms) and a thing done (discursive conventions that frame our interpretations), between someone's body and the conventions of embodiment we have access to cultural meanings and critique'.[9] That is to say, performances have the potential to make visible the process of performativity. As an example, let's consider the work of Cindy Sherman.

Cindy Sherman

Over a career spanning thirty years Cindy Sherman has assumed the role of various female identities found in Western culture. The central motif of Sherman's work is the serial self-portrait. However, this description is perhaps misleading for few of her images assume the conventional format of the portrait, nor do they serve the traditional function of portraiture, that of presenting the self. As Douglas Crimp has summarized, 'Her photographs reverse the terms of art and autobiography. They use art not to reveal the artist's true self but to show the self as an imaginary construct.'[10] Sherman's strategies of performance, repetition and disguise are widely theorized in relation to the constructed nature of identity, and in particular gendered identity.

For many theorists, Sherman's early series *Untitled Film Stills* (1977–80) remains a key work. This series of sixty-nine black-and-white photographs is regarded by many as a landmark in feminist and postmodern art.[11] The political import of Sherman's performances in this series has led to considerable debate among feminist critics.[12] What emerges as a key concern in these debates is whether the Sherman's use of gender stereotypes is politically progressive or if it is reductive, serving only to entrench these stereotypes further. Butler's work allows us to approach these debates differently. Butler's understanding of gender as produced through a set of material practices is one that recognizes that dominant formations of gender cannot simply be 'undone' by positive representations as these leave gender as a category unchallenged. Instead of challenging particular iterations of gender, she argues that agency lies in repetition.

Butler proposes that the possibility of re-signification is opened up by the compulsory repetition of gender's norms: because the individual references norms in both seeking to achieve them and seeking to contest them, repetition produces both gender and the possibility of its undoing. As Butler expresses it, 'If a subject were constituted once and for all, there would be no possibility of a reiteration of those constituting conventions or norms. That the subject is that which must be constituted again and again implies that it is open to formations that are not fully constrained in advance. Hence, the insistence of finding agency as resignification.'[13] Indeed, what Butler calls 'subversive repetition' only exists within the identity categories that require compulsory repetition. As Alecia Youngblood Jackson explains, 'It is when we are *within* the categories that we can be *against* them because the limits of a category are intelligible only *within* the rules governing that category, *within* the constituted effects of that category.'[14] It is not possible to stand outside of the discourses that constitute us, but by exposing the *functioning* of discourses it is possible to derive agency. This is why, for Butler, repetition is central to a politics of performativity.

If we return to *Untitled Film Stills* we can see that the repetitions of Sherman's self-portraits show not only that it is through a process of repetition that gendered subjectivity is produced but also that these repetitions are distinct. The category of 'woman' is varied; however, certain repetitions are dominant, and these produce a cumulative consistency to the category. Over seeking a 'positive' iteration of gendered identity, it is the act of repeating identity so that it cannot become fixed or essentialized that offers the key to a progressive politics for both Sherman and Butler.

Amalia Ulman's work would seem to share these concerns. Indeed, she has stated: 'I wanted to prove that femininity is a construction, and not something biological or inherent to any woman.'[15] Like Sherman's work, *Excellences & Perfections* has drawn criticism from some for the way that it seems to simply reproduce stereotyped images of women.[16] However, others have argued that 'Ulman continues the artistic tradition, established by women artists, of examining the connections between gender, art, the gaze, and the body, and her investigation breaks new ground in terms of how these ideas re-emerge in the digital age.'[17] In order to understand Ulman's work fully, we need to situate it in relation to not only social media and digital technology but also post-feminism and a particular iteration of contemporary subjectivity: that of the girl.

The girl

In keeping with the discursive approach outlined by Butler, the girl should not be understood in terms of biology – a young woman – but rather, a particular subject position that has emerged with neoliberalism. A key text that examines the emergence of the girl as a privileged subjectivity is *Preliminary Materials for a Theory of the Young-Girl* by a collective of French scholars calling themselves Tiqqun.[18] First published in France in 1999, it appeared in English translation in 2012 and has attracted critical praise, criticism and parody.[19]

In their introduction, Tiqqun argue that in order to forestall the threat of revolution, capitalism incorporated those who were not central to production by involving them in consumption. These previously excluded subjects were called upon to not only consume products but also see their consumption as a form of liberation. Tiqqun thus propose that the girl is a historically specific subject position marked by a particular relation to capital. To indicate that the young girl is a performative and not a biological category, Tiqqun use the neologism 'Young-Girl'.

While Tiqqun's writings have attracted criticism, there is nonetheless a consensus that the girl is an emergent subject position in contemporary culture. The work of writers such as Rosamund Gill and Angela McRobbie who are concerned with foregrounding the gendered impact of neoliberalism is important here. These writers are interested in mapping the complex ways in which feminism has a renewed presence in social and cultural life but only as something that belongs to the past. 'Post-feminism' is the term used to describe the assumption, articulated in a number of different ways, that gender inequality has been resolved, and thus the need for continued feminist action is a thing of the past. In post-feminism inequality between men and women is acknowledged only to be disavowed, or rather, it is displaced by being accounted for in individual terms. For example, in post-feminist discourse the pay gap between men and women is not a structural inequality but the result of individual choices or flaws: the choice to have a family; the lack of ambition necessary to earn a promotion. As Gill writes, in post-feminist culture, 'women are interpellated as active, autonomous and self-reinventing subjects, whose lives are the outcome of individual choice and agency.'[20]

The grammar of individualism that predominates in post-feminism displaces previous notions of the social and the political. Thus, a key concern for feminist theorists such as Gill and McRobbie is the way in which post-feminism produces a particular kind of female subject that appears to be the realization of the feminist project, but without being inscribed within a collective context. Here terms central to the feminist project such as empowerment have become commodified and reconfigured as properties of individuals – something that women achieve through consumer choices and not through organizing politically. As Gill writes, 'Using key liberal terms, such as equality, opportunity, and free choice, while displacing and replacing their content, neoliberal feminism forges a feminist subject who is not only individualised but entrepreneurial in the sense that she is oriented towards optimising her resources through incessant calculation, personal initiative and innovation.'[21]

In post-feminism, choice, agency and freedom are commodified and remain firmly lodged in traditionally feminine products such as make-up and clothes. As Mary Celeste Kearney notes, the 'twist here is, within postfeminist logic, women are doing it for themselves rather than men. That is, we are agentically "choosing" to participate and find pleasure for ourselves in the same consumer-driven, hyperfeminine, glamorized body projects long used to construct us as passive spectacles for the male gaze.'[22] Indeed, despite a rhetoric centred on freedom and empowerment, the fashioning of female body in contemporary culture continues to be centred on highly normative ideas of what constitutes a desirable body. What distinguishes contemporary discourses of femininity is not only the rhetoric of choice that accompanies these practices but also that they are now inscribed within the logic of the perpetual makeover in which femininity is produced through a process of *continual* improvement and refashioning in service of an appropriately feminine self that is never quite achieved.[23]

This logic might be seen in the extension of the procedures deemed appropriate for women to participate in, for example, the mainstreaming of surgical procedures such as breast augmentation, liposuction and Botox. In addition, established practices such as applying make-up have undergone an intensification and extension. As an example of the way in which make-up now includes both more specialist products and more exacting routines Elias and Gill give the example of Mac's eight-step routine for colouring the lips.[24] These demanding and time-consuming procedures are championed under the banner of post-feminist liberation in which women are 'freed' to 'invest' in their appearance and bodies as ongoing projects, encapsulated by the long-running L'Oreal campaign tagline, 'Because You're Worth It.'[25] What is often obscured by these aspirational and celebratory discourses is the way in which 'the postfeminist sensibility requires not only regular self-surveillance, but also self-regulation through the consumption of products that promise to correct whatever flaws might be present, whether physical or socioeconomic.'[26] This underlying demand is tied to the economic context of neoliberalism in which it is the flexible and autonomous subject – the subject who is able see constant change in work, income and lifestyle not as forms of insecurity, but as 'opportunities' – who is prized. As such, new modes of subjecthood centred on labour, measurement, comparison and self-transformation are emerging. Young women occupy a key position within this new discourse; indeed, they became its exemplary subjects. McRobbie uses the phrase 'the perfect' to describe the space of subjectivity occupied by the girl in contemporary culture.

The perfect

In 'Notes on the Perfect',[27] McRobbie explores the way in which the notion of 'perfection' has entered into the discourse of contemporary femininity. For McRobbie, the perfect designates the heightened form of self-regulation that young women and girls are asked to adopt as a key tenant of their subjectivity. Under the regime of the perfect, young women's bodies come under hitherto unprecedented degrees of scrutiny. McRobbie uses the term 'the perfect' to reflect the seriousness with which the goals of successful domesticity and successful sexuality are pursued 'on a par with taking an exam':[28]

> Various technologies bring the perfect into life, or vitalise it as an everyday form of self-measurement. How well did I do today? Did I manage to eat fewer calories? Did I eat more healthily? Did I get to the gym? Did I achieve what I aimed to achieve at work? … Did I maintain my good looks and my sexually attractive and well-groomed body?[29]

McRobbie argues that the regime of the perfect replaces domestic labour for young girls. Although the discourse is markedly different, the constraints of heteronormative femininity remain firmly entrenched, and the work of the perfect is nonetheless mundane, routine and does not confer status on the doer. Indeed, the labour of contemporary femininity, just like the labour of housework or childcare, remains a form of daily unpaid labour that women are expected to perform or face social repercussions.[30] We might see *Excellences & Perfections* as an attempt to make visible the space of the perfect.

Amalia Ulman: *Excellences & Perfections*

Ulman's work is situated at the interlocking logics of post-feminism, neoliberalism and self-help culture. Using the construction and ongoing maintenance of an *Instagram* account to illustrate the way in which young women must navigate the regime of the perfect and engage with the often contradictory narratives of gender and sexuality that have emerged under neoliberalism.

The selfie is a key component of Ulman's work, and it should be distinguished from the repetitive self-portrait that was mobilized as a critical device by Sherman. The selfie on social media sites serves as both a form of self-presentation and as an integral part of the young girl's self-monitoring and self-management. As Anne Burns has succinctly stated, the selfie 'occurs at the nexus of disciplinary discourses of photography, gender, and social media'.[31]

Here it is useful to briefly return to Foucault's writings on power. Foucault does not characterize power as purely repressive – rather, power produces identities, activities and ways of thinking as much as it constrains them. Power is diffuse, and the individual positions themselves within, and adheres to, certain discourses by regulating their acts, manners, and conduct with reference to dominant norms or what are called hegemonic ideals. This is a process that relies on self-discipline and the negotiation of social and cultural norms. Therefore, we might better describe the selfie as a strategy of self-representation that has a formative as well as a repressive function.

Sarah Gram has argued that the selfie is a way for young girls to both participate in femininity and document that participation.[32] Indeed, we might see social media sites like *Instagram* and *Facebook* as offering an opportunity for the public recognition of the previously invisible labour of femininity. However, as the comments posted in response to Ullman's images show, the subject position of the girl is one that is charged and difficult to negotiate successfully.[33]

In addition to appropriate feminine behaviour in relation to dress, conduct and sexuality, the young girl must also maintain her authenticity. On social media, femininity is an ongoing project that must be enacted in relation to the norm; however, if it is reproduced too exactly, in too formulaic[34] a manner the subject will be deemed inauthentic. Thus, contemporary subjects must continually offer new iterations of the girl. There are a number of responses to Ulman's work that show the hostility that is directed at subjects who do not fulfil these demands. These range from comments such as the dismissive 'You're an idiot with way too much money and no real interests'[35] to the sexually charged hostility that accompanied the images of Ulman in tears.[36]

Ulman's work clearly marks out the space of the perfect, but does it offer critique? The most common description of *Excellences & Perfections* is as a hoax, a characterization which seems to suggest that it has limited impact as a critique. However, as Emma Maguire has observed, there is an object of critique in a hoax – the audience: 'It doesn't necessarily matter what the author's intentions are in perpetrating the hoax, what's really interesting about hoaxes is that they expose cultural assumptions, they unsettle tropes and conventions of life narrative, and they make norms visible.'[37] In revealing her posts to be fictional, Ulman asks the viewer to reconsider how they read and consume such images. As such, we can see that, rather than a critique of the *Instagram* Girl, Ulman seeks to critique of the discourses and technologies that produce and sustain her. It is interesting to note here that many of the critical responses distanced themselves from this critique by locating its target as audience of which *they* were not a part.[38]

A further aspect that is overlooked in Ulman's work is the way in which her performance is not just of femininity but of whiteness. In her mapping of the contours of contemporary girlhood, Ulman asks us to be attentive not only to the complex narratives of gender that emerge under neoliberalism but also to the way in which the subjectivity of the girl is raced. While the popular rhetoric of post-feminism celebrates the girl's capacity for agency, liberated (hetero)sexuality and financial independence, it rarely acknowledges that the agency of girlhood is not an equally distributed privilege.

8

Race, history and time

In this chapter we will be looking at photographers who use performance as a means of both challenging the way we think about race and engaging with how racial thinking is produced through the photographic record. What does it mean to think about race in terms of performativity? While recognizing that there are important differences, a number of critics have used Judith Butler's writings on gender as performative to think about how we are formed as racial subjects.[1] For example, Nadine Ehlers has reworded Judith Butler's seminal statement on gender to propose that

> there is no racial subject that can be said to exist prior to power and that is then retroactively acted upon by power. Rather, the racial subject comes into being precisely through their discursively constituted identity *as raced*. In this way, then, there is no subject that can be viewed as 'black' prior to the discursive mark that designates them as such.[2]

Understanding race as performative engages with the way in which race as a category is discursively produced, how particular iterations of this discourse become dominant and how certain bodies come to be assigned particular meanings. It is important to stress that a performative approach differs from seeing race as a performance which would suggest race is only related to bodily difference. A performative approach is one that recognizes the complex ways in which racial discourse groups together attribute which do not have a natural relationship such that 'a series of traits linked to whiteness (civilized/intelligent/moral/hardworking/clean) and blackness (savage/instinctual/simple/licentious/lazy/dirty) have been concatenated in the service of specific social hierarchies'.[3] Here race is understood not as a static biologically given attribute but as an ongoing disciplinary practice which requires subjects to reiterate the norms associated with their particular racial designation through bodily acts such as speech, dress and gestures.

While we might think of how we dress or speak to be individual choices, what gives racial discourse its tenacity is the way in which it is reproduced in both individual acts and material practices embedded within specific institutional sites of power such as schools, hospitals and courtrooms where bodies are routinely classified and hierarchized in terms of race. It is through these everyday enactments of race as difference that the demarcations of race appear as natural. However, because race must be continually enacted there arises the possibility for challenging the hegemonic norms that hold individuals in place as raced subjects. As John T. Warren writes,

> The generative power of performativity – the potential of locating race in its own process of reiteration – offers us the possibility of interrupting the discursive process of racial formation, as well as the naturalization and sedimentation of those racial categories. The ability to see how race gets accomplished in everyday life might just present the possibility of constituting race differently. Performativity makes space for possibility and in that lies its strength.[4]

While Butler's writings are important for establishing the framework of identity as performative, Warren, Ehlers and others have shown that it is necessary to be attentive to the distinctive mechanisms through which race operates. These include the complicated ways in which norms of gender, sexuality, class and citizenship are articulated through race. The examples we consider in this chapter use photography and performance to show how race is not an isolated 'truth' about the self but a discursive construction.

Shadi Ghardian: *Qajar*

Shadi Ghadirian's series *Qajar* (1998) is a set of thirty-three sepia-toned photographs in which Ghadirian recreates the painted backdrops, frontal poses and Qajar-style dress characteristic of late nineteenth- and early twentieth-century Iranian studio portraits. However, many of the photographs contain an item, such as a *Pepsi* can, sunglasses or telephone, which is both out of place and out of time in the image (Figure 8.1).

A number of critics have read these works as a comment on the tensions between tradition and modernity in Iranian society. However, Melissa Heer argues that such a reading – in which the contemporary objects are aligned with modernity and the studio set and costume with tradition – is too straightforward and ignores the politics of time at stake in the series. Heer proposes that 'instead of the image representing two separate eras or times, it rather represents a performance'.[5] For Heer the chronological ambiguities in Ghadirian's work are a critical device that asks us to reflect upon 'how time itself is arranged and performed'.[6] In particular, Heer is interested in exploring the way that Ghadirian's portraits direct us to the role that time plays in the production of categories of difference. As Heer writes, in *Qajar* 'time, and its relationship to "tradition and modernity," is held up to a more a scrutinizing lens' in order to 'unsettle the conventions of a progressive, linear, coherent model of time and the categories that depend upon its framework'.[7]

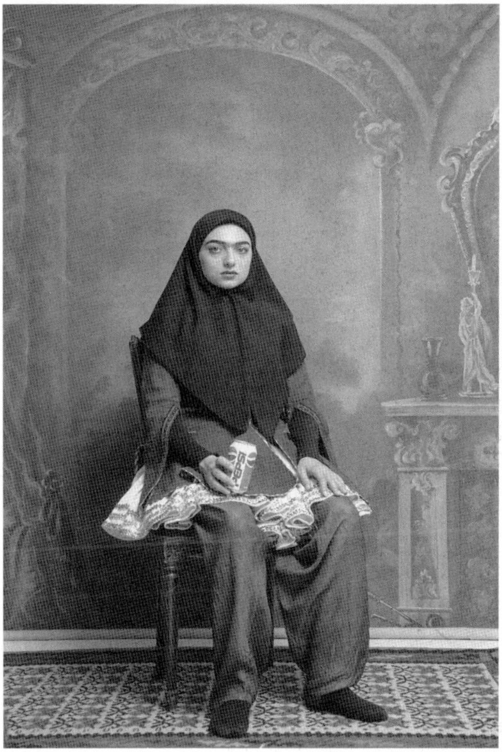

Figure 8.1 Shadi Ghadirian, *Qajar* #1, 1998. © Shadi Ghadirian. Courtesy of the artist.

Time might seem marginal compared to race or gender when considering identity; however, time plays a key role in making certain iterations of identity seem natural. Most simply, certain ways of being acquire their status through precedence – the understanding that 'things have always been this way'. As Butler reminds us, performativity does not refer just to particular acts but also to the reproduction of norms which is a material accomplishment within a specific temporal frame: '*There is no reproduction of the social world that is not at the same time a reproduction of those norms that govern the intelligibility of the body in space and time.*'[8]

However, in her writings on 'temporal drag' Elizabeth Freeman draws attention to the way in which linear time is privileged in Butler's account. Freeman argues that, for Butler, those repetitions with a difference that are seen to be transformative are always 'future-orientated': 'Repetitions with any backwards-looking force ... are merely "citational," and can only thereby consolidate the authority'[9] of current formations of subjectivity. Noting the 'interesting threat that the genuine *past*-ness of the past sometimes makes to the political present',[10] Freeman challenges Butler's account by proposing that backwards-orientated performances may be just, if not more, unsettling than future ones. For Freeman, performances that reference those iterations that we used to believe in but now seem alien offer a way of destabilizing our investment in current formations. Freeman uses the term 'temporal drag' to describe a strategy that uses 'disruptive anachronisms'[11] to challenge hegemonic formations. Freeman describes performances in this mode as being neither reconstructions nor deconstructions, but those in which we simultaneously experience 'minor failures of historical authenticity and the sudden *punctum* of the present'.[12] For Freeman the value of such performances is that they might 'work against the neoconservative tendency to consign to the irretrievable past anything that challenges a dominant vision of the future'.[13]

Just as gender is premised on male and female as binary terms, our understanding of time relies on the binary past/present. By placing past and present within the same frame, Ghadirian draws attention to the ways in which gender and race are produced in relation to discourses of modernization and colonialism. In light of Freeman's argument we might see that the dissonances of Ghadirian's atemporal performances serve to challenge the assumption of gender and race as timeless, universal categories.

Omar Victor Diop: *Project Diaspora*

Project Diaspora (2014) by Omar Victor Diop is a series of self-portraits in which he restages paintings from the fifteenth to the nineteenth centuries. The subjects of these portraits are men of African descent who lived in Europe, the Americas and South Asia who, although many are unknown today, all achieved social recognition within their lifetime. In his reconstructions Diop draws not only on the history of Western art but also on the colonial archive, as well as his own family's collection of portrait albums as a means of reflecting on how contemporary racial identity is structured through personal, social, historical and cultural encounters.

Diop's restagings are both accurate and irreverent copies. In each photograph Diop approximates the clothes and background of the original and the titles remain the same; however, he makes no effort look like the sitter. Further, each image includes an incongruous prop associated with football. Our example will be 'Jean-Baptiste Belley (1746–1805)' (Figure 8.2).

To begin it is important to understand the subject and the painting on which Diop's restaging is based. Jean-Baptiste Belley was born in Senegal in 1746. Sold as a slave at the age of two, he went on to become an educated man who bought his own freedom. He served as a captain and commander in the French Revolutionary Army and was the first man of African descent to hold national elective office when he held the position of deputy to the French National Convention for the colony of Saint-Domingue from 1794 to 1797. Although slavery was abolished in France the year that Belley took up this post, this was short-lived. Napoleon Bonaparte seized power in 1799 and reinstated slavery in May 1802. This was followed by a number of new

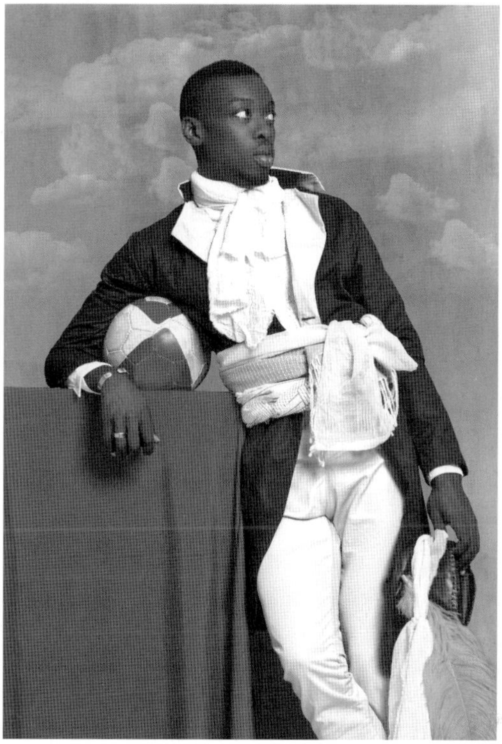

Figure 8.2 Omar Victor Diop, Jean-Baptiste Belley (1746–1805), from *Project Diaspora*, 2014.

Jean-Baptiste Belley was a native of Senegal, born on the Island of Gorée and former slave from Saint-Domingue in the French West Indies who bought his freedom with his savings. During the period of the French Revolution, he became a member of the National Convention and the Council of Five Hundred of France.
He was also known as Mars.
Original painting by Girodet.

laws including the dismissal of all black officers from the army. Belley was imprisoned without charges or trial in the military hospital Belle-Ile-en-Mer where he died on 6 August 1806.

Diop's photograph is based on Anne-Louis Girodet's painting, *Portrait of Citizen Jean-Baptiste Belley, Ex-Representative of the Colonies* (1797). This well-known painting depicts Belley leaning against a bust of the philosopher Abb Guillaume Raynal. Belley is painted in an honorific style, and Girodet uses the signifiers of wealth and learning attributed to European nobility. That an African was depicted in the honorific style by a European artist marks a remarkable moment in the history of painting, and the work is widely interpreted as symbolizing the French Revolutionary ideals of liberty and equality and as a celebration of the abolition of slavery in the

French colonies. However, it is important to note that the abolition of slavery in France was 'less a result of Revolutionary ideals than of political exigency'.[14] Slave rebellions in Saint-Domingue and threats to the French colony from both the Spanish and the British meant the French troops needed the support of the slave population. Thus, on 29 August 1793 the French commissioner in Saint-Domingue unilaterally declared the abolition of slavery. With the abolition of slavery there was a need for new forms of distinguishing between subjects. As Nicholas Mirzoeff notes,

> Under slavery people were legally different. Now a new means of classifying human bodies was devised. An extraordinary volume of scientific and artistic work was produced in the effort to define and make visible the supposed eternal differences of race. Everything from skin colour to the shape of the skull, nose and breasts, and every aspect of culture was used as evidence to prove that humans were biologically distinct.[15]

This sheds new light on the meaning of Girodet's painting; rather than a celebration of liberty and equality, we can see that it reflects the concerns of French Imperialism with 'defining and creating an image of a new colonial subject'.[16] As Mirzoeff has summarized, 'It is a remarkable evocation of the tensions of the period expressed through one person's body.'[17]

Here it should be noted that the markers of status that appear in the painting are modified in significant ways in order to distinguish between their traditional use. At first glance, Belley's representation is that of a dignified French citizen during the Directorial period. However, critics have drawn attention to the way in which the work is marked by a subtle feeling of theatre and excess where 'the deputy's costume can also be read as too new and brightly coloured, the watch at his waist as a fraction too polished, and the *chamois* of the trousers as too clinging, too velvety, and as a shade too yellow.'[18] In this way, the meaning of the signs of privilege that appear in the painting is modified. Rather than symbols of authority, they are depicted as fashionable accessories and thus shown to reflect an acquired status rather than an innate quality. Hence we can see that 'in Girodet's painting French civilization is inscribed onto the body of the black deputy, but in such a way as to convey the message that the essence of that civilization is still lacking'.[19]

In Girodet's presentation of Belley we might see an example of how black subjects are required to adopt white norms of style and behaviour. Catherine Rottenberg argues that this is a key distinction that we must be attentive to when understanding race as performative. While both gender and racial norms are sustained by hierarchical oppositions – male/female and white/black – there is a difference in the identifications subjects are asked to make in respect of these binaries: 'Identification with "being a woman" almost always implies (and is inextricably intertwined with) the desire to "be a woman," that is, a desire to live up to the norms of femininity in a particular symbolic order. Femininity is posited as desirable and as something that "women" should approximate; wanting to "be a woman" is coded as positive.'[20] In comparison, Rottenberg argues that 'black-identified subjects, in order to sustain a nonmarginal existence, are compelled and encouraged to privilege and thus "desire-to-be white," that is, to live up to attributes associated with whiteness'.[21] Therefore, Rottenberg proposes, in racial discourse there is 'really only one norm'.[22] It should be further noted that whiteness paradoxically remains something that cannot be achieved because racial discourse 'assumes that "non-whiteness" has inherent characteristics that preclude black subjects from ever really becoming "white"'.[23]

In Diop's restaging we see the bust of the philosopher Abb Guillaume Raynal replaced with a football. This change signals that the concerns of the work are firmly in the present day, and Diop himself has located the meaning of the work in relation to contemporary narratives of race and citizenship. When asked if the images were self-portraits, Diop replies: 'I'm not that comfortable with that term, no. They are metaphorical portraits in which the idea of black identity is central.'[24] Here, football is employed as a means of exploring contradictory ideas about race in contemporary culture. As Diop has stated in an interview,

> Soccer is an interesting global phenomenon that for me often reveals where society is in terms of race. When you look at the way that the African soccer royalty is perceived in Europe, there is a very interesting blend of glory, hero-worship and exclusion. Every so often, you get racist chants or banana skins thrown on the pitch and the whole illusion of integration is shattered in the most brutal way. It's that kind of paradox I am investigating in the work.[25]

The paradox that Diop refers to is one that is embedded in the postcolonial history of citizenship in Britain. In 1981, the British Nationality Act signalled a decisive break with the previous model of citizenship. British citizenship, once enshrined in liberal ideas of 'social justice, welfare and mutual obligation',[26] become one in which the individual citizen must 'demonstrate or buy their "right" to state protection and care'.[27] As Aihwa Ong writes,

> The elements that we think of as coming together to create citizenship – rights, entitlements, territoriality, a nation – are becoming disarticulated and rearticulated with forces set into motion by market forces. On the one hand, citizenship elements such as entitlements and benefits are increasingly associated with neoliberal criteria, so that mobile individuals who possess human capital or expertise are highly valued and can exercise citizenship-like claims in diverse locations. Meanwhile, citizens who are judged not to have such tradable competence or potential become devalued and thus vulnerable to exclusionary practices.[28]

Here the portrait that Diop draws upon is particularly significant; while the painting is titled *Portrait of Citizen Jean-Baptiste Belley, Ex-Representative of the Colonies*, we have seen how the presentation of Belley shows his status as a citizen to be marked by exclusions, exceptions and limits. In turn, Diop's work addresses migration in relation to the 'hierarchies of belonging'[29] that attend contemporary notions of citizenship. While these replay aspects of colonialism this is often obscured by the understanding, ushered in by neoliberalism, that we are living in a post-race era.

As an economic and political ideology concerned with issues such as market relations, deregulation and privatization, neoliberalism would seem to be 'colourblind'. However, a number of critics have mapped the way in which race invisibly permeates the project of neoliberalism. As Darrel Enck-Wanzer has observed, in spite of a dominant rhetoric of multiculturalism and racial diversity, neoliberalism is 'marked, first and foremost, by an active suppression of "race" as a legitimate topic or term of public discourse and public policy'.[30] Kevin Feldman has similarly argued that the post-racial 'names the condition within which racism's structural violence operates flexibly both within and beyond the logic of the colour line, while routinely disavowing its properly racial character'.[31] Racism is expunged in a number of ways, but principally through the assertion that race no longer matters. Here 'racism is treated as an anachronism'[32] and only permitted to appear in the form of specific incidents concerning racist individuals, something that is therefore beneath public concern and outside the remit of institutions or political systems to address. As Noah De Lissovy has summarized, 'Insisting on race-neutrality at the level of law and policy, neoliberalism in effect privatizes racism.'[33] In this way, race is both 'extricated from the sociality that gives it form and meaning'[34] and rejected as the basis for structural inequalities.

Instead of using explicitly racial boundaries, contemporary populations are divided into 'worthy' and 'unworthy' on the basis of adherence to neoliberal scripts. Here social mobility is understood to be determined by individual qualities such as ambition, determination and risk-taking such that self-reliance and individual entrepreneurialism become the new markers of belonging. As Jodi Melamed observes, neoliberalism ushers in a 'differentiated experience of citizenship' where 'governments protect those who are valuable to capital, whether formally citizens or not, and … render vulnerable those who are not valuable within the circuits of capital, whether formally citizens or not'.[35] In short, in the neoliberal era, the desirable migrant is constructed as someone who subscribes to market values regardless of their race. As such, neoliberalism creates new privileged subjects. Although traditional categories of racial identity can occupy both sides of the privilege/stigma divide, racialized scripts nonetheless continue to determine their positioning *within* these new discourses of citizenship. Here, the figure of the migrant, as racially scripted form of personhood, is an example of the way in which neoliberalism 'confers privileges on some racial subjects (the white liberal, the multicultural American, the fully assimilable black, the racial entrepreneur) while stigmatizing others (the "born again" racist, the overly race conscious, the racial grievant, the terrorist, the illegal)'.[36]

In Diop's work the inclusion of a contemporary object (a football) and the improvised nature of his costume are used as a means of engaging with the demands placed on migrant subjects in the present day. In particular, it shows that the relationship between 'the state and the black subject, in many instances, is still a highly contested political reality'.[37]

As we saw in our discussion of Girodet's painting, the theatrical presentation of the black body served to show the colonial subject as out of place. Diop's restaging comments upon the way in which African players find themselves caught between the promise of a global meritocracy and the reality of tightly enforced social, cultural and legal boundaries of inclusion and exclusion. More complexly, because some populations are subjected to conditional movement, while others circulate freely, neoliberalism can be seen to produce 'contradictory spatio-temporal configurations'[38]. Here as Beth Buggenhagen has argued, 'Diop's use of football props point to dislocations of migrants in space and time.'[39] Despite neoliberalism's promise that racism belongs to the past, Diop shows that the migrant is a subject position fraught with ambivalences. Over the promises of post-identity meritocracy *Project Disapora* asks us to consider how the dynamics of colonial racism are relevant to our time and to remain attentive to the new forces that divide, rank, order and exclude.

Nona Faustine: *White Shoes*

Nona Faustine's *White Shoes* (2012–ongoing) is a series of self-portraits in which Faustine poses at sites around New York City linked to its past involvement in the slave trade. In many of the photographs she is naked except for a pair of white shoes – a reference to the United States' roots in white patriarchy. In some she additionally wears shackles on her wrists and, in more recent images, a skirt slip. Faustine's poetic captions and use of her body direct us to a set of concerns that includes the black body, history, and gender.

While Diop's and Ghardian's imagery is playful, Faustine's work is direct and confrontational. As critics have noted, 'There is a visceral punch to Faustine's images.'[40] Here the tone is one of 'terrible vulnerability ... and courageous defiance'.[41] For example, in an image titled 'From Her Body Sprang Their Greatest Wealth', Faustine stands naked on a box at the site of the colonial slave market that existed on Wall Street. Her hands are clasped in front of her and she is wearing shackles. The wide-angle lens means that her body both appears larger than life in relation to the cars, yet is dwarfed by the buildings. There is a taxi behind Faustine and repair marks to the road that draw a set of parallel lines linking her body and the path of the car. Susan Silas has argued that the taxi is central to the meaning of the photograph because 'it shows the artist as visible, not just to us, but to others within the frame of the photograph. It makes her performance in the street public, makes her vulnerability and seen-ness literal.'[42] Through these elements, Faustine comments not only on the suppressed history of slavery in New York but also on the vulnerability of the black body in day-to-day life in contemporary America. A number of critics have made connections to the recent shootings of black men by police in the city. As Danielle Moodie-Mills writes,

> The imagery of her standing naked on the steps of City Hall and on Wall Street with the past juxtaposed against the present, where we like to believe we've evolved from such savage treatment of other humans – and yet not too far from these locations black bodies lay dead in the streets, shot to death, strangled of life because of the perceived threat of their very existence.[43]

By connecting events that are seen to belong to the past to current events of state violence, Faustine asks us to see both slavery and police killings of unarmed black men as belonging to an ongoing system of economically predicated racialized violence.

The writings of Henry Giroux are useful here. Giroux has theorized contemporary race politics in the United States in terms of disposability: 'As the social state is displaced by the market, a new kind of politics is emerging in which some lives, if not whole groups, are seen as disposable and redundant.'[44] Giroux argues that, under neoliberalism, 'the category "waste" includes no longer simply material goods but also human beings.'[45] Those who are unable to participate in the global economy because they are unable to make a living or consume goods are 'reified as products without any value to be disposed of'.[46] For Giroux, the first task in engaging with and challenging neoliberalism involves making clear how it functions as a historical and social construction. Key for Giroux is not just examining the social and cultural effects of neoliberalism but also addressing the 'kind of history it ignores'.[47] As such, he argues that 'it is crucial that the history of slavery, civil rights, racial politics, and ongoing modes of struggle at the level of everyday life be remembered and used pedagogically to challenge the historical amnesia that feeds neoliberalism's ahistorical claim to power and the continuity of its claims to common sense'.[48]

In her article 'Visualizing Disposability: Photographing Neoliberal Conflict in the United States' Clorinde Peters draws on Giroux's work to argue that the challenge for photography is not only to make the disposable or historically excluded visible (as is the goal of traditional social documentary photography) but also to picture 'the processes and effects of disposability itself'.[49] Peters argues that a practice that seeks only to correct or reverse the public visibility of its subjects allows the history of their erasure to remain 'hidden from sight, and with it the means necessary to remain historically literate and accountable'.[50] In Faustine's work, we might see a powerful example of the visualizing of disposability called for by Peters.

The three artists considered in this chapter have used historical time as a means of drawing attention to the way in which disavowed histories continue to impact upon the present. In this way, they have each sought to disrupt the hegemonic discourses concerning race, history and time.

9

Performativity and disability

In this chapter we will be looking at work by photographic artists who engage with issues of identity and representation through performances of disability. We have already explored how artists have used performance and photography as a means of 'troubling' representations of gender and race; however, that disability could be understood as performative is a contentious statement. Disability is a complex category that is used to describe a wide range of physical, mental and emotional conditions. As Petra Kuppers notes, 'The term "disability" is problematic, since it designates identity for a wide range of different forms of embodiment, and because it continues to be used as a tool of subjection.'[1] However, for the artists discussed in this chapter, performing disability offers a vital way of critiquing dominant understandings of disability and illness.

In understanding how disability might be understood in terms of performance, the writings of Rosemarie Garland-Thompson are useful. Garland-Thompson proposes that we understand disability as 'a culturally fabricated narrative of the body, similar to what we understand as the fictions of race and gender'.[2] In her article 'The Story of My Work: How I Became Disabled', Garland-Thompson recounts that 'I became disabled … similarly to the way I had become a woman'.[3] As with the discursive understandings of gender and race that we have already explored, it is important to be attentive to the material effects of the 'culturally fabricated narrative' of disability. For example, the ways in which the differentiating and marking of bodies both produces subjects and legitimatises the distribution of resources, status, and power within a biased social and architectural environment'.[4]

Just as subjects are required to perform gender and race with respect to the dominant understanding of them, the behaviours permitted of disabled subjects are tightly circumscribed. As Kuppers writes,

> Disabled people have been forced to act in pre-determined scripts: the child with short arms has to parade in front of an audience of doctors, the woman who hears voices has to faint in the arms of the male psychiatry professor, or drown as Ophelia in flowers and water. The person with cancer has to see her or his body imaged as a battleground, and the person with AIDS has to see his or her body colonised as a metaphor rather than understood to be a lived experience.[5]

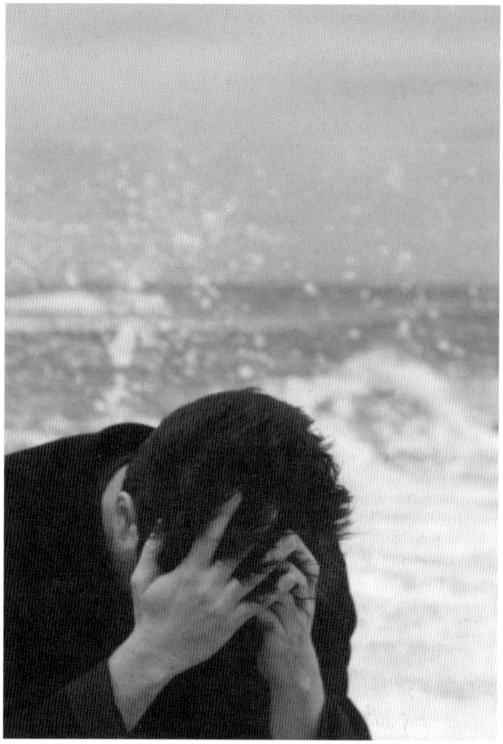

Figure 9.1 David Horvitz, *Mood Disorder*, 2012–ongoing. Openly circulating high resolution image file. Courtesy of the artist & ChertLüdde, Berlin.

David Horvitz's *Mood Disorder* (2015) takes the cultural scripts for depression as its subject. In this work Horvitz took a self-portrait of himself holding his head in his hands with a wave crashing in the background (Figure 9.1). Horvitz then uploaded the image to Wikipedia as a copyright free image. *Mood Disorder* traces the image across the internet as it is repeatedly used in news and medical stories to illustrate depression. As George Pendle has written, 'The effect is like looking at the medical chart of a disease spreading through a body – a truly viral image – yet it also shows how shared our visual vocabulary is, how common our common denominators are'.[6]

The writings of Tobin Siebers have also drawn attention to the rigidity of the scripts of disability and the consequences of failing to fulfil these. Drawing on his personal experience of the long-term effects of childhood polio Siebers begins his article 'Disability as Masquerade' with the following passage:

> In December 1999, I had an altercation at the San Francisco airport with a gatekeeper for Northwest Airlines, who demanded that I use a wheelchair if I wanted to claim the early-boarding option. He did not want to accept that I was disabled unless my status was validated by a highly visible prop like a wheelchair. … I answered the gatekeeper

> that I would be in a wheelchair soon enough, but that it was my decision, not his, when I began to use one. He eventually let me board and then chased after me on an afterthought to apologize. The incident was trivial in many ways, but I have now adopted the habit of exaggerating my limp whenever I board planes. My exaggeration is not always sufficient to render my disability visible – gatekeepers still question me on occasion – but I continue to use the strategy, despite the fact that it fills me with a sense of anxiety and bad faith, emotions that resonate with previous experiences in which doctors and nurses have accused me of false complaints, oversensitivity, and malingering.[7]

Although Siebers is ambivalent about exaggerating his limp, he concludes his discussion by arguing for its critical potential of performing disability: 'Exaggerating or performing difference, when that difference is a stigma, marks one as a target, but it also exposes and resists the prejudices of society.'[8]

The contribution of a performative approach is that it shows the way in which – in spite of the tendency to reduce disability to the individual's body – disability is a social construction. Garland-Thompson has proposed that we might understand disability as having four aspects: 'First, it is a system for interpreting bodily variations; second, it is a relationship between bodies and their environments; third, it is a set of practices that produce both the able-bodied and the disabled; fourth, it is a way of describing the inherent instability of the embodied self.'[9] For Garland-Thompson, the category of disability serves 'to exclude the kinds of bodily forms, functions, impairments, changes, or ambiguities that call into question our cultural fantasy of the body as a neutral, compliant, and predictable instrument of some transcendent will.'[10] Indeed, a number of writers have argued that disability can be mobilized as a critical category to explore the intersectionalites of difference. By locating able-bodiedness as the primary disciplinary vector, a new set of political affiliations may emerge. As Kim Hall observes,

> Seemingly unrelated technologies such as orthopedic shoes, cosmetic surgery, hearing aids, diet and exercise regimes, prosthetic limbs, anti-depressants, Viagra, and genital surgeries designed to correct inter-sexed bodies all seek to transform deviant bodies, bodies that threaten to blur and, thus, undermine organizing binaries of social life (such as those defining dominant conceptions of gender and racial identity) into docile bodies that reinforce dominant cultural norms of gendered, raced, and classed bodily function and appearance.[11]

Drawing on the writings of Judith Butler, Robert McRuer has proposed the need for 'ability trouble': a performative strategy that challenges compulsory able-bodiedness. McRuer's work seeks to unsettle the dominance of the able-bodied/disabled binary by 'imaging bodies and desires otherwise.'[12]

It is important to note that, unlike gender, disability is often seen to be an isolated and exceptional deviation from the norm. Yet, despite the consistent characterization of disability as anomalous, as Garland-Thompson reminds us, it is perhaps 'one of the most universal, fundamental of human experiences. After all, we will all become disabled if we live long enough.'[13] Indeed, most of us will move in and out of disability in our lifetimes, through illness, an injury or merely the process of aging. This distinctive aspect of disability is expressed in Sarah Lochlann Jain's proposal that we are all 'living in prognosis'.[14] While Alison Kafer uses the anagram TAB (temporarily able bodied). For all of these writers, the critical project lies in contesting and debating the discourses that cast disability as a 'monolithic fact of the body, as beyond the realm of the political and therefore beyond the realm of debate or dissent, and makes it impossible to image disability and disability futures differently'.[15]

Laura Swanson: *Anti-Self Portraits*

In her series *Anti-Self Portraits* (2005–8) Laura Swanson plays with the viewer's desire to look at her variant body by partially hiding behind domestic objects such as a coat, pillow and record cover. Swanson's acts of hiding in plain sight produces a visual dynamic that might be usefully read in relation to Rosemarie Garland-Thompson's writings on staring. For Garland-Thompson, staring is the dominant mode of looking at disability, 'Disabled people have variously been objects of awe, scorn, terror, delight, inspiration, pity, laughter, and fascination – but we have always been stared at.'[16] Garland-Thompson describes the stare as 'a more forceful and sustained form of looking than glancing, glimpsing, scanning, contemplating, surveying, gazing, and other forms of casual or normative looking, staring starkly registers intense interest and endows it with meaning'.[17] In the act of staring something particular takes place; the starer is constituted as normal and the object of the stare as different, as such 'it is one of the cultural practices that creates disability as a state of absolute difference, rather than as simply one more variation in human form'.[18] Staring is not socially acceptable and produces discomfort for the viewer and the viewed. However, Garland-Thompson argues that photography offers the possibility of staring without social censure. In the photograph, the spectator is offered 'the pleasure of unaccountable, insistent looking'.[19] This is a criticism that is often made of the work of photographers such as Diane Arbus and Joel-Peter Witkin.[20] Swanson explicitly locates her work in opposition to such an approach and has stated: 'This might be putting it too simply, but the title for this series could have been "Anti-Diane-Arbus," especially if I wanted to be didactic.'[21] As Kristin Lindgren has observed, 'Swanson explicitly critiques the enfreakment of bodily difference, but her photographs talk back to Arbus while working with some of the same elements: domestic space, masking, the play of gazes.'[22]

Swanson's photographs explore what Garland-Thompson calls the 'visual paradox' of the disabled body: that it is 'at once to-be-looked-at and not-to-be-looked-at'.[23] By frustrating the viewer's ability to gaze at her body, Swanson pushes the viewer towards 'questioning the desires behind wanting to look at difference'.[24] Further, through her playful hiding and revealing of her body, Swanson's asks us to consider her body in dialogue with her environment. The disjuncture between Swanson's body and everyday objects and environments draws attention to how disability is produced through social systems, infrastructures and institutions. Rosemarie Garland-Thomson's use of the terms 'misfit' and 'misfitting' to theorize the lived experience of disability is useful here.

In Garland-Thomson's writing, a misfit describes 'an incongruent relation between two things: a square peg in a round hole. The problem with a misfit, then, inheres not in either of the two things but rather in their juxtaposition.'[25] Garland-Thomson argues that 'misfitting' is a performance in Butler's sense because it foregrounds the way in which disability is produced as a material arrangement located in time and space. We might see that Swanson's humorous and theatrical performances draw attention to her body as misfitting rather than the body as spectacle.

For example, in *Pillow* (2008) Swanson is pictured sitting in the middle of a large bed holding a pillow in front of her obscuring everything but her lower arms, hands and feet. There seems to be a straightforward comparison at stake: the pillow is large, the person is small. If we understand the misfit in opposition to the norm of the 'fit' then lack of fit exposes the shape of the normative body for which the space was originally designed. However, there is a play with scale within the confusing architecture of the hotel room with its oversize headboard and abundance of pillows. Thus, Swanson's staging of her body as out of place is not singular but an act that exposes both the misfit and the fit to be contingent. As Garland-Thompson expresses it, 'The body is dynamic, constantly interacting with history and environment; sometimes it fits and at other points or moments, it does not.'[26] Swanson's photograph raises the question of what kind of body would fit here. In this way we might see that Swanson's act of performed misfitting troubles the able-bodied/disabled dichotomy that often informs popular, medical and many photographic representations of disability.

Sam Taylor-Johnson: 'Self Portrait in a Single Breasted Suit with Hare'

Sam Taylor-Johnson's 'Self Portrait in a Single Breasted Suit with Hare' (2001) was taken following her treatment for breast cancer which included six months of chemotherapy, a mastectomy and breast reconstruction. Taylor-Johnson's photograph is notable because it is a departure from both representations of breast cancer that appear in the public realm and those by artists such as Jo Spence, Kerry Mansfield and David Jay.

There has been a significant increase in the visibility of breast cancer as a result of a number of high-profile campaigns by charities such as *Breast Cancer Now* and *Wear it Pink*. Breast cancer maintains a high level of visibility not only in charity advertising but also in the marketplace through collaborations with a number of companies to produce pink goods including items such as GHD 'Electric Pink' hair straighteners and a 'Petal Pink' Dualit toaster. However, as Nadine Elhers has observed, despite the 'prevalence of breast cancer awareness, there has been a hardening of only a few representational figures or tropes that stand in for the reality of the disease within the aesthetic field' such that 'the realities of breast cancer are reduced to an abstracted symbolism to be consumed'.[27] The focus on ephemeral concepts like 'awareness' and 'cure' means that there is little space in the public realm for the realities or a politics of cancer. Indeed, despite the enormous numbers of sufferers, cancer is still taken to be a tragic exception seen primarily as a personal problem afflicting individuals who are expected to 'take on the mantle of "survivorship," consider the "gift" of cancer, and increase their life chances with positive attitudes'.[28] As Samantha King notes, the 'image of the woman with breast cancer that has emerged with the pink ribbon industry – youthful, ultrafeminine, slim, light-skinned if not white, radiant with health, joyful, and proud – leaves little room for recognition that people still die of the disease'.[29]

In short, the dominant discourse of breast cancer centres on a set of narrative and aesthetic tropes which privilege heterosexuality, femininity and survival. In response, works by David Jay, Jo Spence, Catherine Lord[30] and Lynn Kohlman[31] have adopted an uncompromising approach that foregrounds the realities of the disease. These works also openly acknowledge the loss of life that is frequently the ultimate outcome of even the most aggressively treated cancers. As Elhers has written of David Jay's documentary work,

> The endless drive for 'the cure', so present in public breast cancer campaigns, functions not only to foreground an elusive biomedical 'promise' but also to deny or suspend the sheer terror, pain, suffering, and death that accompanies breast cancer diagnosis, treatment, and the experience of life in prognosis. In defiance of such erasure, these images highlight that there is no quick 'cure' for breast cancer but, rather, a range of disabling effects that follow from the disease and its treatment.[32]

Taylor-Johnson's photograph (Figure 9.2) offers a different – allegorical – approach. Dressed in a black suit and trainers, holding a dead hare in one hand and a cable release in the other, Taylor-Johnson stares directly at the camera. Taylor-Johnson's self-portrait complicates our understanding of what the cancer survivor looks like

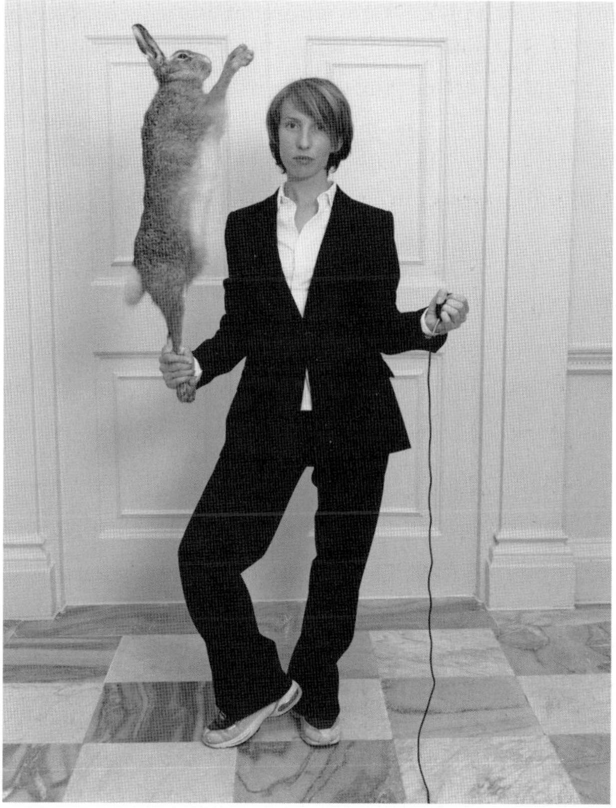

Figure 9.2 Sam Taylor-Johnson, 'Self Portrait in a Single Breasted Suit with Hare', 2001. © Sam Taylor-Johnson. All rights reserved, DACS 2019.

by troubling the visual tropes for the representation of the disease. As Stella Bolaki notes, the first impression is 'that it is not about breast cancer or illness at all. Or, to put it better, it is difficult to decode this picture because it does not draw on the kind of imagery (such as the surgical scar or other markings on the body) associated with … representations of breast cancer.'[33] How then can we locate this portrait as a politicized representation of the post-cancer, post-mastectomy body? Like Swanson, the politics of Taylor-Johnson's performance lies in the way that it elicits and frustrates our gaze.

As Garland-Thompson has noted, staring at disability 'intensely telescopes looking toward the physical signifier for disability. Starers gawk with abandon at the prosthetic hook, the empty sleeve, the scarred flesh, the unfocused eye, the twitching limb.'[34] In Taylor-Johnson's portrait there is nothing within the image to suggest that the viewer is looking at a single-breasted woman. However, the caption, which 'foregrounds the single-breasted suit, shatters the unity of the body and astonishes its viewer by exposing the misrecognition involved in the contemplation of the photo'.[35]In Taylor-Johnson's photograph we are unable to 'see' cancer, and this directs us to the recognition that even the marks on the body that result from the invasive treatments of breast cancer are not the disease itself. Indeed, Sarah Lochlann Jain has argued that cancer 'materializes as much in cultural interchanges as in its biological form; it can only be located in, culled from, cultural interstices: not only from pathology reports but also in conversations with oncologists, support groups, get-well cards, coffee shop gossip, wig shops, clinical trial reports, medical malpractice opinions'.[36] In Taylor-Johnson's work cancer remains abstract, and this guides us to understanding that cancer has a discursive as well as a biological existence.

While Taylor-Johnson is young, white and thin, her black suit and trainers challenge the dominant aesthetic of sentimentality and infantilism that pervades mainstream representations of the cancer survivor. Jeremy Millar has described this portrait as an example of 'contemporary dandyism',[37]and this is helpful in understanding the ways in which this portrait challenges the limitations of existing imagery offered to those living with and after cancer. Taylor-Johnson's playful use of clothing and pose presents both the suit and the body as citational. Through the figure of the dandy, both femininity and disability are 'cited' as discourses, thus blurring the categories upon which traditional narratives of pathology, disorder and femininity depend.

Amy Brandzel has argued that 'the stripping down of the body in breast cancer treatment highlights the ways in which gendered, racialized, and sexualized performativities are opportunities for negotiation as much as they are violent demands for conformity'.[38] Bradzel gives Eve Kosofsky Sedgwick's account of dressing after a mastectomy as an example. In 'White Glasses', Sedgwick reflects on the 'dizzying array of gender challenges and experiments [that] come with the initiations of surgery, of chemotherapy, of hormone therapy. Just getting dressed in the morning means deciding how many breasts I will be able to recognize myself if I am wearing (a voice in me keeps whispering, *three*).'[39] For Brandzel, the forcefulness of breast cancer discourse is an effort to quash these intersectional possibilities.

The black suit has a further significance in Taylor-Johnson's performance of the cancer survivor. As Bolaki has observed, coupled with the hare and white shirt, the suit evokes the female magician.[40] Here, like the dead hare that magically 'stands' upright, Taylor-Johnson has magically survived. However, by foregrounding survival as a performance, Taylor-Johnson shows it to be contingent and temporary. Taylor-Johnson's performance of the cancer survivor is finely balanced, referencing both life and death. As such, it participates in the uncertainty associated with what Sarah Lochlann Jain has described as 'living in prognosis'.[41] Arguing that it is not possible for cancer, or suffering more generally to be understood 'cleanly through a politics that tries to disavow death (as the survivor politics does), or cheer it up (as the pink-ribbon rhetoric does), or deny or defer cancer suffering (as does the "drive for the cure")'.[42]

Jain argues that 'living in prognosis' offers 'an uneasy alternative, one that inhabits contradiction, confusion, and betrayal'.[43] Prognosis here 'emerges as a technology of mourning, holding together the future and the past. Prognosis stands as a small monument to those who will not make it through the five- and ten-year marks.'[44]

Hannah Laycock: *Awakenings*

Hannah Laycock's practice is concerned with representing the experience of living with multiple sclerosis, a disease that is often characterized as 'hidden'.[45] Although its cause is known, the immune system attacks the myelin coating of the nerve fibres around the spinal cord, the effects of MS are unpredictable; they not only vary between different people but can also change daily. Stella Bolaki argues that Laycock's practice seeks to make the person with MS 'visible and experiential without making [him or her] fully knowable'.[46] For Bolaki, Laycock's portraits and landscapes, which are suffused with uncertainty and ambiguity, seek to articulate states and experiences that medicine and science are largely resistant to. This quality is furthered by the presentation of the photographs which are untitled and do not articulate a narrative. Bolaki thus proposes that Laycock's work should be read in relation to a countering of the 'dehumanising and objectifying aspects of medical care'.[47]

Laycock's work might also be usefully read in relation to an articulation of a particular temporality. As Laycock has stated, the work addresses 'the intangible nature of the future: whether you've got MS or not, you don't really know how your future is going to unfold. But MS adds another uncertainty; because you don't know what journey your MS will take.'[48] As Alison Kafer has noted, time plays a key role in formulations of disability:

> The medical field in particular has a long tradition of describing disability in reference to time. 'Chronic' fatigue, 'intermittent' symptoms, and 'constant' pain are each ways of defining illness and disability in and through time .... 'Frequency', 'incidence', 'occurrence', 'relapse', 'remission': these too, are the time frames of symptoms, illness, and disease. 'Prognosis' and 'diagnosis' project futures of illness, disability, and recovery. Or take terms such as 'acquired', 'congenital', and 'developmental', each of which is used to demarcate the time of onset or impairment.[49]

Kafer's writing points to the way in which the temporal orientation of 'the future' is deployed in the service of compulsory able-bodiness and able-mindedness. As Kafer notes, time is used in relation to a curative temporality focused on a future with*out* disability. This is seen in the questions that often accompany a diagnosis such as: 'How soon before you recover?' or 'How long before they find a cure?' As opposed to the use of time in relation to race, in which the past is used to establish

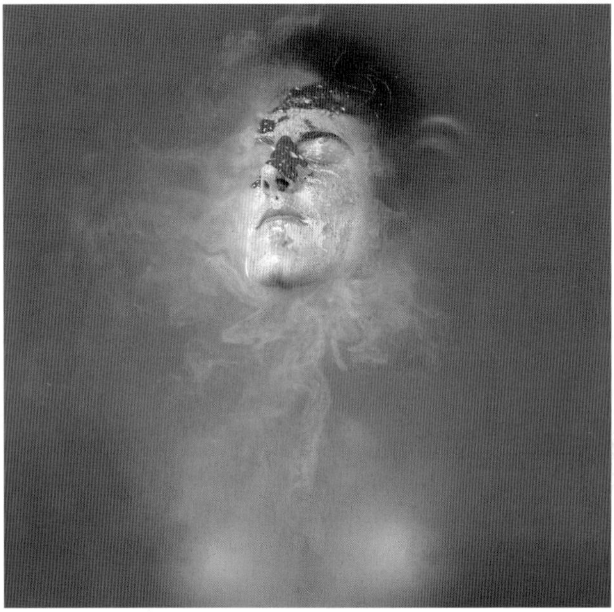

Figure 9.3 Hannah Laycock, *Untitled 01 (Forced to Gasp [Blue])*. © Hannah Laycock, www.hannahlaycock.com. Courtesy of the artist.

the hegemonic ideals of the present, here the future is used as a time frame that serves to cast disabled people as 'out of time, or as obstacles to the arc of progress'.[50] Kafer thus argues that it is important to 'engage in the process of articulating other temporalities, other approaches to futurity beyond curative ones'.[51]

In Laycock's work photography plays a particular role in articulating a suspended temporality. This can be seen in her focus on moments such as the picturing of a 'cloud' covering her face or paint leaving the surface of skin; transient moments that photography is privileged position to capture. In our example (Figure 9.3), Laycock appears to be both emerging from the water and sinking beneath its surface. The paint that covers her face seems both primitive and futuristic; her body appears to be simultaneously melting away and materializing. Unlike the performances considered so far that have sought to destabilize particular iterations, here Laycock seems to occupy a space between one iteration and another. Thus, the importance of performance as a critical strategy in Laycock's work is that it maintains a space and time in which alternative iterations of subjectivity might (yet) be articulated.

Part Four

Photography and psychoanalysis

In this section we will be looking at how psychoanalytic theory can help us to understand photographic art works and their reception. The central premise of a psychoanalytic approach to photographic images is that photographs operate in psychic space. In short, what we see when we look at an image is not only informed by optics but also determined by our unconscious. While we may consider ourselves to be rational beings, psychoanalysis asks us to recognize that our relationship to the visual is determined by desire. This is why Joan Copjec has argued that analysts of culture must 'become literate in desire'.[1]

To begin, we will consider the work of Lucas Blalock and how his playful use of digital editing produces a very particular effect that can be usefully theorized in relation to Lacan's concept of *objet a*. In Chapter 11 we will compare the work of Jemima Stehli and Laurel Nakadate as a way of exploring the gaze in relation to some of the key feminist writings on psychoanalysis and gender. To conclude, in Chapter 12 we will discuss Richard Prince's series *New Portraits* in relation to writings on psychoanalysis and ideology. The aim throughout this section is to show how psychoanalysis allows us to ask different questions about photographs and the way they affect us.

10

Psychoanalysis, representation and desire

Lucas Blalock is a photographic artist who has been celebrated for his strategically poor use of Photoshop. As Chris Wiley has summarized, 'He's horrible at it.'[1] In Blalock's work the labour of post-production is made visible and our relationship to the objects depicted becomes disturbed. As one reviewer notes, 'Blalock's images are weird, inventive and ultimately persuasive. In them, situations and objects hover on the edge of familiarity while remaining strange, and sometimes even wondrous.'[2] Blalock himself has also reflected upon the way in which objects acquire new meaning and function in his work. For Blalock the 'making strange' he is engaged with is a response to the very particular way in which photography and capitalism change our relationship to objects:

> One of photography's greatest impacts in the 20th century is that it played a central role in transforming everything into a commodity. It is a condition that narrows the terms of our relationships. So, in turn, I'm more interested in objects that fail to do a good job in that system. I'm also interested in alternative ways objects can become circuits for energy, that they can connect to us through other kinds of value.[3]

What we can see from these comments is that there is an agreement that Blalock's work changes our relationship to objects through the way he represents them.

Our example, 'Two Lettuces' (2014) (Figure 10.1), is an image of two lettuces: a 'real' lettuce and a badly drawn lettuce added in post-production using digital editing software. Incongruously, Blalock has used Photoshop not to craft a more perfect representation of the lettuce but to reproduce it. One way of reading this visual pun would be to argue that Blalock is directing us the contingency of the signifier.

The signifier appears to simply give a name to an object (the signified): there is a green leafy object that grows in the ground and someone decides to use the word 'lettuce' to describe it. However, the signifier is not identical with the signified. This

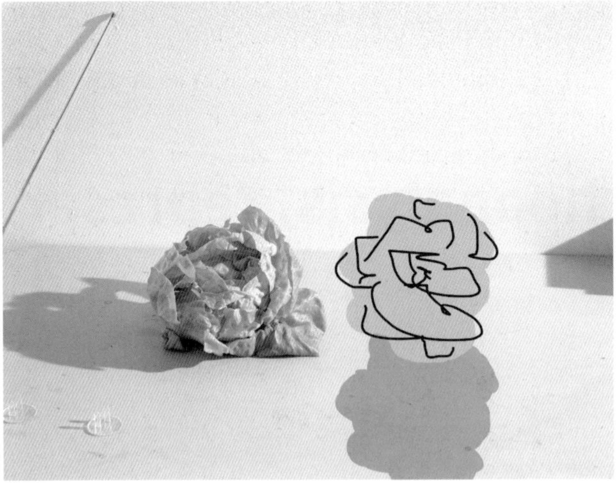

Figure 10.1 Lucas Blalock, *Two Lettuces,* 2014. Courtesy of the artist.

noncoincidence is crucial – for linguists it is where meaning emerges, for capitalism it is where value emerges and for psychoanalysis it is where desire emerges.

Signifier, signified, sign

For linguistics, the signifier is an element such as a word, gesture or sound that gives meaning. The signified is the element; for example, an object, feeling or idea which is given meaning through being attached to the signifier. Together, the signified and signifier make a sign.

Although the relation between the signifier and the signified seems to be self-evident, it is arbitrary. The relationship between signifier and signified, and therefore the possibility of meaning, is only produced through convention. Indeed, meaning is neither self-evident nor straightforward; a number of signifiers can be used to describe the same thing, and a word can have more than one signified. Vernacular expressions often deliberately break with the conventionalized relationship between signifier and signified; for example, the use of the word 'bad' within hip-hop terminology to mean good. While the naturalized relationship between signifier and signified can be disturbed as a means to signal a cultural, social or generational difference, Blalock's work seeks a different effect – rather than challenging the authority of particular meanings, his work plays with the contingency of meaning.

One of the ways he does this is through repetition. Blalock's stylized and 'unskilled' use of repetition can be seen to expose the way in which meaning adheres solely in the movement of the signifying chain: the way in which none of the individual signifiers that make up the signifying chain have any positive meaning; rather, meaning arises as a result of their interaction. For example, in his series of photographs of hot dogs in which the same object is repeatedly arranged in different ways and given titles such as 'Six', 'Weight', 'Circle', 'Relation of Relations', 'Night Drugs' repetition is pushed to absurdity and meaning put in doubt: with only doubles of themselves to interact with, the meaning of both signifier and signified falters.

What does this have to do with psychoanalysis though? Jacques Lacan is famous for inaugurating a return to Freud through an approach to psychoanalysis that incorporated linguistics, anthropology and mathematics. In his writings, Lacan emphasizes the pivotal role of language in the unconscious processes of the subject formation.

For psychoanalysis, the unconscious can be found in the gaps and slippages between signifiers: 'That signifiers can signify more than one thing or concept ... is a condition of possibility for the fact that unconscious meanings and desires can and do erupt in everyday speech.'[4] For psychoanalysts, dreams, slips-of-the-tongue and jokes are all examples of 'irregular' forms of signification that can be used to derive unconscious meaning. As Derek Hook explains, 'One way of understanding the traditional psychoanalytic notion of repression – i.e. the process whereby unacceptable ideas or impulses are rendered unconscious – is through the idea that particular signifieds have been split off from those signifiers that would bring them into consciousness.'[5]

For Lacan, the acquisition of language plays a pivotal role in the formation of the subject. Signification introduces an experience of loss into all of our interactions. This is because signification is an act of substitution in which a word replaces a thing. As Lacan expresses it, 'The symbol manifests itself first ... as the murder of the thing.'[6] Lacan theorizes this loss as a castration

This initially sounds like a strange characterization of the acquisition of language. However, Lacan modifies Freud's account of the castration complex to suggest that castration is not related to perceptions of anatomical difference, but rather entry into the Symbolic. For Lacan castration 'is the recognition by the subject of a kind of lack. Thus, women, no less than men, must undergo castration.'[7] This is why, in his vocabulary of symbols, Lacan represents the subject as '$\not{S}$'. The bar is used to indicate that the subject is divided, split and lacking. As Alain Vanier expresses it, 'The subject of psychoanalysis is a barred subject, subordinated to the signifier, represented in the signifying chain without figuring in it, and, at the same time, unable to be pinned down by a signifier *qua* signifier. The subject of the unconscious is an evanescent subject without wholeness.'[8]

As speaking subjects, our relation to objects becomes mediated by the structure of loss. Even objects necessary for our survival such as food and shelter are not objects of need as they are for animals, but objects of desire. As Todd McGowan explains,

> As an object of need, the apple is just an apple and can satisfy the need. But after the introduction of the signifier, the apple's self-division [between signifier and signified] enables it to signify something beyond itself. A supplement attaches itself to the apple in the form of the signifier, and this excess remains irreducible to the object. The subject in the world of signification can never just eat an apple but eats instead what 'keeps the doctor away', what is juicy and delicious, or what connotes original sin.[9]

The supplement, the 'something more', that the apple embodies is not something that we can have – it is not 'in' the object. Lacan theorizes this supplement through a very particular kind of object that he terms *objet a*.[10]

Objet a

Despite its name, *objet a* is not coincident with an object at all. As Joan Copjec explains, *objet a* is not an object in our everyday sense of the term: 'It has neither an essence nor a signification. It cannot be communicated or exchanged. It has, in short, no *objectivity*.'[11] Absolutely unattainable, *objet a* is 'the remainder of an operation that Lacan calls the causation of the subject'.[12] Sometimes referred to as the lost object, it is that which is 'lost' by the constitution of the subject as a speaking subject. However, it has not been lost in any conventional understanding of the term, rather the process of signification, by substituting signifiers for objects, has 'absented' it. This is why Lacan argues the apparently chimerical position that the *objet a* is by definition an object that has come into being by being lost. Although *objet a* is lost and cannot be 'refound', 'all of the subject's multifarious activity within the world of signification centres around the attempt to rediscover this object that it never possessed'.[13]

Here it is perhaps useful to explain the difference between an object and *objet a* in terms of their relation to desire. In Lacanian terminology, *objet a* is the object-cause of desire. This means that *objet a* precedes desire. The object of desire is that which comes to be desired as a result of desire.[14] In being motivated by *objet a*, psychoanalysis asks us to rethink our understanding of desire; desire is not a relation to a presence – the wish for some*thing*, but rather a relation to lack. Indeed, desire is predicated on absence to the extent that 'desire's *raison d'être* … is not to realize its goal, to find full satisfaction, but to reproduce itself as desire'.[15] Despite the huge number of cultural texts – from songs to adverts – that suggest otherwise, desire can never be satisfied.

This means that it is necessary for us to revise our conventional understanding of fantasy as the imagined satisfaction of the desire for a specific object. It is not that we desire an object and this sets in motion a fantasy about this object, but that fantasy structures desire in relation to a particular object. As Žižek expresses it, 'It is precisely the role of fantasy to give the coordinates of the subject's desire, to specify its object, to locate the position the subject assumes in it. It is only through fantasy that the subject is constituted as desiring: *through fantasy, we learn how to desire*.'[16] In short, it is only through fantasy that desire can be attached to a specific object and thus appear to the subject as something that can be realized. This is why Lacan argues that 'fantasy constitutes the pleasure proper to desire'.[17]

While the fantasy scene may employ socially conventional objects of desire, it is not the aspirational qualities of the scene that distinguishes it as a fantasy, but the unconscious function that it fulfils. Within the fantasy, desire appears as something that can be fulfilled. That is to say, the role of fantasy is *defensive*; it provides relief from the repetitions of desire. As McGowan succinctly expresses it, 'We do not turn to fantasy for happiness or for respite from reality; we turn to it for respite from the enigmatic torments of our desire.'[18]

Fantasy is a defence that serves to mask the subject from the impossibilities of desire by offering a symbolic possibility in which the absolutely unattainable *objet a* is represented by a specific object that is available except for a particular spatial or temporal obstacle (as we all know, we do not fantasize about what we have).[19] While desire only offers perpetual failure, fantasy offers the possibility of satisfaction. However, the pleasures of fantasy always fall short of fulfilment. In short, the resolution of desire offered by fantasy is only ever fantasmatic. As McGowan succinctly expresses this, 'One thought that one was obtaining the impossible lost object, but one ends up with just an ordinary empirical object that pales in comparison. I believed that the piece of chocolate cake that I just ate embodied the lost object itself before I ate it, but after having done so I realize its underwhelming ordinariness.'[20] Nonetheless, we constantly seek *objet a* through the fantasies we construct around objects, and this is where capitalism installs itself.

Capitalism

As our discussion so far has shown, no object is fulfilling for the subject. Although it can't make objects 'whole', by presenting objects to us in the form of commodities, capitalism offers subjects the ability to relate to objects through a fantasy that holds out a promise of satisfaction, of completion. Capitalism is particularly skilled at presenting objects in a way that the satisfaction of desire appears to be possible (at least temporarily). As Žižek has described the commodity, 'A commodity is a mysterious entity full of theological caprices, a particular object satisfying a particular need, but at the same time the promise of something more, of an unfathomable enjoyment whose true location is fantasy.'[21] In the world of the commodity, cream is 'naughty, but nice', a Mars bar 'helps you work, rest and play'. As commodities, these objects have a 'ready-made' fantasy frame. Of course, not all objects are successful commodities. As McGowan notes, 'The inventors of failed commodities such as *Pepsi Clear* did not adequately carve out an appealing fantasmatic position. … Even products that endure, like *Coke* or *Apple* electronics, must constantly renew themselves in order to remain within the prevailing fantasy.'[22]

It is important to recognize here that the fantasies offered by capitalism about a particular object cannot make the object satisfying. Capitalism cannot undo the effects of signification. However, capitalism is able to sustain itself because it does not matter that the commodity never satisfies. In fact, it is essential that it does not. Even though it repeatedly sells us dissatisfying objects, capitalism is effective because it engages with the crucial insight of psychoanalysis 'that the subject's satisfaction is located in how it desires and not what it obtains'.[23] The movement from one dissatisfying commodity to another which is often characterized as an empty, consumer experience is actually a satisfying repetition for the subject because what we desire is not the object itself but the object in its absence.[24]

Blalock does not work with consumer objects; his interest lies in those objects that are 'out of the limelight or not made explicitly to be desired visually'.[25] Blalock's comments on his early work are interesting here: 'When I started making photographs of cigarettes as still life objects it became clear that they carried too much baggage – that we all had too much of a readymade relationship to these things already, and that previous relationship was louder than any conversation I could create.'[26] In terms of our argument so far, we might say that Blalock is interested in those objects that do not have a particular visual or narrative fantasy attached to their mode of presentation. It is not that there is anything particular about a lettuce per se that precludes it from appearing as an object of desire; however, it does not currently have a fantasy script that renders it as a prized object of desire. Blalock could photograph the lettuce in a way that elevated it to an object of desire, but he does not do this. What kind of objects are the lettuces in Blalock's photograph then? There is another category of psychoanalytic object that is useful to consider here: the object of anxiety.

The object of anxiety

To briefly reprise our discussion so far, *objet a* is the name given to the remnant produced by the subject's submission to the Symbolic order. *Objet a* designates that which is 'lost' by the constitution of the subject as a barred subject ($\$$). The function of fantasy is to figure this lack in the subject as a loss. As Yannis Stavrakakis has noted, 'The structure we always find in fantasy is this relation between the split subject, the lacking subject and the promise of the elimination of this lack or of a compensation for it amounting to its structural neutralisation.'[27] As a means of inscribing this relationship, Lacan offers a 'matheme', or formula, of fantasy:

$$\$ \Diamond a$$

This matheme shows the way in which when we are at some remove from it – represented in the formula by the *poiçon* (◇) – *objet a* (*a*) appears as a lost part of ourselves, that which prevents the subject ($) from becoming whole.

In anxiety, our distance from *objet a* is reduced and that which 'completes' the subject appears as a disfiguring surplus. In short, when the distance (◇) between the subject ($) and *objet a* (*a*) is collapsed, *objet a* no longer functions as the object-cause of desire, but as the object of anxiety. In anxiety, instead of

$$\$ \diamond a$$

we get

$$\$ a$$

a 'shrivelling up of the distance separating the two terms [which] results in the collapse of the fantasy structure'.[28]

Put another way, within the fantasy scenario the subject does not suffer anxiety because the fantasy scene consists of not only the anticipated pleasures of obtaining the object but also the obstacles to this pleasure. As Parveen Adams expresses it, 'I do not suffer anxiety because I am waiting for the object of my desire.'[29] The fantasy scene is pleasurable not because it promises the attainment of the object, but because it keeps *objet a* at a pleasurable distance. However, when the fantasy scenario which positions *objet a* at a distance is disrupted, an anxious relation takes hold. Contrary to what we might expect, anxiety is not provoked by the loss of a particular object, but by the appearance of the 'lost' object, *objet a*.

In Lacanian terms, anxiety is caused by the lack of a lack. The appearance of *objet a* finds popular expression in the horror film in, for example, Freddie Kruger's disfigured face, the vampire's fangs or the doppelgänger.[30] However, it is important to be clear that anxiety does not relate to particular kinds of objects, but describes a particular relation to the object: 'Anxiety describes a relation of overpowering proximity to the object [*a*].'[31] Mladen Dolar offers the example of looking at your own reflection in a mirror and seeing one's mirror image close its eyes. What this example shows is the way in which the double is 'me plus the object *a*, that invisible part of being added to my image. In order for the mirror image to contain the object *a*, a wink or a nod is enough.'[32] Is Blalock's use of Photoshop not just such a nod or wink? We might say that Blalock gives us both the lettuce and its double. However, Blalock's work does not make the viewer feel anxious. Indeed, Blalock talks about his work in terms of love: 'You could say that making these pictures is about trying to have a love relationship with these things. … I'm trying to love them all. I don't think I'm succeeding. My work is about an attempt at love.'[33] Yet these two descriptions of Blalock's work are not as far apart as they might seem, for there is one kind of encounter in which we are able to tolerate the alterity of *objet a* in proximity: love.

Lacan famously describes love as 'giving what one doesn't have [*objet a*] to someone who doesn't want it'.[34] Love depends on the subject embracing *objet a*. This can be illustrated by the way in which the first sign that one is falling *out* of love is that the unique quality that one attributed to the love object regains its troubling status. As McGown recounts: 'This occurred to me when I began to find a distinctive mark on my romantic partner's face repulsive, whereas before I had always viewed it as a sign of her singularity.'[35] Love depends on the embrace of what is undesirable in the object, and thus the love object is completely opposed the object of desire central to capitalism. Although the promise of love is a key component of many of the fantasies constructed about commodities – diets, cars, clothing are all imbued with the fantasy of finding true love – capitalism's ideological operation is to remake 'love, which involves an object we can't have, into romance, which involves an object that we can'.[36] In Blalock's work we are not just asked to engage with those objects that have been overlooked by capitalism, we are asked to love them in all their repulsive singularity.

11

Psychoanalysis, spectatorship and the gaze

In this chapter we will be considering how psychoanalytic writings on the gaze can help us to understand the dynamics at stake in viewing photographs. This has been an area of particular concern for many female artists. Psychoanalysis might seem an unusual choice for this task; many critics have argued that psychoanalytic theory essentializes gender, rather than accounting for it in terms of culture and ideology as with the poststructuralist or discursive approaches considered in Chapter 7. However, in the mid-1970s there was what Joan Copjec describes as a 'global warming' that 'began to melt the icy resistance of feminists to psychoanalysis'.[1] This shift was inaugurated by a number of key publications: Juliet Mitchell's *Psychoanalysis and Feminism: A Radical Reassessment Of Freudian Psychoanalysis*;[2] the journal *m/f* edited by Parveen Adams and Elizabeth Cowie and Laura Mulvey's article 'Visual Pleasure and Narrative Cinema'.[3] Written in 1973 and published in the journal *Screen* in 1975, Mulvey's essay is perhaps one of the most widely read writings on psychoanalysis and the politics of spectatorship. Mulvey is explicit about the political aims of her text and begins by stating thus:

> This paper intends to use psychoanalysis to discover where and how the fascination of film is reinforced by pre-existing patterns of fascination already at work within the individual subject and the social formations that have moulded him. … Psychoanalytic theory is thus appropriated here as a political weapon, demonstrating the way the unconscious of patriarchal society has structured film form.[4]

Drawing on the key psychoanalytic insight that ideology is operative at the level of the unconscious, Mulvey proposes that the cinematic apparatus (specifically of classical Hollywood cinema) puts the spectator in a masculine subject position, where the figure of the woman on screen functions as the object of desire. Mulvey argues that the only way to annihilate this form that serves to naturalize patriarchy is to radically deconstruct traditional filmic strategies, and she calls for a new feminist avant-garde filmmaking that will rupture the pleasure of classical Hollywood filmmaking.

Mulvey's work has been incredibly influential,[5] and the idea of the male gaze is now routinely invoked in describing a wide range of media forms including photography. In this chapter we will be considering the work of two artists: Jemima Stehli and Laurel Nakadate.

Jemima Stehli: *Strip*

Jemima Stehli is a British artist who uses photography and the self-portrait to explore issues of representation in relation to the female nude. Stehli's photographs often reference existing works by male artists such as Helmut Newton, Allen Jones and Francis Bacon.[6] Stehli's strategy of presenting herself in the position of '*to-be-looked-at-ness*'[7] identified by Mulvey while also signalling her command of the situation has been described as critical strategy that serves to 'underscore the ambivalence of women's investment in their own objectification within patriarchy'.[8]

Stehli's series *Strip* (2000) is perhaps her most well-known work. For this piece Stehli performed a striptease for several men chosen from the art world including a writer, critic and curator. The performance took place in the studio where, positioned against a number of brightly coloured backdrops, each man was asked to photograph Stehli as she undressed. The camera was not held by the men, but located on a tripod facing them. Thus, when they pressed the cable release the photograph taken is not from the point of view of the male subject, but rather shows him in the act of looking. It is a sophisticated and humorous work that has garnered critical praise. For example, Ruth Rosengarten argues that 'Stehli's work succinctly plays out and makes visible the dynamics of power and eroticism in traditional studio representations of the female nude'.[9] While Heather Anderson praises Stehli for the way in which her work parodies 'her own status as sexual object and foreground her ambivalent relation to the male (art) economy'.[10] Criticisms of Stehli's work – as with many female artists working with their own bodies – have turned on the question of whether the desirability of her body negates the critique she seeks to advance. As Anderson admits, 'It is arguable whether Stehli's *Strip* Series would register as critique in the pages of *GQ* or *Loaded*'.[11]

Laurel Nakadate: *Lucky Tiger*

Laurel Nakadate works across photography, film and video. Her work explores uncomfortable, ambiguous encounters between herself and men. The male subjects of Nakadate's work are often marginalized, middle-aged men, and the encounters are disturbing in their tentative intimacy. For example, for *Happy Birthday* (2000) Nakadate would ask strangers to celebrate her birthday with her in their apartments and film the two-person party. As Vivian L. Huang has noted of the work, 'The mood of the scene is unclear; neither attendee seems particularly joyful or sure of their role.'[12]

Our example is taken from *Lucky Tiger* (2000), which is a series of small, cheaply printed photographs of Nakadate in poses based on the kind of calendars found in gas stations and garages. Nakadate, a Japanese-American, is pictured in front of typical American provincial scenery, sometimes on horseback, sometimes in a pickup truck. She wears variously a Superman T-shirt, cowboy hat and a two-piece bathing suit, which has the head of a tiger printed on the crotch and gives the series its title. These poses, belonging to the history of women's objectification, are overlaid with other elements that show the way in which gender intertwines with race, class and national identity to produce certain bodies as desirable. In our example, *Lucky Tiger #63* (Figure 11.1), Nakadate adopts a pose common to 'pinup' photographs: her arms are raised above her head, leaving her body exposed. One hip is raised, accentuating her abdomen and legs, and her face is turned slightly to the side. Yet, there is also something intimate about the photograph. Nakadate's pose is held gently. Further, the sun is positioned behind her producing a 'sunburst' and lending the image a romantic feel – as if it were taken by, or for, someone in particular. The photograph is criss-crossed by black marks which further this sense of the photograph as a keepsake that has been handled. However, the marks are fingerprints produced when Nakadate gave the photographs to a group of men that she had contacted via *Craigslist*. Each of the men had to press their fingers on an ink pad, then pass around the *Lucky Tiger* photographs. Across the series, these fingerprints acquire an amorphous but insistent presence.

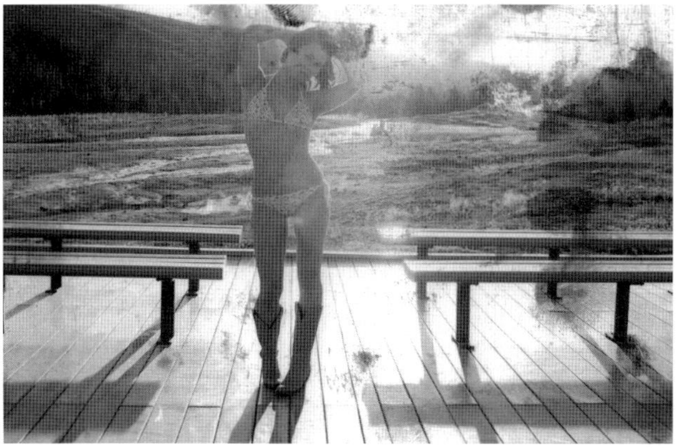

Figure 11.1 Laurel Nakadate, *Lucky Tiger #63*, 2009. Type-C print and fingerprinting ink, 4 × 6 inches. © Laurel Nakadate. Courtesy of Leslie Tonkonow Artworks + Projects, New York.

As with Stehli, there is an explicit engagement with the male gaze as theorized by Mulvey in Nakadate's work. Both artists use photography to record a collaborative performance in which an act of voyeurism is granted in exchange for the recording of it on the artist's terms. However, while Stehli recreates fine art images and uses representatives of male power such as the critic and the curator in her work. Nakadate complicates the sexualized tropes of pop culture by drawing on vernacular imagery of pin-up calendars, and her collaborators are marginalized, anonymous men.[13] Unlike Stehli's work which has been critically praised, Nadakate's work, in particular her ten-year survey show *Only the Lonely* (MoMA, 2011), has attracted disparate reviews.

Broadly, the criticisms of Nakadate's work assert that it is exploitative and derivative.[14] What is interesting about these reviews is the intensity of feeling generated in discussions of her work. For example, Karen Rosenberg of the *New York Times* describes Nakadate's work as 'reeking of exploitation: hers, theirs, and ours'.[15] Elsewhere, Nakadate is spoken of as a tease or a provocateur[16] and chastised for crossing the line into an uncritical objectification of her body.

However, some responses are more nuanced. For example, Ken Johnson observes that 'the simple enjoyment one might feel in the display of the female body is complicated by a sense of emotional disconnection, of a displacement that feels troubling' and goes on to conclude that 'the feeling of uneasiness provoked by the work is not always edifying or pleasurable.'[17] Another reviewer remarks that 'voyeurism, exhibitionism, and hostility merge with gullibility, cunning, and folly in Nakadate's work. Not only is this creepy, it's confusing and complicated'.[18]

We can see that while both Stehli and Nakadate position themselves as the object of desire, their work produces very different effects. Psychoanalysis offers a way of understanding these differences by directing our attention away from an analysis of the content of scene to thinking about how it organizes the viewer.[19]

The Lacanian gaze

Mulvey's theorization of the male gaze has been hugely influential and generated a vast and varied literature including calls to recognize the female gaze as well as the significance of sexuality, class and race in determining the spectator's position. However, many of these responses have departed from the psychoanalytic theory that informed Mulvey's argument[20] and have failed to take account of new writings that have emerged in this field. A significant contribution to the psychoanalytic line of enquiry initiated by Mulvey's article has been Joan Copjec's essay 'The Orthopsychic Subject: Film Theory and the Reception of Lacan'[21] and the writings of theorists such as Todd McGowan, Slavoj Žižek and Jennifer Friedlander.[22] Together these works have produced a second generation of Lacanian film theory.

Contemporary Lacanian film theory is based on an understanding of the gaze that differs significantly from Mulvey's. In Mulvey's writing, which draws on Lacan's essay 'The Mirror Stage as Formative of the *I* Function as Revealed in Psychoanalytic Experience',[23] the gaze is understood in terms of the exercise of power. In short, the gaze belongs to the subject who looks. Or in the terms of Mulvey's argument, the male gaze belongs to an active subject whose point of view organizes and dominates the field of vision. However, in his later writings, Lacan begins to theorize the gaze in a way that differs significantly. In *The Four Fundamentals Concepts of Psycho-Analysis*[24] the gaze is not an action, but an object. One way of understanding this difference is that the Lacanian gaze is opposed to the Mulveyian gaze in that it does not belong to a determinate subject: the reference to a specific person remains in suspense in an encounter with the gaze. As Joan Copjec expresses it, '*There is no bearer of the gaze, there is only the gaze*.'[25] Slavoj Žižek gives the following example:

> Let us recall the archetypal scene from Hitchcock: a heroine (Lilah in *Psycho,* Melanie in *The Birds*) is approaching a mysterious, allegedly empty house; she is looking at it, yet what makes a scene so disturbing is that we, the spectators, cannot get rid of the vague impression that the object she is looking at is somehow *returning the gaze*. The crucial point, of course, is that this gaze should not be subjectivized: it's not simply that 'there is somebody in the house', we are, rather, dealing with a kind of empty, a priori gaze that cannot be pinpointed as a determinate reality – she 'cannot see it all', she is looking at a blind spot, and the object returns the gaze from this blind spot.[26]

Here we can see that, contra-Mulvey, the gaze is related neither to the point of view of the camera, the male protagonist, nor to the power structures that inform it, but to an unsymbolizable point at which the image seems to look back at the viewer.

The example given by Lacan is of Hans Holbein's painting *The Ambassadors* (1533). This well-known painting pictures two richly dressed men with a number of objects that indicate wealth and learning such as books, a globe and musical instruments. In addition, there is an object that we cannot visually resolve in the foreground. This object is anamorphotic, it is only when it is viewed from an oblique point of view that it is revealed to be a skull. Lacan describes the painting in the following way: 'The secret of this picture is given at the moment when, moving slightly away, little by little, to the left, then turning around, we see what the magical floating object signifies. It reflects our own nothingness, in the figure of the death's head.'[27] The skull reflects our own nothingness in an allegorical sense; however, for Lacan, it also offers a description of the way in which an encounter with the gaze involves a desubjectification: 'The gaze is the point at which the subject loses its subjective privilege.'[28] The relationship between the subject and the gaze is not one of objectification in which the spectator is dominant, but one that radically disrupts the mastery of the viewing subject.[29]

Hence we can see that Lacan's notion of the gaze offers a very different understanding than that proposed by Mulvey. While this revised understanding of the gaze has been very productive for film theory, it does not seem to have much to offer to a feminist theory of photography that is interested in how the figure of woman unconsciously organizes patriarchy. In order to develop a theory of spectatorship that incorporates both psychoanalysis and the political aims set out in Mulvey's paper, we need to understand some key Lacanian terms.

Imaginary, Symbolic, Real

Lacan proposes that there are three categories that constitute our experience: the *Imaginary*, the *Symbolic* and the *Real*. The *Imaginary* realm offers the subject the illusion of fullness, completeness and mastery. Associated with the child's early experience of the world, it is pre-verbal and pre-social. In the *Imaginary* 'no clear distinction exists between the "self" and other, between internal and external worlds. There is no clearly defined "I" at this point, rather a loosely bounded and undifferentiated mass of sensations in which the body, much like the emerging ego, has not taken on a coherent form.'[30] The *Symbolic* is the order of language, it structures and gives meaning to our experiences. The third category, the *Real*, marks the point at which the *Symbolic* fails.

It is important to stress that the *Imaginary*, *Symbolic* and *Real* are three mutually entangled levels rather than discrete phases the subject passes through. Although the *Imaginary* does predominate in the infant's early life, these three orders are 'ever-present and underscore all aspects of human experience'.[31] Further, although the *Real* can neither be represented in the *Imaginary* nor inscribed in the *Symbolic*, it is not 'beyond' these orders. Rather, all three orders are interrelated. This interdependence of the *Imaginary*, *Symbolic* and *Real* is represented by Lacan in the form of a Borromean knot.

The *Real* has become a central category for contemporary Lacanian theorists who are interested in exploring the limits of ideology. As a point of failure, the *Real* 'marks ideology's vulnerability'[32] thus, 'when we call ideology into question, we do so from this real point within it'.[33] With this in mind, let's briefly return to Mulvey's argument. Mulvey proposes that the cinema puts the spectator in an imaginary position of mastery. This position is organized narratively/symbolically around the figure of the male protagonist to produce a particular form of spectatorship that she theorizes through the term 'the male gaze'. Mulvey concludes that the destruction of the pleasures associated with the male gaze offers a way of challenging patriarchy. In particular, Mulvey calls for a politics of filmmaking that would include freeing 'the look of the audience into … passionate detachment'.[34] However, as McGowan argues, psychoanalysis shows us that 'our ability to contest an ideological structure depends on our ability to recognize the point at which it breaks down, not on our ability to distance ourselves from that structure through the process of conscious reflection'.[35] In short, the passionate detachment argued for by Mulvey does not call the ideology of patriarchy into question from the *Real*. How then do we 'find' the *Real*? Lacan teaches us that 'there is no other entrance for the subject into the real than the fantasy'.[36]

Fantasy 'fills in' the gaps in ideology, and this is why theorists such as Mulvey are critical of it. However, this criticism of fantasy only addresses one aspect of the relationship between fantasy and the *Symbolic*. It does not take into account that if ideology and the *Symbolic* order were not haunted by the *Real*, there would be no need for fantasy. Fantasy thus simultaneously denies and declares the constitutive incompleteness of the *Symbolic* order. When we understand this, we can see that fantasy not only acts in the service of ideology but also has the potential to disrupt it. As Žižek states in *The Sublime Object of Ideology*, 'The fundamental level of ideology ... is not that of an illusion masking the real state of things but that of an (unconscious) fantasy structuring our social reality itself.'[37]

What then is the fantasy that structures the social reality of patriarchy? Although fantasies take many forms, Žižek argues that 'fantasy is ultimately always the fantasy of a successful sexual relationship'.[38] We might recognize this fantasy as one that is often mobilized by Hollywood, capitalism and the compulsory heterosexuality of patriarchy. However, Lacan's understanding of the sexual relationship is rather different. As he famously states in *Encore*, 'There is no sexual relation [*Il n'y a pas de rapport sexuel*].'[39]

Psychoanalysis and sexual difference

The Lacanian account of sexual difference does not relate to anatomical difference but to the limits of the *Symbolic*; woman and man mark the two ways in which the *Symbolic* fails. As Jennifer Friedlander has summarized, woman and man 'refer not to biological categories, nor to their cultural overlays, but instead to the two positions that a subject can take in response to the failure of the symbolic system to confer an identity'.[40] Sexual difference in Lacan's writing relates to what is unsymbolizable within *every* subject as opposed to symbolic differences between subjects. As such, in Lacanian theory, sexual difference is not the same as racial, class or ethnic differences. As Joan Copjec explains, 'Whereas these differences are inscribed in the symbolic, sexual difference is not: only the failure of its inscription is marked in the symbolic. Sexual difference, in other words, is a real and not a symbolic difference.'[41]

Psychoanalysis would therefore seem to have little to offer feminism. While feminism is concerned with questioning and challenging the symbolic value that is accorded to the biological differences between men and women, psychoanalysis insists on the primacy of sexual difference. This understanding of woman and man as radically opposed seems to be politically regressive. However, what psychoanalysis asks us to do is to invert our thinking and recognize that, contrary as it may seem to say it: insisting on sexual difference is the only guarantee we have against sexism.[42]

Here it is important to introduce a distinction between the poststructuralist position which stresses the particularity and diversity of the categories woman and man (among others); the notion of the universal that underpins the essentialist thinking exemplified by popular psychology texts such *Men Are from Mars and Women Are from Venus*[43] and Lacan's demand that we read universality and particularity together. Lacan's position is not a compromise where the merits of both are embraced, rather what is articulated in Lacan's formulas of sexuation is an insistence that the 'either/or choice between universal and particular proves not only insufficient, but also erroneous'.[44] That is to say, Lacanian psychoanalysis asks us to recognize that a feminist politics lies not in challenging the way in which woman and man are positioned in the *Symbolic* but in challenging the binary logic that conceives the universal and the particular as exhaustive possibilities. In Lacan's account of sexual difference, male and female are different positions that *both* declare the constitutive incompleteness of the *Symbolic* order. What is important to understand is that this failure of the *Symbolic* order to confer an identity is not binary; although the subject must adopt one of these two enunciative positions, the relation between these two possibilities is not complementary. As Copjec explains,

> Rather than defining a universe of men that is complemented by a universe of women, Lacan defines man as the prohibition against constructing a universe and women as the impossibility of doing so. The sexual relation fails for two reasons: it is impossible and it is prohibited. Put these two failures together; you will never come up with a whole.[45]

We are now in a better position to understand Lacan's assertion that there is no sexual relation. This statement encapsulates the asymmetrical relation between male and female structures. What is key here is that these two modes of impossibility 'are not transcended; there is no harmonious coming together, no balanced relationship emerges between them'.[46] It is not the conception of the terms male and female as different, but the characterization of them as complementary binaries that serves the aims of heterosexism: the complementary relation is a fantasy that conceals the fundamental impasses of sexual difference.[47]

Understanding the relation between the antimonies woman and man in this way relocates the terrain of a feminist politics of spectatorship. It allows us to see that patriarchy is underpinned by a fantasy of the successful sexual relationship which replaces antinomy with eroticized difference. That is to say, it offers an account for the failure of the sexual relation in symbolic terms. It is what the fantasy of the sexual relationship conceals – 'the fundamental deadlock of symbolization'[48] – and not the symbolic valency of how we attribute meaning to biological difference that forms the proper terrain for a feminist response. With this in mind, if we compare our examples, we can see that they form two different responses.

In *Strip*, Stehli positions herself as the object of desire in a way that positions men and women in a complementary binary. *Strip* complicates dominant modes of representing the female body; it illuminates ideological formations and directs the viewer towards recognizing the constructed nature of gendered viewing positions. However, reflecting on the female body as an object of desire in this way does not challenge the understanding of men and women as complementary opposites. Changing the content of the fantasy scene, for example, so that the woman assumes a dominant role, does not change the function of the fantasy which is to present the sexual relationship as possible. In *Strip* the symbolic categories of male and female are played with, but the fantasy of the successful sexual relation is sustained, and the viewer remains comfortably within the boundaries of ideology. This is reflected in the reviews which show that viewers feel secure looking at this work; we know how to locate ourselves within it. Its disruptions are humorous rather than *Real*. In short, by organizing the relationship between male and female in novel, but nonetheless complementary ways, Stehli's work only addresses the *Symbolic* dimensions of patriarchy.

By contrast, we can see that Nakadate's work is concerned with the non-relation between sexes – they seem to exist in completely different spaces.[49] This is reflected in the audience responses where the relationship between the audience and the work remains irreducible to comfortable point of identification. As one reviewer expresses this disorientating experience, 'I was never certain who it was directed at.'[50] The thread 'the-afc-guide-to-disliking-laurel-nakadate-without-hating-women'[51] is another example of the troubling position Nakadate puts viewers in, and of the impasses generated by her work. Instead of a work that consolidates ideology, Nakadate's work is structured around points of symbolic failure. By engaging with sexual difference as *Real*, the work effects a disturbance in the functioning of ideology. It is not that Nakadate's work 'undoes' patriarchy, rather it shows us where the ideology of patriarchy falters, the antagonism that it seeks to cover over. In short, it disturbs the fantasy of the successful sexual relation. And this returns us to Mulvey's argument, for the name that Lacan gives to disturbances of fantasy when they occur in visual field is the gaze.

12

The politics of enjoyment

In this chapter we will consider Richard Prince's *New Portraits* (2014) as a way of exploring psychoanalytic writings on fantasy, enjoyment and the social.

Richard Prince: *New Portraits*

Richard Prince's *New Portraits* is a series of screenshots from *Instagram* that have been printed on large canvases measuring 65 × 48 inches. The posts chosen tend to be from accounts of artists, models, musicians and socialites who have a significant social media following. The screenshot includes the uploaded photograph – most often a portrait – and some of the comments, including one by Prince himself who posts as @richardprince4.

The reception to *New Portraits* has included public outrage, demands for personal compensation and critical dismissal. For example, after noting that 'possible cogent responses to the show include naughty delight and sincere abhorrence', the *New Yorker*'s Peter Schjeldahl stated that his own response on seeing the work was 'something like a wish to be dead'.[1] The response on *Twitter* has been particularly virulent and includes the following succinct verdict – retweeted by Prince himself – that 'Richard Prince is a jerk and he sucks'.

This is not the first time that Prince's work and his practice of appropriating images have attracted a negative response. While appropriation was welcomed by a number of critics who argued that it was a critical strategy that subverted the notions of originality and authorship associated with modernism,[2] it was not universally welcomed. For many, works such as Prince's seminal *Cowboy* series did not partake in the labour or self-reflection necessary to produce art. That these works were to eventually sell for vast sums of money – in 2005 *Untitled (Cowboy)* (1989) sold for more than $1 million at auction – only attracted further derision. As Douglas Eklund has noted of postmodern practices of appropriation, it 'rivals in effect and inspires a perhaps even deeper revulsion and contempt than the most perverse of pornographic transgressions'.[3] Although it has been argued that we are now in a post-postmodern era, Prince's work – like pornography – continues to attract visceral public, legal and critical responses.

With *New Portraits*, the charges levelled against Prince are threefold: that he has asserted authorship over a work he did not produce, that he has made money from someone else's labour and that he is a misogynist. As Jerry Saltz has summarized the negative responses,

> First, he's making money from these things, a lot of money, and given how easy they seem to be to make, that seems like theft, or at least a con; second, he's using other people's *Instagram* feeds without their permission; and most prevalently, he's a lech for looking at and making art with pictures of young girls.[4]

However, the 'wrongs' of Prince's work are not as tangible as they may first appear. For example, although Prince has been called 'a dirty old man', 'creepy' and 'a pervert', his comments do not differ significantly from many of the other posts found underneath these images. As Megan M. Gallagher has observed, 'Prince is definitely not the only American male with an imaginary relationship with Pamela Anderson. In fact, Anderson's social media accounts are littered with comments of similar tone and subject.'[5]

While many have framed the issue of authorship in relation to copyright laws (and in particular to *Cariou v. Prince*), the issue of copyright is not straightforward regarding online material. In addition, the logic that informs copyright laws is that copying disperses the value of the original. However, in *New Portraits* Prince turns something that was freely distributed into something that he profits from. Therefore, although some have tried to quantify Prince's actions in terms of individual losses, the value of the work is produced by Prince's act of 'stealing' it; he does not steal it because it is valuable. As such, Prince's strategy might be seen to replicate *Instagram*'s own strategy of converting what is freely given into valuable content and data. It is notable that the most common response given by those whose images had been used relates not to legal copyright, but the claim that using images from another person's stream goes against the 'spirit' of the *Instagram* community. As Missy Suicide wrote of her response to seeing her portrait in the gallery, it felt like 'a violation by someone who doesn't get it'.[6] In understanding why *New Portraits* has caused so much anger, the work of Jodi Dean is useful. Dean's use of psychoanalysis to theorize communicative capitalism shows us that we need to take seriously the role of enjoyment if we are to grasp what underpins the *Instagram* community and recognize what is at stake in Prince's contravention of it.

Communicative capitalism

In her writings on communicative capitalism Jodi Dean draws attention to the way in which the discursive construction of the internet as a forum in which people are free to express their individuality masks the requirement to exhibit certain forms of behaviour including what has been termed 'affective labour'. This is a familiar argument; what distinguishes Dean's work is that she argues that we not only need to understand the internet as a space that is deeply implicated in capitalism but also need to be attentive to the psychic dynamics of the internet.

For Dean, the repetitions of social media, the constant updates, likes and posts are key: 'Repetition exerts a force, a compulsion; repetition has effects *independent* of the meaning of what is repeated.'[7] We can see this in recent research that has shown that as many as 59 per cent of links shared on social media have never actually been clicked or read by the person sharing them.[8] As Dean observes, 'The movement from link to link, the forwarding and storing and commenting, the contributing without expectation of response but in hope of further movement (why else count page views?) is circulation for its own sake.'[9] As such, Dean argues that there are two elements to networked communications: the content of the communication and the fact of its being sent. Dean proposes that we are witnessing a displacement of content by contribution where the *exchange* value of messages overtakes their *use* value. As she summarizes, 'Old media sought to deliver messages. New media just circulates.'[10]

This offers a way of understanding Prince's often baffling comments which range from jokes and quotes to random emojis. They are generic, often awkwardly sexual, sometimes nonsensical comments written under the username richardprince4. What has angered many who have responded to Prince's work is their unskilled nature. As Clay Cubitt succinctly expresses it, 'Watching Richard Prince do *Instagram* is like watching your dad try to rap'.[11] However, rather than a lack of skill, what we might see in Prince's comments is a foregrounding of the post as contribution and not content. It is also notable here that many people were critical of the production quality of the work. However, the pixilation of the images not only references the technological conditions of their production and circulation[12] but also demonstrates that Prince's work is not concerned with images in themselves, but with the image-as-contribution.

The image-as-contribution asks us to understand *New Portraits* in a different way to Prince's earlier work. While postmodern strategies of appropriation targeted modernist notions of authenticity and originality by challenging the hierarchical relationship between copy and original, there is no such privileged origin here. As Dean observes,

> A message is no longer primarily a message from a sender to a receiver … the message is simply part of a circulating data stream. Its particular content is irrelevant. Who sent it is irrelevant. Who receives it is irrelevant. That it needs to be responded to is irrelevant. The only thing that is relevant is circulation, the addition to the pool.[13]

This allows us to see that it is not copying per se that is the issue, but the stopping of circulation and the depletion of the pool. The removal of contributions from the pool is the critical gesture that Prince enacts. Here it is interesting to note that the popular response to

Prince's work – from posting selfies in front of the work to Missy Suicide offering reprints of her post used by Prince for $90,[14] is to put the images back into circulation.

However, this still leaves a key question unanswered: Why should this matter? After all, there are more messages circulating than anyone can quantify. However, Dean argues that there is something very particular at stake in contributions. By undergoing circulation, an image or post becomes itself and something more. As Dean expresses it, 'The additive dimension of communication for its own sake designates an excess. This excess isn't a new meaning or perspective. It doesn't refer to a new content. It is rather the intensity accrued from the repetition, the excitement or thrill of more.'[15] Participation is not compulsory so what compels us? Acknowledging that affective attachments to media are not in themselves sufficient to produce actual communities, Dean's answer is that 'communicative capitalism relies on networks that generate and amplify enjoyment.'[16]

The Lacanian term for the anxious enjoyment that Dean argues is central to the pleasures of social media is *jouissance*. Derek Hook's description is useful here:

> We may speak of someone *flying* into a rage or of a person *wallowing* in despair. The verb in each case, 'to fly', 'to wallow', indexes the factor of *jouissance*. The enjoyment involved here is to be distinguished from the everyday (banal, pleasurable) sense of *enjoying*; it refers, instead, to more illicit gains, to 'getting off' in ways one would not readily admit to … the possibility that once I have flown into a rage I find myself greatly excited, exhilarated by this; that in the midst of wallowing in despair I find myself painfully gratified by own misery.[17]

While such an enjoyment would seem to be an intensely individual experience, it is in fact a social product. As Hook goes on to explain, 'Enjoyment, far from being reductively individual … is always linked to the symbolic. How so? Well, by virtue of its relation to socially prescribed limits.'[18] Enjoyment not only structures online behaviour, it is central to any social group. Indeed, psychoanalysis asks us to recognize that ideology works 'via the currency of enjoyment'.[19]

Psychoanalysis and enjoyment

In *Totem and Taboo*[20] Freud illustrates the foundational role of enjoyment in structuring the social order by offering a mythic account of the birth of civilization. Freud imagines a primal horde ruled by a primal father who keeps all the enjoyment to himself until one day the sons band together to kill and devour the father. Freud describes this murder as the first social act. However, this act does not produce a social order in which everyone can enjoy, for, in order to guarantee that no one will take the place of the dead father and that the sons will all be equal, 'what had up to then been prevented by his actual existence was thenceforward prohibited by the sons themselves.'[21] As such, society is installed under the banner of the son who 'stands for the evacuation, or drying up, of excess enjoyment and thus for the possibility of pleasure's even apportionment.'[22] This narrative dramatizes, on a social or group level, the way in which the sacrifice of enjoyment is the price that must be paid for entry into the social realm.

It is important to recognize that this narrative is a construction and that the enjoyment embodied in the primal father is something that does not exist prior to its renunciation. As McGowan notes, 'In giving it up, … we in effect retroactively create, through our presupposing of it, an enjoyment that we never had.'[23] Democratic societies are able to perpetuate themselves because they are structured in a way that allows subjects to derive pleasure from the sacrifice of their enjoyment. Indeed, social coherence depends on the pleasure that subjects derive from the sacrifice of their private enjoyment on the understanding that it is for the greater good of society. This pleasure in sacrifice is additionally supplemented by the pleasure that is derived from various minor transgressions that are permitted by the social authority such as drinking, gambling and so on. Todd McGowan describes societies that are structured in this way as a 'society of prohibition': 'A society of prohibition requires all its members to sacrifice their individual, private ways of obtaining enjoyment for the sake of the social order as a whole. That is to say, one receives an identity from society in exchange for one's immediate access to enjoyment, which one must give up.'[24]

What must be added here is that there is in fact no such thing as enjoyment; 'There are only distributions, articulations of enjoyment as structured by fantasy.'[25] We are used to thinking of fantasies as both individual and opposed to reality; however, as we saw in Chapter 11, fantasy plays a key role in the organization of the social. Fantasies concerning enjoyment are central to group identity. However, as Freud's example demonstrates, the fantasies that constitute a group are not about the enjoyment of enjoyment, but rather concern its absence. This absence is normally narrated in relation to a theft.[26] This apparently undesirable set of fantasies function to conceal from us 'that *we never possessed what was allegedly stolen from us*.'[27]

Although the fantasies produced and circulated to mask this traumatic fact vary immensely, what is key is that the social is not produced by shared interests or needs: the social is a group bound by a shared fantasy of an enjoyment that would fill the gap left by their sacrifice. As Žižek expresses it, 'A nation *exists* only as long as its specific *enjoyment* continues to be materialized in a set of social practices and transmitted through national myths or fantasies that secure these practices.'[28]

Now, *Instagram* isn't a nation, but nonetheless, the community of *Instagram* is defined and distinguished by a particular organization of enjoyment that is expressed by its members as the 'spirit' of the *Instagram* community. While some of Prince's transgressions have been subject to public law, most are transgressions of unwritten codes of conduct.

Psychoanalysis shows us that there are always two sides to the law: the public, written law, and the obscene, unwritten underside to this law. While public law is enforced through prohibitions, the obscene law operates through commandments. Slavoj Žižek uses the film *A Few Good Men*[29] as an example. The film's drama centres on the court-martial of two marines accused of murdering a fellow soldier. The defence argues that the murder was carried out under the auspices of a 'Code Red' which authorizes the disciplining of a fellow soldier who fails to respect the chain of command. As Žižek notes, the 'function of this "Code Red" is extremely interesting: it condones an act of transgression'.[30]

What is significant here is not only the way in which prohibition is always accompanied by an unwritten understanding of the conditions under which it might be transgressed but also that it is the transgression of the law that constitutes the social bond. As Žižek writes, 'The deepest identification that holds a community together is not so much an identification with the Law that regulates its "normal" everyday rhythms, but rather identification with the specific form of transgression of the Law, of its suspension (in psychoanalytic terms, with the specific form of enjoyment).'[31] In short, 'Transgression is a form of ideological inscription that is central to the maintenance of … social bonds.'[32]

Here it is interesting to note that, when questioned, many of the users who criticized Prince's work had themselves copied content. So how are Prince's transgressions different to the condoned transgressions that bond *Instagram* together? How do we determine who belongs to a group, especially when it is as vast and diffuse as *Instagram?* Here enjoyment plays a key role. To understand the forms of enjoyment particular to *Instagram* further, we need to address the distinctive form that fantasies of enjoyment acquire under neoliberalism.

The society of enjoyment

A number of critics have pointed to the way in which there has been a shift in the fantasy narrative that underpins capitalist societies. The shift from the public citizen to the private consumer advanced as the model of social belonging under neoliberalism has precipitated a move from a society of prohibition to what McGowan calls the 'society of enjoyment'.[33] In the society of enjoyment the private enjoyment of individuals that must be sacrificed in the society of prohibition becomes a stabilizing force. Indeed, enjoyment acquires the status of a social duty: my position as a citizen requires the unending display of my enjoyment.

Without the narrative of sacrifice which governs the society of prohibition, in the society of enjoyment there appear to be no obstacles to the subject's enjoyment. However, commanded enjoyment is not the same as enjoying freely. The command to enjoy only produces a sense of obligation to enjoy oneself; it does not produce enjoyment. Indeed, the reversal of the permissive 'You May!' into the prescriptive 'You Must!': the transformation of permitted enjoyment into ordained enjoyment is one 'with which it is impossible to comply'.[34] As Yannis Stavrakakis has noted, 'The seemingly innocent and benevolent call to "enjoy!" – as in "Enjoy *Coca-Cola*!" – embodies the violent dimension of an irresistible commandment'.[35] Indeed, the apparent presence of enjoyment is paradoxically more oppressive than its absence. The society of enjoyment commands the subject to an impossible enjoyment: to find complete fulfilment in work, relationships, exercise, a holiday, a party, a new dress, a cup of coffee and so on.

Social media is a good example of this. Posting online concerns the display of our enjoyment to others. We feel the need to do this constantly. However, our posts – no matter how celebratory – always seem to pale in relation to everyone else's. Enjoyment seems to be everywhere on social media, yet for the individual it remains out of reach: we are only pretending to have fun at a party while everyone else is *really* enjoying. As McGowan reminds us, 'The fundamental thing to recognize about the society of enjoyment is that in it the pursuit of enjoyment has misfired: the society of enjoyment has not provided the enjoyment that it promises.'[36] The shift from prohibition to enjoyment does not designate a change in social reality but a shift in the fantasies that constitute the social bond. As McGowan notes of this change, it is 'merely a transformation in the way subjects experience the social order, ... it occasions no substantive change in the relationship between society and enjoyment'.[37] The question then becomes for whom are we pretending to enjoy?

The Other

Lacan proposes that in addition to the others that form a social group, there is the Other: 'A figure of social authority that represents the social order as a whole and makes demands on the subject.'[38] Thus, whether our settings are private or not, when we post on *Instagram* we are presenting ourselves not only to discrete others but also to the Other. The Other is key to understanding the ways in which fantasies of enjoyment circulate and the forms they take.

Lacan has famously stated that 'man's desire is the desire of the Other'.[39] Lacan expresses this dynamic in the form of a question – '*che vuoi?*' (What do you want?)[40] Although there can be no answer to this question, fantasy offers an imagined scenario in which the desire of the Other becomes clear. Unlike the popular understanding of fantasy as an intimate, personal form of wish-fulfilment, for psychoanalysis, fantasy is always constituted in relation to the perceived desire of the Other. The intersubjective dimension of fantasy becomes apparent in the following example, cited by Žižek, of a child's fantasy of eating strawberry cake. As Žižek writes

> what we have here is by no means a simple case of the direct hallucinatory satisfaction of a desire (she wanted a cake, she didn't get it, so she fantasized about it ...). What one should introduce here is precisely the dimension of intersubjectivity: the crucial feature is that while she was voraciously eating a strawberry cake, the little girl noticed how her parents were deeply satisfied by this spectacle, by seeing her fully enjoying it – so what the fantasy of eating a strawberry cake is really about is her attempt to form an identity (of the one who fully enjoys eating a cake given by the parents) that would satisfy her parents, would make her the object of their desire.[41]

What is key here is that although the fantasy scene may employ socially conventional objects of desire – strawberry cake, a relationship, a new car – it is not the aspirational qualities of the scene that distinguishes it as a fantasy, but the unconscious function that the scene fulfils. As Žižek explains, 'What we encounter in the very core of fantasy is the relationship to the desire of the Other, to the latter's opacity: *the desire staged in fantasy is not mine but the desire of the Other*.'[42] Or, in McGowan words: 'Fantasy provides the subject guidance about what the Other desires and thus constitutes this desire as knowable. Without this guidance, these would be no way of approaching this desire or beginning to make sense of it.'[43]

In the society of prohibition, the desire of the Other was articulated through social regulations. Lacking such guidance in the society of enjoyment we interpret the desire of the Other through the lens of consumerism. As McGowan summarizes, 'When I feel as if I must have a new product, at that moment I fully immerse myself in the fantasy of what the Other desires.'[44] While some of the choices we might make are straightforward – the latest car, the most expensive and obscure new kind of coffee – because we must interpret the desire of the Other, fantasies can also take unexpected and novel forms. McGowan's example of fashion trends is useful here. Remarking on the trend for leaving the tags on new clothes, McGowan argues that it 'began not with one subject's desire but with the interpretation of the desire of the Other.'[45] Similarly, when we post online, we are responding to and interpreting the question of the Other's desire. Whether we post about a party, reading a book, visiting a gallery or going the gym we are immersing ourselves in the fantasy of what the Other wants.

If we take one of the most frequent forms of post, the selfie, as an example. When we take a selfie we adopt the pose and location that we think will speak to the Other. Likes indicate if others think the Other would like it or not. And this is how certain types of post evolve. If I doubt what the Other wants, I need only follow the likes. Each post is an opportunity for subjects to prove that they have the kind of enjoyment that the Other wants. What underlies this is a demand that the Other acknowledge us as enjoying subjects.

We can, of course, account for many of the popular elements of the selfie through ideology: poses that accentuate youth or showcase an expensive new watch or stylish haircut can all be placed within the coordinates of a society orientated around consumption. However, this does not explain the repetitive, cyclical nature of the selfie. As Dmitry Uzlaner notes, 'The subject takes one selfie after another, as if each time trying and each time failing to reach something through his same repeated action.'[46] The repetitions of the selfie show us that they concern an elusive object. Uzlaner argues that what is sought in the selfie is not just social recognition but the gaze of the Other. For Uzlander, the selfie is a repetitious longing to both 'receive that very gaze and at the same time to give this gaze what it needs'.[47] This, Uzlaner proposes, is the 'selfie-fantasy'. It is important to note that 'no matter how successful the resulting image, however many likes or enthusiastic comments it gets – all the same it is not enough. The subject must again dress up, again put on makeup in the hope of finally catching that same gaze of that same Other. In this sense the selfie, like any other fantasy, is endless.'[48]

The empty gesture

As Žižek has noted, belonging to a society involves a paradoxical point at which each of us is ordered to embrace freely, as the result of our choice, what is anyway imposed on us. This paradox finds form in the empty gesture. The empty gesture is an offer which is meant to be rejected: 'What the empty gesture offers is the opportunity to choose the impossible, that which inevitably will *not* happen.'[49] The example Žižek gives is as follows: 'When, after being engaged in fierce competition for a promotion with my closest friend, I win, the proper thing to do is to offer to withdraw, so that he will get the promotion, and the proper thing for him to do is to reject my offer.'[50] However, what if the offer is accepted? A situation like this is, in Žižek's words, 'properly catastrophic' causing a dissolution of the social link. Let's return to *New Portraits* to consider this further.

Prince's comments have attracted much commentary, and the responses are particularly charged in relation to those posts in which Prince implies a physical relationship with the women who have posted. For example, under singer-songwriter Sky Ferreira's portrait of herself in the passenger seat of a red sports car he posts, 'Enjoyed the ride today. Let's do it again. Richard.' Under an image of Nightcoregirl he writes, 'Now I know.' Under a post by Pamela Anderson he writes, 'Let's hook up next week.' In all of these cases Prince takes the 'offer' of the post literally.

The nature of the posts becomes clear if we compare it with the comments made by others. For example, under the image of Pamela Anderson in a white bathing suit acidayn writes: 'Makes me wanna watch your not so famous home movies. WOW!'

Though misogynistic, this is the correct response. In common with many celebrity posts, Anderson is not offering herself in the image, but rather using the personal address of the post to suggest an intimate encounter that will be declined so that the boundary between the celebrity and her audience appears permeable but remains intact. To phrase it in terms of enjoyment, the possibility of enjoyment is presented as something that is possible but save for an obstacle – she is geographically 'out of reach'. acidayn's response turns down the 'offer' made by the post. However, Prince takes it literally. The act of taking the empty gesture literally enacts what Lacan calls 'traversing the fantasy'. Let's return to the reviews to better understand this idea.

> My own [response] was something like a wish to be dead.[51]
>
> . . .
>
> I can't help thinking that I've never, ever been to a show and been so unmoved. So underwhelmed. So *what's-the-point*?
>
> I got nothing.[52]
>
> . . .
>
> What, exactly, is there to say about any of this? Virtually nothing.
>
> . . .
>
> Don't go see it. Don't ever buy the work.[53]

Critics argue that Prince's work does nothing, yet the anger in the responses show that it is deeply effecting. So, what is the 'nothing' that it does?

In order to challenge ideological structures it is necessary traverse the fantasies that sustain our psychic investment in them. As such, a truly political act is one which alters the subject's mode of enjoyment. If we take the reviews at their word, we might see that Prince's work is not without meaning, but rather without fantasy. This is the offensive nothing that Prince does in *New Portraits* – he asks us to experience *Instagram* without the fantasies that sustain our belief in the possibility of enjoyment. Confronting the fantasies that organize our enjoyment destroys our sense of self – who 'we' are. By accepting the empty gesture Prince's work confronts us with unbearable realization that there is no Other and no enjoyment. We literally 'get nothing'. It is not enjoyable; indeed some of us would rather die than encounter it.

Part Five

Photography and the event

In this section the relationship between photography and the event will be considered. To begin, we will be looking at examples of work that engage with new lines of thought on historical violence, memory and trauma. Works by David Levinthal, Alan Schechner and Marc Adelman will be used to explore the role that photography might play in mediating our relationship to past events of which we have no direct experience. Chapter 14 addresses the work of a number of contemporary photographers working within what might be termed 'post-photojournalism'. We will consider the work of three photographers, Christoph Bangert, Richard Mosse and Antonio Denti, as examples of how photographic artists have responded to debates on the representation of conflict and the ethics of representing violence in relation to recent events. Finally, Chapter 15 will consider how a new aesthetic – that of the aftermath – is being used by artists such as such as Simon Norfolk, Rosemary Laing and Heungsoon Im.

13

Photography, memory, history

In this chapter we will address some of the key debates surrounding photography, memory and history with particular reference to artists whose work addresses the Holocaust. To begin, we will address the ethics of witnessing in relation to David Levinthal's series *Mein Kampf*. Second, we will consider Alan Schechner's 'Self Portrait at Buchenwald: It's the Real Thing'. In this photograph Schechner uses the photographic archive and digital technology to draw attention to the way in which the reproduction and circulation of Holocaust photographs always take place under particular ideologically inflected conditions. To conclude, we will look at Marc Adelman's *Stelen* as a way of engaging with contemporary debates around technology and multidirectional memory.

To begin, it is necessary to consider the significant shift that has taken place how we think about and conceptualize the past. As Kerwin Lee Klein notes, '*Memory* is replacing old favourites – *nature, culture, language* – as the word most commonly paired with history, and that shift is remaking historical imagination.'[1] Across a range of disciplines, memory, in particular traumatic memory, has become a key way of theorizing the links between history, individual experience and cultural representation.

The emergence of traumatic memory as a way of thinking about history was the result of research conducted into what was to become known as post-traumatic stress disorder within the fields of psychology and psychiatry. In 1990s this research started to be incorporated into writings by academics working in the humanities. The now vast literature that makes up the multidisciplinary field of trauma and memory studies combines concepts of trauma developed in psychoanalysis and psychology with a deconstructive approach to language, philosophical reflections on historical trauma as well as subject-specific knowledge from disciplines such as literature, film and cultural studies.

Writings by Shoshana Felman and Dori Laub[2] and Cathy Caruth[3] are considered to be canonical texts of trauma studies. Caruth proposes that trauma should be understood as a 'pathology of temporality' and argues that the 'enigmatic core' of trauma is 'the delay or incompletion in knowing, or even in seeing, an overwhelming occurrence that then remains, in its insistent return, absolutely *true* to the event'.[4] Through this characterization of traumatic memory as 'true to the event', trauma theory promises a unique mode of access to the past.

The writings of Marianne Hirsch, which privilege the role of photography and visual media in acts of remembrance, are also useful to consider here. Hirsch uses the term 'postmemory' to describe a very particular form of memory that is connected to its source not through recollection but through an imaginative investment. Distinguished from memory by generational distance and from history by deep personal connection, the term is chosen by Hirsch as a means of conveying 'its temporal and qualitative difference from survivor memory, its secondary, or second-generation memory quality, its basis in displacement, its vicariousness and belatedness'.[5] For Hirsch the mediated nature of postmemory is central; indeed, she argues that postmemory is 'a powerful form of memory *precisely* because its connection to its object or source is mediated not through recollection but through representation, projection, and creation – often based on silence rather than speech, on the invisible rather than the visible'.[6] The concept of postmemory offers an important way of thinking about the complex relationship that the children of survivors have to the Holocaust; however, because it opens acts of remembrance out beyond a direct connection to the event, Hirsch's work also offers a means of thinking through artistic representations by second-generation and third-generation artists.

While the work of Hirsch, Caruth and Felman and Laub remains popular and influential, the model of witnessing employed in the early writings of trauma theory has been subject to criticism. Although the turn to memory was influenced by incorporating sources such as life writing, diaries, photographs and art works by subjects previously excluded as historical witnesses on the basis of their gender, class or race, critics have argued that there is a universalizing force in trauma theory's characterization of the witness and the survivor such that the account of the survivor has come to carry with it 'a connotation, if not of precise factual accuracy, then of moral innocence and a drive to serve the truth'.[7] In recent critiques of memory studies, or what might be termed critical memory studies, there is a concern articulated that witnessing becomes 'scripted' and therefore simply reproduces a particular set of ideologically inflected 'truths'. As Debartai Sanyal writes, 'The dislocation of the event's particularity and of the traumatized subject's specificity has fostered a dehistoricized, catastrophic vision of history that may become a cultural master narrative in its own right.'[8] As such, recent writings have stressed the need to entertain other forms of engagement. In this chapter we will address three artists who use photography to ask us to engage in acts of viewing that are difficult and conflicted as a means of drawing attention to the complexity of witnessing history.

David Levinthal: *Mein Kampf*

In his work *Mein Kampf* (1994–6) David Levinthal seeks to complicate the way in which we think about memory, history and the representation of traumatic events by drawing attention to the ways in which the Holocaust circulates as a representation.

In *Mein Kampf* Levinthal uses toy figures to stage scenes referencing the visual legacy of Nazi military spectacle and the Holocaust. As Anne Chapman notes, 'In employing toys ... Levinthal reminds us that what we consider to be our knowledge of the reality of the Holocaust is in fact partially constructed by our imagination: we take representations of the Holocaust and cannot help but "animate" them.'[9] This play between truth and fiction is furthered by Levinthal's use of a very shallow depth of field, his choice of 20 × 24 inch Polaroid film and dramatic lighting which produces highly cinematic images characterized by deep, vivid colours. As Chapman summarizes, 'Levinthal is representing something other than the Holocaust itself ... he is interested in the "cultural transformation" in the ways it has been imagined'.[10]

Levinthal's staging of how he experienced the knowledge of the Holocaust as a child provocatively shows that his relationship to the Holocaust is contaminated by personal desires and cultural fantasies. The discomfort we experience viewing this work is heightened in those images where we are asked to take up the viewpoint of the perpetrator (Figure 13.1). Here, Levinthal's images draw attention to what is often marginalized in discussions around the reproduction of photographs from the Holocaust; many of the photographs we are most familiar with are perpetrator images taken by the Nazis.

Marianne Hirsch is one of the many critics who have drawn attention to the way in which the same few images have come to be seen as emblematic of the Holocaust. Hirsch argues that these photographs, reproduced across museum exhibits, educational texts and artworks often without details or context, have come to be employed 'more for their symbolic or affective than for their evidentiary or informational power'.[11] Hirsch is particularly critical of those images in which the photographer, the perpetrator and the spectator share the same space of looking. Hirsch argues that in such works 'the genocidal gaze of the Nazi death machine'[12] is also being reproduced. However, recent writings in trauma theory have advocated the importance of doing just this.

Susannah Radstone argues that it is important to recognize that 'the position of witness is a complex one that can exceed an empathic identification with victimhood to include identifications with other positions available within any given scenario, including, especially, those of perpetration'.[13] Indeed, Radstone proposes that 'an art-work's ethical value lies in its capacity to move its spectator through fantasy identifications with perpetration as well as with victimhood'.[14]

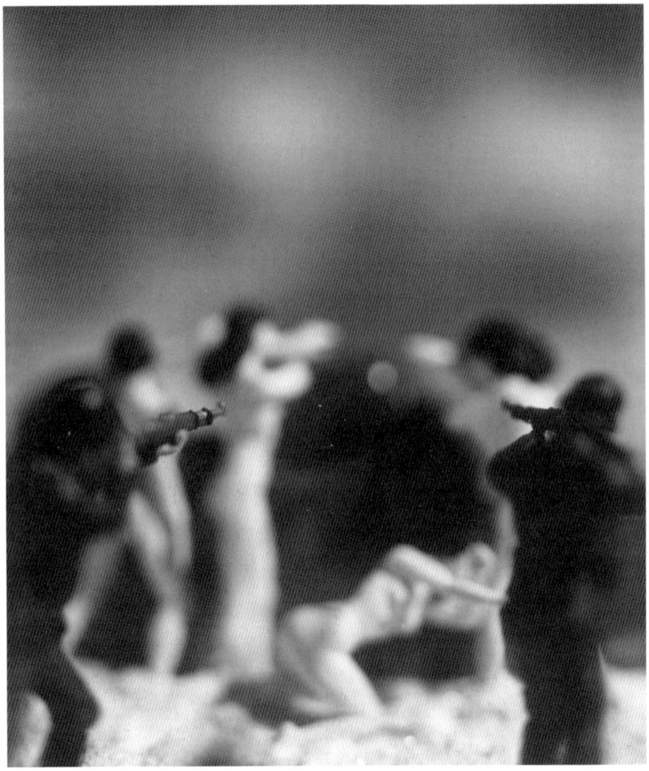

Figure 13.1 David Levinthal, *Untitled* from *Mein Kamf*, 1994. © ARS, NY and DACS, London 2019.

The identifications that we are asked to take on in Levinthal's images are nonetheless disturbing. As Claudia Eppert recounts, 'I was horrified and repulsed by the images, and by what they seemed to be asking of me.'[15] Despite the difficulties of viewing Levinthal's work, Eppert argues that assuming the position of the perpetrator is an important spectatorial position because it 'challenges us as viewers to face the potential of our own role in and capacities for violation and violence'.[16] Eppert argues that an ethical relationship between the present day witness and a historical moment of suffering is one in which we are held answerable, and proposes that those representations best suited to allowing us to do this are those that challenge us, 'alerting us to our responsibilities, not because they embody our responsibilities but because they may, in fact, neglect or violate them.'[17]

The importance of work such as Levinthal's is that we are not given the possibility for 'self-validation', and 'heroic confirmation'. Thus, Eppert argues, by 'toying with history' Levinthal's work asks us to reflect upon the limitations of dominant modes of engagement with traumatic past events: 'Toying with history also encompasses toying with those conventions, and the emotive and intellectual habits through which we access the past.'[18] Thus, while uncomfortable, we might see that Levinthal's work offers an important counter to the idealized model of witnessing invoked in relation to the Holocaust: it directs us to the crucial task identified by Radstone and Eppert of questioning dominant representations and the way in which they position the spectator.

Alan Schechner: 'Self Portrait at Buchenwald: It's the Real Thing'

Like Levinthal, Alan Schechner's work is concerned with how Holocaust images circulate in contemporary culture. In particular, Schechner engages with the way in which Holocaust is present as a part of contemporary American culture from Hollywood films and advertising, to museum exhibitions and textbooks. As Gary Weissman has noted 'because writings on the Holocaust are replete with such phrases as "imagining the unimaginable," "speaking the unspeakable," and "expressing the inexpressible," considering the subject in these terms has come to seem natural to both authors and readers'.[19] However, the discursive construction of the Holocaust as unrepresentable ignores how photographs from the Holocaust routinely appear in a range of contexts and thus serves to conceal the specific ways in which the Holocaust has been mobilized within American culture.

In our example, 'Self Portrait at Buchenwald: It's the Real Thing' (Figure 13.2), Schechner digitally inserts his own image into a famous photograph by Margaret Bourke-White of the liberation of Buchenwald. Schechner's intervention raises a number of issues. First, the obvious manipulation along with the title undercut authenticity of photograph as a historical document. Buchenwald appears only as a background to an ad for *Coke*, a device which draws attention to the fact that Holocaust photographs are a commodity; they are reproduced to fulfil a demand for understanding Holocaust in a particular way. As Nancy Weston succinctly notes, '*It's the Real Thing* refers not only to the reality of Buchenwald but the commodification of this reality.'[20] As Weston continues, the purpose of Schechner's intervention is that it 'transforms the standard Holocaust iconography of the Bourke-White image into an image that demonstrates the overuse of such images, so that they no longer shock us as they should, and the way they have been exploited for political gain'.[21] Lutz Koepnick offers a similar interpretation and argues that this work seeks to 'render problematic the way in which contemporary media culture makes use of the Shoah, the way in which images of the Nazi period and the Holocaust have become some of the most enduring commodities of postwar visual culture'.[22]

In addition, the inclusion of a can of *Coke* might reference the ways in which the Holocaust has been mobilized within American culture. A number of writers have

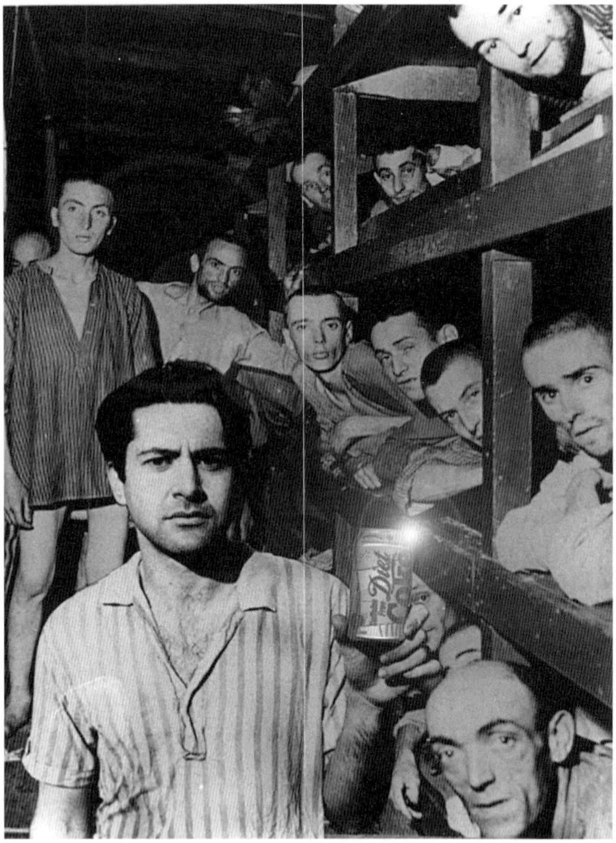

Figure 13.2 Alan Schechner, *Self Portrait at Buchenwald: It's the Real Thing*, 1991–3. © Alan Schechner. Courtesy of the artist.

theorized what has been termed the 'Americanization of the Holocaust'. Writings by Alvin Rosenfeld, Hilene Flanzbaum and Peter Novick[23] have all drawn attention to how 'America's adoption of European Jewish history is part of a process by which the story of the Holocaust – and America's presumed role in ending it – is incorporated into the fundamental tale of pluralism, tolerance, democracy, and human rights that America tells about itself'.[24] Indeed, Efraim Sicher has argued that, in the United States, 'the Holocaust entered popular culture as an American experience'.[25]

Schechner's work thus draws attention to how 'the unknowable, unspeakable, and unrepresentable can also function as alibis for identification and appropriation'.[26] In particular, his work asks viewers to recognize the extent to which Holocaust photographs have aided a writing of history that is in service of political and ideological aims. As Michael Rothberg notes, 'While a given memory rarely functions in a single way or means only one thing, all articulations of memory are not equal; powerful social, political, and psychic forces articulate themselves in every act of remembrance'.[27]

Marc Adelman: *Stelen*

Stelen (Columns) (2007–11)[28] by Marc Adelman is a collection of over 100 images of men posing at the Memorial to the Murdered Jews of Europe in Germany that Adelman sourced from various gay dating websites. Adelman spent several years collecting the photographs and notes that

> when I first saw the images I thought they were captivating but somewhat inexplicable; why did each of these men pose in the Holocaust Memorial and upload the image to their dating profile? Why strike these playful, flirtatious, and times overtly sexual gestures at such a historically vested public monument? I honestly did not know what to make of the images in the first several years of collecting them other than feeling that something was indeed being communicated across the series.[29]

As with our previous examples, Adelman's work asks us to reconsider the traditions and practices of witnessing in light of shifting cultures of remembrance. In particular, *Stelen* asks that we do this through the optic of social media.

While taking selfies at all memorial sites would seem to be an exceptional violation of traditional modes of witnessing, the sheer number of images collected by Adelman shows that it is an emergent trend that deserves attention. One way of thinking through these images is in relation to broader shifts about what constitutes witnessing.

As a number of critics have observed, publics are increasingly incited to participate in documenting history. As Sophia Drakopoulou notes, 'In global events, amateur photographs can create a collective memory of the event by crossing the public–private boundary.'[30] When shared publicly, amateur images become personal, public and historical at the same time. Indeed, Kari Andén-Papadopoulos has proposed that the camera-phone permits entirely new performative rituals of bearing witness. Examples given by Andén-Papadopoulos include the amateur footage of the September 11 attacks (2001), the London bombings (2005), the post-election protests in Iran (2009) and the Arab uprisings (2011–12). In all of these cases, we can see the way in which a wide range of ordinary people including 'local residents, holiday makers, soldiers, democratic activists, insurgents and terrorists – are now enabled to bypass established editorial and censorial filters and turn their personal record of an event into a public testimony that might disrupt "official" perspectives carefully crafted and provided to the mainstream news media'.[31]

Although witnessing encompasses a range of technologies, Andén-Papadopoulos stresses the visual aspect of these new forms of witnessing, arguing that witnessing is increasingly 'camera-mediated'. As Andén-Papadopoulos notes, photography is the 'standard response to crisis, serving to at once authenticate and screen the experience of a hurtful reality'.[32] However, we should also note that alongside the egalitarian rhetoric of citizen journalism, witnessing can be both a political act and a commodity.

14

Post-photojournalism and contemporary images of conflict

In this chapter we will be considering how photographic artists have responded to debates on the representation of conflict and the ethics of representing violence. In particular, we will be looking at how, in an era characterized by continuing cycles of wars, armed conflicts and ongoing states of terror, a number of contemporary photographers are seeking out new ways of depicting violence. Although the work of the photographers we will consider has a conscious relation to the goals and aesthetics of traditional photojournalism, it is tempered by the recognition that depiction of violence and the cultivation of empathy are no guarantees of social justice. Indeed, contemporary photographers must respond to the way in which citizen photojournalism, technological advances and the concentration of press ownership have all produced shifts in the role and status of photojournalism. The effect of these shifts has been so significant that a number of writers have been led to assert that 'photojournalism is dead'.

In this chapter we will be following Liam Kennedy's proposition that, rather than analysing the reasons for its 'death', we should be attentive to the new forms that photojournalism is taking. Post-photojournalism, anti-photojournalism, fine art photojournalism[1] are just some of the names that critics have given to the new ways that photographers are engaging with the representation of war.[2]

In 'Photojournalism and Warfare in a Postphotographic Age', Kennedy argues that contemporary conflict photographers 'are working to build visual vocabularies of documentation and representation that are less idealized than those that have preceded them, less burdened by assumptions about the truth value of the image'.[3] Through this new vocabulary photographers are seeking to present a critically engaged account of the changing nature of war. In Kennedy's words, 'Photographers are seeking answers to not only formal problems of visualization but ideological problems: ways of seeing war and state violence.'[4]

The ironic spectator

As Julian Stallabrass has noted, the ideals of liberal humanitarianism central to photojournalism 'seem unsuited to a neoliberal climate'.[5] The object of photojournalism to reveal, bear witness and prompt action is often compromised by the commodified frames through which we encounter such images. Thus, when addressing photographs of modern conflict we also need to consider the conditions of spectatorship that frame our encounter with such images: we need to place moral subjectivities and spectatorship in their social and historical context. This allows us to see that 'photojournalism is only in "decline" to the degree that it is still perceived as a late-modern, predigital form of image making performing to outmoded assumptions about the evidentiary authority of the documentary image and the existence of a knowledgeable, engaged citizenry'.[6] In moving away from a framework based on liberal humanism and developing ways of thinking about spectatorship in a neoliberal age, the writings of Lilie Chouliaraki are useful.[7]

In her book *The Ironic Spectator: Solidarity in the Age of Post-Humanitarianism*,[8] Chouliaraki argues that there has been a paradigmatic historical shift in moral subjectivities from a spectator whose solidarity is embedded in grand narratives to a framework of irony. Chouliaraki proposes that three key forces have been responsible for the shift to post-humanitarianism and the formation of ironic moral sensibilities: the waning authority of grand narratives, technology and commercialization. These changes have shaped the ways in which Western spectators are invited to imagine other people's suffering and act upon it. In the age of post-humanitarianism the rationale for action is frequently framed in terms of individual participation, the 'point and click' activism of adding a donation to a pizza order, buying a wristband or attending a concert.

Chouliaraki argues that in contemporary forms of spectatorship there is a disengagement of witnessing from emotions, such as empathy, anger or shame[9] that have traditionally been used to mobilize social action, in favour of a reflexive engagement with oneself.[10] Chouliaraki's writing thus directs us to recognize that it is not that images have lost their power to move, but rather that spectators are no longer ideologically constituted in a way that allows them to be moved.[11] As Chouliaraki summarises, 'As long as our relation to others is only accomplished through an imagination *of ourselves*, solidarity can never become a matter of commitment and justification.'[12] That is to say, the political disengagement with images of conflict is not produced by 'image fatigue' but by the absence of frameworks[13] that help us to locate ourselves in relation to the violence, abuses and destruction they document.

As a way of thinking about how we can foster alternative, more engaged and socially aware subjectivities, Chouliaraki puts forward the figure of the ironic spectator: 'An impure or ambivalent figure that stands, at once, as sceptical towards any moral appeal to solidary action and, yet, open to doing something about those who suffer.'[14] While the ironic spectator might seem to reproduce the cynical disengagement that Chouliaraki seeks to challenge, she argues that ironic subjectivities 'are not pure subjectivities of neo-liberal morality but hybrid subjectivities that contain contradictions. Their utilitarian and self-centred orientation is mixed with realizations that the world is unfair, that human suffering needs to be addressed and that minor actions can make a difference.'[15]

For Chouliaraki irony has the potential to allow us to imagine alternative forms of spectatorship because it directs us to being more reflexive about the way in which we engage with mainstream representations of suffering. Thus, Chouliaraki advocates a communicative structure that she calls the 'solidarity of agonism'. Based on agonistic theatre, Chouliaraki asserts that such a structure serves to mobilize the two key requirements of solidarity: empathy *and* a distance between self and other.

Christoph Bangert: *hello camel*

Published in 2016, *hello camel*[16] is a collection of photographs taken by Christoph Bangert over a ten-year period in Iraq and Afghanistan. While previous works, such as *War Porn*,[17] have documented the horror, *hello camel* explores the strangeness and absurdity of armed conflict. In *hello camel*, Bangert adopts an irreverent approach which uses irony to subvert the dominant representation of war. These images – including the cover image of a camel amid a cordon and search operation – challenge our expectations both of photojournalism and of war. As Bangert notes, the absurdity of war is rarely represented 'because it's confusing for the viewer and these sorts of images can be very dangerous – no publication wants to be seen as making fun of war'.[18] However, the purpose of Bangert's incongruous images is to direct us to recognizing that the dominant representation of war is not definitive.

This is a timely project; David Campbell and Fred Ritchin are just some of the many critics who have called attention to the limited vocabulary of conflict imagery.[19] The vocabulary mobilized by Bangert is specific to the military interventions in Iraq and Afghanistan: his compositions register 'the lack of comprehension about the meanings of this "war"'.[20]

As Laurence Cornet has observed of Bangert's image of an Afghan policeman examining his target during a training session (Figure 14.1), it feels very much like this man is part of an incarnation of war that he doesn't understand: 'The same feeling that soldiers experience when parachuted from their native countryside to such a foreign context, that readers undergo when facing the anonymous flow of images that comes from conflict, and ultimately that photojournalists feel while covering it.'[21]

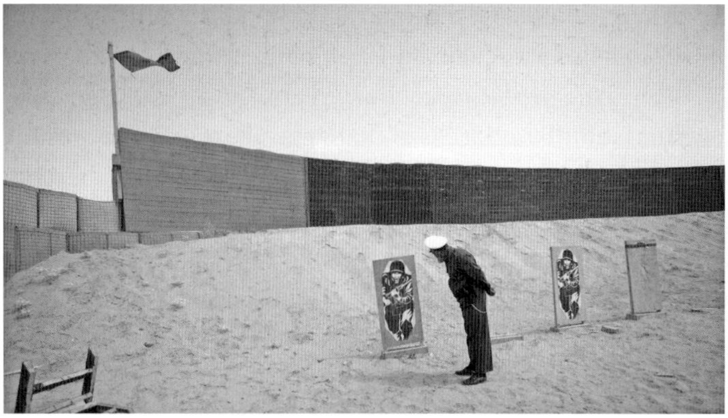

Figure 14.1 Christoph Bangert, from *hello camel,* 2016. An Afghan policeman searches for bullet holes he was supposed to have created on a paper target during a training session conducted by Royal Canadian Mounted Police officers at Camp Nathan Smith in Kandahar. Police training efforts are hampered by corruption, incompetence and illiteracy in the existing Afghan police force. 8 May 2010, Kandahar, Afghanistan. © Christoph Bangert. Courtesy of the artist.

It is through his presentation of the military that Bangert is able to develop an alternative dialogue on the conflict in Afghanistan and Iraq. Rather than the traditional presentation of the soldier as an icon of patriotic duty and heroism, here soldiers are often confused, disorganized and bored. In addition, Bangert includes a number of images of soldiers practising or in training. This, along with the inclusion of minor ceremonies such as cutting a cake or a graduation ceremony, develops a theme of performance. That many of these performances seem inept, surreal or arbitrary challenges the dominant rhetoric of the involvement of the military forces as an organized intervention with a clear set of goals. Finally, the performed nature of many of these images draws attention to the way in which, in Bangert's words, 'war is also something that is set up for journalists.'[22] As Bangert continues, 'Of course violence and fighting would happen no matter what, but I am not a neutral observer; I am also part of this war. It's troubling and makes it morally difficult but you have to acknowledge it.'[23] Indeed, Thomas Keenan has argued that 'we cannot understand, nor have a properly political relation to, invasions and war crimes, military operations and paramilitary atrocities … if we do not attend to the centrality of image production and management in them.'[24]

The representation of war tends to draw on established imagery, such as the spectacle of military power or the grief of the civilian population. This restricted repertoire of imagery serves to activate 'institutionalised sites of spectatorship'[25] that organize the public around the narrative of military intervention as required, just and successful. *hello camel* is a significant example to consider in relation to contemporary debates about the imaging of conflict for, through his use of irony, Bangert challenges us to see the ideological function of the visual record of war.

Richard Mosse: *Infra*

Infra[26] by Richard Mosse (Figure 14.2) is concerned not with challenging the dominant imagery of a war but with making visible a conflict that has failed to elicit the attention of the international community: that of the complex and ongoing violence in the Democratic Republic of Congo. The work has been described as 'haunting, surreal and beautiful'[27] and 'an arresting mash-up of fashion photography, military surveillance stills, and psychedelic dream imagery'.[28] What has solicited these unexpected comments for a work documenting such a brutal conflict is Mosse's use of colour infrared film, specifically, *Kodak Aerochrome III*. The film was originally developed for the US military to use for surveying bombing targets during the Vietnam War. The false colour-reversal film is sensitive to the infrared spectrum, and thus allowed the military to detect camouflage installations in dense forest during aerial reconnaissance. The film was also available to civilians and was used to produce album covers for, among others, *The Jimi Hendrix Experience* and *The Grateful Dead*. Production of the film ended in 2010.

Mosse's work has won critical acclaim for the way in which the vibrant images produced by using this film open up a new set of questions for the viewer. As Aaron Rothman has observed, the altered coloration evokes

> the profound sense of dislocation that people must feel in a place of continual war. The magenta hillsides are somehow fitting, the landscape inverted by the incomprehensibility of the human activity that it holds. The colors seem more than symbolic. If the land were red, we could say, tritely, that it is soaked in blood and move on. But the electric pink is harder to pin down. It overtakes everything, leaving us without reason or explanation.[29]

Mosse's vibrant images seem to be saturated with violence, but what kind of violence? The violence in the Congo stems from a notoriously complex set of causes that include long-standing ethic conflict, vast wealth and the absence of an adequately functioning national government. Susie Linfield's writings are a useful aid when trying to understand the nature of war in the Congo. In *The Cruel Radiance: Photography and Political Violence*,[30] Linfield shows how, since end of the cold war, violence has become 'less tethered to political aims'.[31] Linfield argues that contemporary conflicts such as those in Somalia, Uganda, Colombia and the Congo are characterized by both their 'astonishing ferocity' and their longevity. Linfield links these characteristics to the absence of political aims where the participants 'have no platforms they seek to

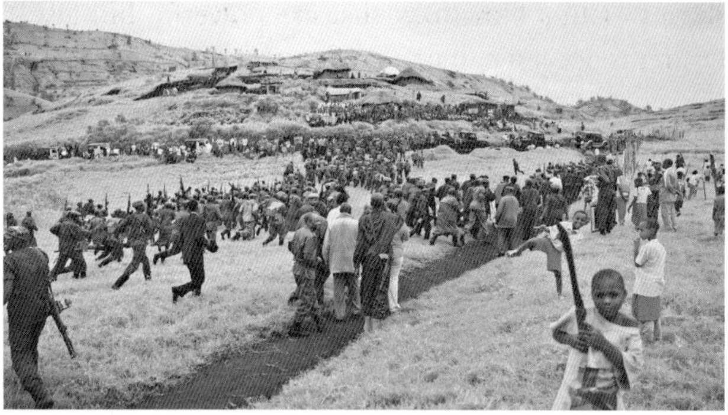

Figure 14.2 Richard Mosse, *Better the Devil You Know*, 2010. Villagers of Bihambwe alongside United Nations Organization Stabilization Mission in the Democratic Republic of Congo (MONUSCO) Indian Battalion troops, observe National Congress for the Defense of the People (CNDP) rebels celebrate their integration into the FARDC. © Richard Mosse. Courtesy of the artist and Jack Shainman Gallery, New York.

carry out, no models of government they seek to realize, no institutions they seek to build, no visions of justice they seek to actualize'.[32] Linfield is careful to stress that this does not mean that these wars do not have causes, nor does she deny that these should be analysed. However, her work seeks to draw attention to what exceeds analysis: 'The ways in which these wars unfold: … the jump from poverty to state collapse …, or from the battle over the Congo's coltan reserves to the carving up of young girls' vaginas.'[33] Our response to such situations is often overwhelming because the absence of political aims and unpredictable escalation of violence can mean that there are no clear channels for political action.

However, Linfield proposes that photographers can play a role in forging a visual vocabulary that can begin to make such violence politically legible. Here, the role of the photographer is to find a way of visualizing, and thus bringing into public discourse, the multitude of small-scale acts that constitute conflicts that are not fought through traditional military means. It is on this point that critics are divided over the value of Mosse's work.

John Roberts has proposed that, 'if the history of photography is a history of its struggle over how practitioners have defined and foregrounded the "event", this struggle is inseparable from photographers' use and adaptation of new photographic techniques'.[34] For some, Mosse's use of Aerochrome offers a new way of looking – and therefore potentially seeing the conflict in the Congo 'beyond meaning-denuded statistics about the three million deaths'.[35] In this reading, Mosse's work serves to 'liberate images from a homogenizing flow and re-inscribe them within a critical discourse emptying the image of elements that make it self-evident and fit into pre-existing discourses and familiar interpretations'.[36] In this respect, it is not just the aesthetic dissonances of this film stock that are powerful but also how the highly unstable film comments upon the uncertainties and volatility of this ongoing conflict. Indeed, it is not simply that the infrared makes 'the invisible' visible; as Mary Walling Blackburn notes, 'What we are looking at never existed (or, rather, was never visible to the human eye).'[37] In this way, Mosse reorders not only our viewing habits but also our visual hierarchy. As Susan Gibb has noted, the effect produced is of a demand to 're-orientate my perception of the image to place equal emphasis on its artfulness as well as its documentary nature'.[38]

However, Mosse's use of both 'artfulness' and 'documentary' is a controversial tactic that has drawn criticism. For example, David Brancaleone has argued that this approach has the effect of drawing the gaze 'away from the literal tragedy of civil war, towards a dreamy subjective fiction, one which overlaps with layers of the West's own cultural history and an appropriation of Conrad's Congo'.[39] These associations, including Mosse's own statements that reference Joseph Conrad's novel *Heart of Darkness*, raise the question of whether – rather than offering a departure – the work further aestheticizes already existing visual tropes of 'African incrutability'. In this criticism, there is a concern that the work conforms to hegemonic discourses of war, the Other and photography.[40] In this regard, it is important to consider not only the aesthetic value of the film stock that Mosse uses but also its history and use.[41] Here, one cannot ignore that the original function of this film stock was to aid military operations, and the kind of 'seeing' it enabled resulted in 46 million litres of Agent Orange being dropped, affecting 5 million civilians in Vietnam.[42]

Yet, perhaps these contradictions are central to the work that these photographs do. As Gibb concludes, 'I remain in a state of conflict about the work that I cannot reconcile. My thoughts are a constant feedback loop of the neat statements that acknowledge its ethical issues and aesthetic pursuits, followed by a frustration at the ambiguity and eventual ambivalence this causes.'[43] This response finds a corollary in Thomas Keenan's writings on the troubled relation between representation and acts of atrocity. Noting that the 'aesthetic finds itself in extreme proximity to the ethico-political now',[44] Keenan proposes that, though this proximity is discomforting for some, 'it is also the condition of any serious intervention'.[45] Tirdad Zolghar's call for intelligent forms of voyeurism is also of use in thinking through the uncomfortable pull between aesthetic distraction and the depiction of violence offered by Mosse. In his article 'Them and Us', Zolghadr concludes his discussion of the difficulties of producing an engaged art practice in the face of increasing commodification of suffering by arguing that the challenge is

> not to summon selfless goodwill or progressive content, but to find intelligent forms of voyeurism – that is, a mode of visual production that faces up to its own strategies of entertainment, infotainment and/or objectification. I think there's much to say for strategies that are blunt without being retrograde, and that elude simple notions of

> solidarity and empathy in favour of an analysis of our very fascination with the outlandish, be it touching or violent or both.[46]

What the arguments put forward by Keenan and Zolghar point to is that, while Mosse's images produce a very different effect to traditional photographic responses to violence, the difficulties we experience when encountering his work might serve to put pressure upon neoliberal viewing habits.

Antonio Denti: *The Surviving Frame*

The Surviving Frame is a body of work made up of stills taken from video footage that Antonio Denti shot over nearly two decades while working as a cameraman for Reuters. As Denti expresses it, 'These images were not born as photographs, … but they have chosen to be photographs.'[47] Denti frames the work as both a very personal project inspired by his young son's growing experience of the world and as universal: 'The frames that survived are the ones where I can see a universal lesson about life and the human condition.'[48] However, the universal in Denti's work is tempered by both humour and hindsight. As in Bangert's work, there is a critical humour that runs through Denti's work with the captions that would normally serve only to describe the event pictured offering historical detail, personal reflection and at times acerbic musings. This approach, where the subjective and the documentary occupy the same space, is a method frequently used by contemporary photojournalists as a means of signalling their implication in the representation of the event depicted. In addition, Denti's captions frequently draw attention to the inability of the participants: press, civilians and military alike to fully understand events of violence as they unfold. For example, the caption beneath the photograph of a US marine includes the observation:

> Sent to guard the scene of a crime, he was sensing – it looked like – the start of a long tragedy. The start of a long war that is now being fought across borders. He – like most of us – did not know who had shot whom and why. This lack of understanding was to make many misinterpret the apparently quiet beginning of a very violent conflict.[49]

Denti's framing of the project through a narrative of retrospective reflection asks us to understand the images not as still, but stilled, and this directs us to the broader understanding that events do not have an intrinsic meaning; rather their meaning and significance are determined after the fact, often with an ideological basis.

It is in this respect that the pixilation of the images serves a critical function. The pixilated image has famously been theorized by Hito Steyerl in her essay 'In Defense of the Poor Image';[50] however, Rebecca A. Adelman has traced a different history that highlights the role of pixilation in the visual culture of the Global War on Terror. In

'Pixelizing Atrocity',[51] Adelman proposes understanding pixilation as a form of editing aesthetics which has a particular connection to the political management of contemporary images of war. Using the images of abuses carried out by US military at Abu Ghraib as a case study, Adelman explores the pixel's political, ideological and epistemological role. By demonstrating that 'pixels and militarized violence intersect in a variety of unexpected and sometimes unpredictable ways',[52] Adelman asks us to recognize that the pixel is imbricated in networks of power. Although it is most frequently used to withhold visual information, Adelman proposes that the pixel has a critical potential in relation to images of atrocity because of its 'incomplete visibility'[53] which simultaneously highlights and obscures elements within the image. Pixelization is thus able to challenge traditional forms of spectatorship: 'Typically, we conceptualize spectatorship within a binary of looking or not looking. In the spectatorship of pixelized images, these two apparently opposite possibilities become intertwined, indistinguishable.'[54]

Unlike the photographs that Adelman analyses, Denti's work rarely pictures acts of violence. These images have been redacted from the news cycle for other reasons. Often they centre on in-between, mundane or seemingly inconsequential moments: the daily routine of a search at a checkpoint, patients at a psychiatric hospital sitting in the sun, relatives patiently searching a mass grave.

What is common to the images Adelman discusses and Denti's work is that by highlighting the incompleteness of the viewer's access, pixelization serves to 'establish a quietly agonistic spectatorial dynamic, a demand for certain information, which the image stubbornly refuses to relinquish'.[55] In Denti's stilling of the events that were recorded for the mass media, the pixelization creates a disturbance, interrupting our habitual emotional engagement with such scenes.

This returns us to the writings of Lilie Chouliaraki. In a recent dialogue, Chouliaraki clarifies her position. 'I firmly believe in the moralizing potential of the spectacles available in our mediated societies. I do not ignore the critique of the spectacle but, rather than rejecting the spectacle of suffering, I insist that we take it seriously and that we engage with it both with our emotions and with our critical thinking.'[56] Through its use of captions, the stilled image and pixelization, *The Surviving Frame* offers the possibility of a spectatorial engagement in which empathy is mobilized in a way that allows for critical reflection.

In this chapter we have addressed the work of three artists using photography to offer new ways of visualizing conflict and of engaging spectatorship in an era marked by profound shifts in the nature of conflict and the way in which moral subjectivities are constituted. However, it is important to note that the critical project outlined by post-photojournalism and critics writing in this area does not seek to enforce a new paradigm: 'The idea is not to replace traditional atrocity images but to balance them; in order to best understand and learn about conflict, we need multiple approaches to its visualization.'[57]

15
Photography, empathy and responsibility

In this chapter we will be addressing the aftermath photograph as a particular form that offers an alternative way of representing war and conflict. The examples we discuss in this chapter explore the way in which this approach asks us to reflect upon a range of issues beyond those provoked by traditional images of conflict. In particular, these works mobilize an ambivalent spectatorial position in order to direct viewers beyond the circumstances of the event itself towards a consideration of systemic causes of violence and conflict.

The late photograph

In recent years there has been intensified interest in the genre of photography variously referred to as 'aftermath photography' or 'late photography'. This work approaches traumatic historical events through an aesthetic of absence. Rather than documenting the event itself, these works focus on its aftermath. Often there is little evidence of what occurred within the frame, and it is only through extended captions, additional contextual material such as archival documents or the viewer's own research that the event is revealed. It is a strategy that asks the viewer to reflect upon historical traumas and the limits of photography's capacity to represent these events. Such work might find a precedent in work by Roger Fenton, Mathew Brady, or more recently, Dirk Reinhartz, Richard Misrach and Willie Doherty. However, the use of this aesthetic in contemporary photographic practice can be traced to a historically specific set conditions. A key text here is David Campany's essay 'Safety in Numbness: Some remarks on the problems of "Late Photography"'.[1]

For Campany, late photography describes the belated relationship of not only the photographer to the event but also that of *photography* to the event: the perceived redundancy of the photograph's capacity to capture the live event, a task which has increasingly fallen to the moving image in the form of video, television and web broadcast. As such, the historical conditions for the emergence of this genre include the location of photography 'at the aftermath of culture'[2] and its subsequent cultural role as 'an undertaker, summariser or accountant'.[3] Rather than compete with video and digital media in reporting events, the late photograph pursues very *photographic* kind of photography. Shot on large format (5 × 4 or 10 × 8), formally composed and employing a neutral palate, these photographs are very different to those which circulate within news sources. In addition, the prints are large – often near life size – which means that they are 'incompatible with the economy of the press'.[4] This resistance to the demands of the news cycle is also seen in the way in which the photographers working in this mode favour a long-term engagement with a particular event or location. As John Roberts has summarized,

> It represents photography trying to reposition its relationship to the event in order to establish a new temporal role for itself by making a case for the necessary *lateness* of the photograph. In a world of the diffuse and mutable image, of instant digital grabs, of the general crisis of documentary culture, photography can only arrive – and perhaps more importantly should only arrive – late.[5]

Although Campany's writings have been influential in defining the genre, he is uneasy about the open nature of the images produced. Describing the late photograph as 'the radically open image par excellence',[6] he concludes his article with a warning:

> The late photograph in all its silence, can easily flatter the ideological paralysis of those who gaze at it with a lack of social or political will to make sense of its circumstance. In its apparent finitude and muteness it can leave us in permanent limbo, obliterating even the *need* for analysis and bolstering a kind of liberal melancholy.[7]

Campany's reservations are well founded: there is no guarantee the late photograph will have its desired effect. Presenting images of conflict in the gallery space does not mean that the work is free of ideological pressures, and political meanings can be muted or transformed by the institution of the gallery as much as by the demands of the press. Nonetheless, a number of critics have argued for the importance and potency of this approach. For these critics[8] the intangible effects of this approach do not mean than such works do not have a political potential. For example, Frank Möller argues that

> if we fail to understand a given photograph or assign meaning to it, we may start both understanding our failure to understand the conditions depicted and questioning the frequent reduction in political discourse of complex social relationships to seemingly straightforward explanations. Thus, aftermath photography complicates; it does not simplify the conditions depicted. Such photography is both precarious … and profoundly political.[9]

Debbie Lisle has similarly argued that we need to expand our understanding of what might constitute a politicized reading and recognize that paralysis, limbo and melancholy are modes of attention that might offer a way out of established viewing practices. Lisle stresses the importance of understanding that such works are not silent but ambivalent. For Lisle, ambivalence is an important mode of engagement which refuses the hierarchal relationship between the subject and the viewer embedded in established interpretive tropes such as pity. Indeed, Lisle proposes that ambivalence is politically productive because it fosters a critical curiosity for the other. In her words, ambivalence 'is politically compelling precisely because of its unruly, open, and contingent character'.[10] As such, she argues that 'ambivalence is not a condition to be ignored or repressed, nor is it a "problem" to be "solved" by established critical viewing practices that lead to political action'.[11] For Lisle, that the late photograph of traumatic events does not look the same, or emotionally move us in the ways we are accustomed to, should not blind us to the important ways in which it can produce feelings that may 'exceed the emotional responses considered "proper" in the face of war, atrocity, and conflict'.[12]

Simon Norfolk: *Bleed*

Simon Norfolk's *Bleed* (2005) is a series of photographs taken in Bosnia many years after the genocide in the 1990s. While there have been many graphic images of this conflict, Norfolk's photographs capture what appears to be a near peaceful aftermath. However, Norfolk's otherworldy images of ice and snow-covered landscapes are the sites of mass graves. Our example, 'Crni Vrh, Untitled No.4' (Figure 15.1), documents one of the largest mass graves from which the remains of 629 people were removed. The bodies were of victims who had been killed and buried at several other sites, but were later moved in order to hide evidence of the massacres from war crimes investigators.

As with many artists using the late photograph, words play an indispensable role in Norfolk's work; without contextual information we would not be able to understand the meaning of these enigmatic images. However, the information provided by Norfolk is not simply descriptive, and the book opens by offering the reader a series of definitions. As Paul Lowe has noted, the delineation of the terms 'solution', 'dissolve' and 'absolution' serves to establish both 'the multiplicity of meaning of the words, and the tension between the states of liquid and solid and answers and guilt'.[13] These descriptions are followed by a series of close-ups of the ice that has formed at the site. These abstract images are unexpectedly captivating and emotive. As Lowe has written, 'These images are strikingly beautiful, … in their monochromatic pallets of pale blue, white and brown; the swirling eddies of the frozen water creating complex

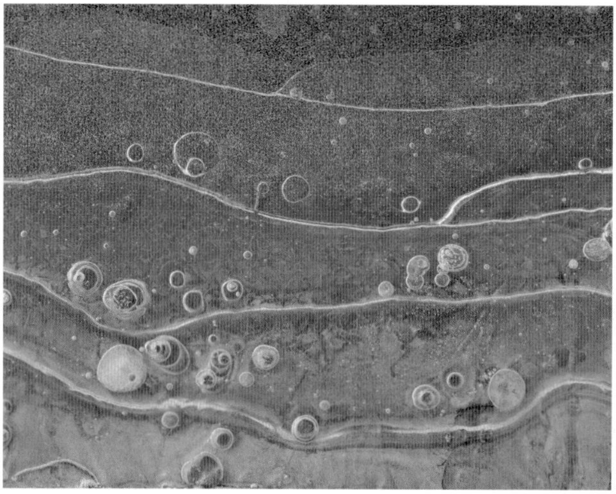

Figure 15.1 Simon Norfolk, 'Crni Vrh, Untitled No.4', from the series *Bleed*, 2005.

Crni Vrh

In 2003, the largest mass grave so far discovered in Bosnia was opened at a remote mountain location known as Crni Vrh between Tuzla and Zvornik. The grave contained the remains of 629 people who had been killed and buried in the Zvornik area and then dug up and moved to this location in an attempt to hide the killers from justice. The bodies were removed to mortuaries in the Tuzla area in the summer of 2003. In the winter of 2004 it was simply a large, newly worked over hole the filled with water that had iced over during the hard winter.

patterns that lead the eye on a dance around the frame.'[14] The unexpected beauty of the work is a critical strategy that Norfolk employs in order to 'put pressure on his viewer's expectations and response'.[15] Norfolk's work does not seek to add to the documentary evidence of what occurred in Bosnia; rather, it asks the viewer to engage with the unresolved legacy of this genocide – for example, the continued violence that exists in the enforced silence of those who witnessed the killings, the bodies that remain hidden and the guilt of the perpetrators.

Norfolk's work is emblematic of how, by documenting the aftermath of the event, the late photograph is able to engage with the ongoing impact of traumatic events by using 'belatedness' as a mode of thinking about trauma and memory. Indeed, memory has a particular status within genocide for ethnic violence includes the destruction of the cultural memories necessary for group coherence. As such, the task of remembrance concerns not just the details of the event but those targets of genocidal violence that are difficult to give form to.

Norfolk's images are open; however, rather than averting meaning, this openness offers space for a range of interpretations, as is reflected in the critical responses to the work. For example, Liam Kennedy has succinctly argued that *Bleed* 'metaphorizes the frozen topography of genocide'.[16] What is key here is that Norfolk does not adopt a redemptive approach but rather directs our attention to the ways in which the aftermath of the genocide continues to resonate through the landscape. This is why, for Lowe, *Bleed* is 'a work about guilt, and the fear that a crime will be uncovered and punished. The frozen landscapes of eastern Bosnia become a powerful metaphor for the secrets that lie buried under the earth, secrets that in time are bound to leech out into the open.'[17]

For others, the absences of Norfolk's work are key. For Antonio Monegal, photographing the empty graves does metaphorical work: 'The fact that there are no human beings depicted in these works ... does not mean the victims are not represented in the picture. Their conspicuous absence is a form of indirect recollection, a gesture of mourning.'[18] For Simon Faulkner, the absences are 'inextricably linked to issues of memory'.[19] Here, the work it does is that of bringing the viewer 'face-to-face with the otherness of the past as something that cannot be grasped in its full complexity'.[20] Rachel E. Cyr has proposed that Norfolk's work seeks to 'emphasize the question and problematic of absence. ... In so doing, Norfolk reminds us that the quest to find the missing men of Srebrenica is not just a presencing of bodies but also confrontation with what it means to find someone missing.'[21]

Roberts has argued that a particular kind of politicization occurs with the late photograph: 'Far from being the recording of the event in all its intense and conflictual unfolding or instrumental horror the moment of its heightened critical temporality is identifiable with those incidents and details that emerge as a result of the *atemporal* recovery of the event.'[22] In these stark yet compelling images of ice and snow-covered landscapes, Norfolk uses the late photograph in order to register photographically a loss that exceeds the details of the event.

Rosemary Laing: 'welcome to Australia'

'welcome to Australia' by Rosemary Laing (Figure 15.2) is a photograph of the Woomera detention centre, an Immigration Reception and Processing Centre (IRPC), taken a year after it closed. Woomera opened in 1999 as part of a government policy of mandatory detention for refugees. Over the four years that it was open reports of abuses circulated widely in the media. These included hunger strikes, attempted suicide and the detainment of children. Under pressure from the United Nations Human Rights Commission, Woomera was closed in 2003.

In Laing's photograph, the 'Woomera Detention Centre appears desolate, peopleless: it is as if history is at a standstill.'[23] Veronica Tello has argued that the palpable absences of Laing's photograph may be seen to comment upon the ban that the Australian government had imposed on images that humanized refugees.

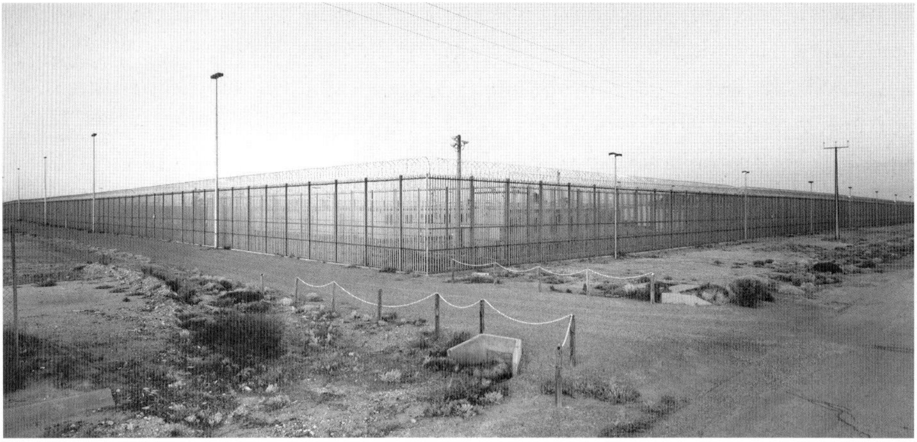

Figure 15.2 Rosemary Laing, 'welcome to Australia' from the series *to walk on a sea of salt*, 2004. C-Type photograph, 110 × 224 cm. © Rosemary Laing. Courtesy of Tolarno Galleries, Melbourne.

However, even without such explicit strictures in place, the representation of refugees tends to adhere to a limited range of approaches. Imogen Tyler's writings are useful here. Tyler argues that the figures of the refugee and asylum-seeker are not invisible, but rather 'hypervisible'. To counter the hypervisibility of refugees in mainstream media as a dehumanized, undifferentiated mass, humanitarian discourses often use portraits and first-person accounts to encourage the public to engage with the 'human face' of the refugee crisis. However, Tyler argues that such an approach often serves to 'exceptionalize the deservingness'[24] of specific categories, such as women or children. Tyler's writings draw attention to the way in which humanitarian responses often work through the same dichotomies of inclusion/exclusion, authentic/inauthentic, deserving/undeserving, us/them, as the xenophobic discourses they seek to critique. Tyler warns that, no matter how well meaning, strategies which seek to mobilize compassion by presenting refugees and asylum-seekers as 'just like us' run the risk of reducing individuals into figures 'through which "we" narrate other cultural fantasies'[25] as such those of benevolence or rescue. As such, photography's capacity to intervene in the visual field and the political order that sustains the uneven distribution of visual and other rights to refugees may not lie in direct representation, but in visualizing the political relations that demarcate the refugee from the citizen. The absence of the figure of the refugee in Laing's photograph serves to direct us away from the familiar terrain of empathetic engagement with the refugee and towards a political engagement with the conditions of possibility that produce the detention centre itself.

Laing's photograph is composed such that the frame is filled by 'the materiality of the architecture of the detention centre, its grid of rectilinear palisade fencing and its vertical strands of razor wire'.[26] As such, Laing's image incontrovertibly asks us to see the detention centre as a camp. In order to explore the troubling, but politically pertinent, associations between the detention centre and the camp made explicit by Laing, we must turn to the writings of Giorgio Agamben.

In *Homo Sacer: Sovereign Power and Bare Life*,[27] Agamben argues that the camp is the paradigmatic form of political space in modernity: 'The camp is the fourth, inseparable element that has now added itself to – and so broken – the old trinity composed of the state, the nation (birth), and land.'[28] For Agamben the camp is not simply a place, but a particular kind of space: 'The essence of the camp consists in the materialization of the state of exception and in the subsequent creation of a space in which bare life and the juridical rule enter into a threshold of indistinction.'[29]

Agamben's theorization of bare life draws on a figure from Roman law, *homo sacer*, a person excluded from religious and political life who can be killed without punishment, but who cannot be sacrificed. As Klaus Ronneberger explains, 'Agamben suggests that inclusion in a political community assumes the simultaneous exclusion of people who are not accorded a legal status. Politics thus commences with a kind of demarcation and the establishment of a space that is removed from protection by law. Agamben terms this space bare life.'[30]

What is key to Agamben's theorization of the camp is that it is not defined by a particular architecture, nor by the particular acts which may occur within it, but the relations of power that the space of the camp enables. The camp is the space in which bodies are reduced to 'bare life' through modalities of power that rely on practices of exception. That is to say, the camp – whether the concentration camp, prison camp or refugee camp – is the space in which the law is suspended. In Agamben's words: '*The camp is the space that is opened up when the state of exception begins to become the rule*.'[31]

The mechanism through which the law is suspended is the state of exception: a state of emergency in which the law and the formal rules of justice are suspended, ostensibly for the purposes of restoring order. However, modern power is distinct in that the state of exception has become a routine, permanent situation. Agamben's work thus provocatively[32] asks us to recognize the camp as 'the hidden matrix of the politics in which we are still living'.[33] This is why he proposes that 'it is this structure of the camp that we must learn to recognize in all its metamorphoses'.[34]

By presenting Woomera as a camp, Laing asks us to reflect not only upon what happened at Woomera but also upon the political space of the camp. Although the openness and abstractions of the late photograph have been criticized, we can see that these attributes are critically mobilized in Laing's photograph. In photographing Woomera as abstracted, Laing – like Agamben – asks us to recognize that the camp is not an exceptional space. As Tello has observed, in Laing's photograph, 'The grid of palisade and razor wire comes to image the sublime proliferation of the camp both here and elsewhere: from Woomera, Lampedusa, Abu Ghraib and Guantánamo to Christmas Island.'[35] Laing thus directs us to reflect upon the political relations exemplified by the camp and to recognize that these persist even though Woomera itself is now closed

However, it is notable that Laing photographs Woomera in a way that it appears as both abstracted and stubbornly *here*. In particular, through the inclusion of a substantial amount of foreground, Laing's photograph of Woomera as a camp presents it as firmly rooted in the Australian landscape. Thus, the abstractions of the camp as a space are bought uncomfortably close. As Tello notes,

> That a camp existed in Australia seemed for many an 'impossible' notion. A common response to the events that transpired at Woomera was disbelief: how could a place like it have manifested in Australia? But the camp and the associated processes of biopolitical violence had always existed in Australia. It is the pervasive, if not also concealed, force underlying the formation of the Australian nation.[36]

Here the temporality particular to the late photograph serves to make visible those relations between place and history that are frequently elided: 'welcome to Australia' potently asks us to consider the resonance of one history of subjugation within another. In this way, the space of ambivalence created by Laing's presentation of Woomera tasks the viewer with reflecting upon 'our own predicament as participants in the reduction of life to bare life'.[37]

Rather than adopting a humanitarian approach to documenting Woomera, Laing uses the late photograph to respond to the need for alternative ways of envisioning modern forms of power. Laing's presentation of the detention centre as an uncanny structure, both alien and familiar, is such that an encounter with this work leaves the viewer with the profoundly disquieting knowledge that 'bare life' describes the potential relationship of all subjects to modern forms of power.

The aftermath

As Frank Möller has noted, the word 'aftermath' is little theorized in the discourse of the late photograph: 'The aftermath of war – when does it start exactly? When does it end? Does it end? War may end but the conflict that triggered it may prevail. Conflict may be resolved but people may still suffer from what they experienced during the war. What comes after the aftermath?'[38]

For some critics, the ambivalence produced by the late photograph is a critical tactic that directs our attention to the particular nature of modern conflict. Here, the limbo of the late photograph can be seen to be a response to the long-term impact of ongoing states of conflict and the state-sanctioned violence of the regime-made disaster. The examples we will consider in this section use the late photograph as a means of presenting the aftermath not as resolution, but as ongoing state. As such, we might see that the late photograph is a form that has evolved through photographers seeking a means to represent some of the aspects of modern war that are denied visualization in mainstream representation.

In *Jeju Notes* (2012) Heungsoon Im uses the late photograph as a means of engaging with what Dong-Yeon Koh has described as 'the paradoxical state of peace in South Korea … as its government and people continue to juggle between militaristic confrontations and economic pragmatism, and between historical consciousness and amnesia.'[39] The title of Im's work references the military conflicts and massacres on Jeju Island during and after the Korean War which resulted in casualties of between 14,000 and 30,000 civilians. However, there is nothing in the images themselves that indexes this violence. Instead Im pictures the tourist attractions and hiking trails that have been constructed for the growing population of international tourists on the island. As Koh has argued, Im mobilizes the ambivalence of the late photography as a means of asking us to critically engage with the way in which the growing influence of tourism in the region is giving rise to a historical amnesia. What is important here is how the open nature of the late photograph – what Faulkner calls it's 'avoidance of instruction'[40] – refuses to 'cater to the full narratives of already obscured and forgotten historical materials.'[41] Rather than historical or political absolutes, in Im's work the 'ambiguous nature of late photography thus runs parallel with the ambiguous state of peace in the Korean Peninsula.'[42]

As Rebecca A. Adelman and Wendy Kozol have noted, living 'in war zones, through state-sanctioned violence, or under occupation by enemy forces – is characterized by temporal extendedness and experiential repetitiousness, which makes the work of survival exhausting and often inhospitable to visual representation.'[43] The difficulties of representing survival means that the visual vocabulary of war often excludes what is perhaps the dominant mode of existence in contemporary zones of conflict. As Adelman and Kozol note, 'It is nearly impossible to quantify the number of people affected by – and hence compelled to survive – militarized violence; even expansive casualty counts do not capture the way that such casualties ripple outward to impact families, children, and other kinship networks.'[44] It is the 'work of survival' that is the topic of Ahlam Shibli's *Occupation* (2016–17). In this work Shibli documents the landscape of al-Khalil in Palestine. However, rather than photographing oppressive military installations such as checkpoints, walls or surveillance cameras, Shibli records the improvised use of the day-to-day materials of occupation (Figure 15.3). As Shibli notes,

> On the one hand, the images indicate how the settlers – who have invaded the Palestinians' territory, preventing them from using their property, and disrupted their freedom of movement – create a prisonlike space for themselves. On the other hand, the photographs reveal how the Palestinians use the hardware of the separation implemented by the Israeli occupation – sheet metal, razor wire, barrels filled with cement, fences, grids, nets, et cetera – to protect their own public spaces and their homes.[45]

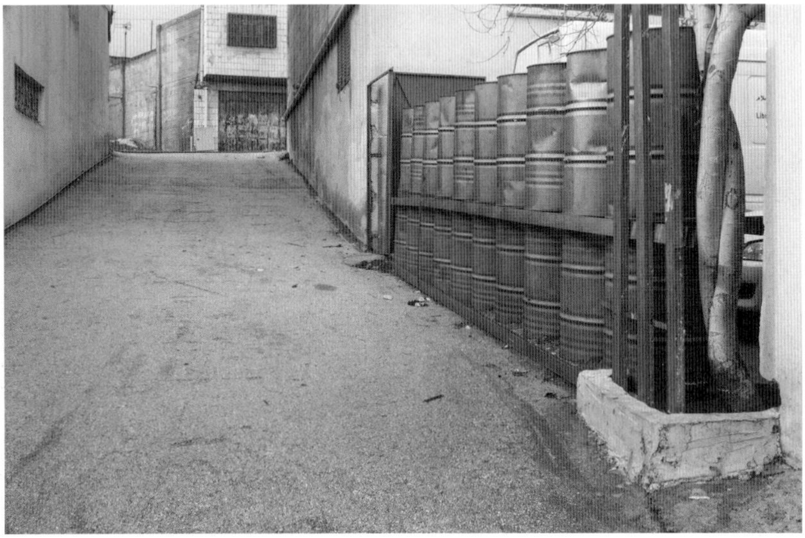

Figure 15.3 Ahlam Shibli, 'Untitled' (*Occupation* no. 18), al-Khalil/Hebron, Palestine, 2016–17, chromogenic print, 40 × 60 cm.

Residential building of the al-Rajabi family, Tareq ben Ziyad Street, al-Mashrqa al-Tahta neighbourhood, Old Town, al-Khalil, 27 January 2017.

The family blocked the entrance to their yard from the byroad of Jabal al-Rahmah that leads to an important road for Israeli settlers. The settler road connects all Israeli settlements in the city, and only settlers are permitted to drive on it. All other streets leading to that road have been blocked with concrete blocks, metal structures, or barrels by the Israeli army. Entire Palestinian neighborhoods are affected by these closures.

Shibli's photographs do not document acts of violence, struggle or protest; indeed, living beings rarely make an appearance. In Ulrich Loock's words, 'The photographs present views of a place locked in a time after the passing of time.'[46] The late photograph as it is used by Shibli offers a means of engaging with the temporality of survival. The 'limbo' that Lisle describes as being characteristic the late photograph allows for a consideration of how visualizing survival might require departing from ideological absolutes.[47] Rather than spectacular incidents of violence or resolved narratives, Shibli presents us with the perpetual uncertainty of daily life under conditions of occupation.

To conclude this chapter, Frank Möller's writings on the 'peace photograph' are interesting to consider. For Möller the peace photograph is one that moves beyond the aftermath to focus on the legacies of the past. This does not mean a forgetting of the past, but rather an engagement with the complexity of what the aftermath is. For Möller, the peace photograph is one that includes a forward-looking perspective visualizing peace or peace as a potentiality: 'It has to succeed in visualising the point in time when expectations of peace replace experiences of violence as the single most important aspect of life from which people, individually and collectively, derive their identities.'[48]

Möller proposes Rineke Dijkstra's series *Almerisa* as an example of a work that takes the evolution of conflict time into peace time as its subject. This ongoing series consists of photographs taken at one- or two-year intervals of Almerisa who arrived with her family in Amsterdam from Bosnia in 1994. Möller proposes that the photograph in which Almerisa is pictured holding her first-born child is a photograph of peace. However, the tentative note offered by an earlier photograph is perhaps a more suitable conclusion to this chapter and our discussion. In the first photograph of the series (Figure 15.4) a young girl is seated on a red plastic chair. Although her face is relaxed, a number of elements are askew; she sits at an angle across the chair which is also at an angle to the camera and her feet did not yet reach the ground. The feeling that she is suspended in space is furthered by Dijkstra's framing which positions Almerisa in the bottom two thirds of the picture. Yet, in its improvised, awkward and strangely solemn photograph perhaps we might glimpse a visualization of peace as a potentiality.

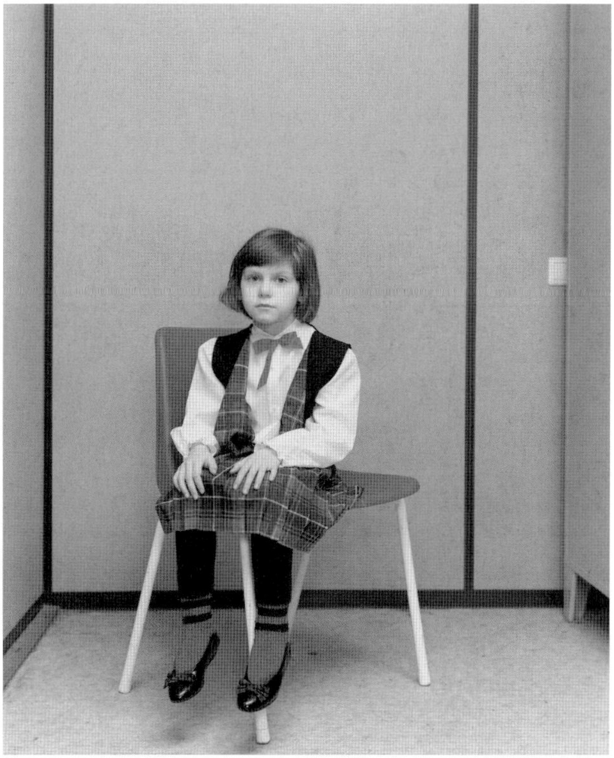

Figure 15.4 Rineke Dijkstra, 'Almerisa, Asylum Center Leiden, Leiden, the Netherlands, March 14, 1994'. Courtesy of the artist and Galerie Max Hetzler, Berlin | Paris | London.

Notes

Introduction

1. John Tagg, *The Burden of Representation: Essays on Photographies and Histories* (Basingstoke: Macmillan, 1988), 63.
2. Jeremy Gilbert, 'What Kind of Thing Is "Neoliberalism"?' *New Formations* 80/81, (2013).
3. Ibid., 12.
4. Noah De Lissovoy, 'Conceptualizing the Carceral Turn: Neoliberalism, Racism, and Violation', *Critical Sociology* 39, no. 5 (2012): 741.
5. Henry A. Giroux, 'Beyond the Biopolitics of Disposability: Rethinking Neoliberalism in the New Gilded Age', *Social Identities* 14, no. 5 (2008): 589.
6. Ibid., 589.
7. Ibid., 590.
8. Ibid., 591.

Chapter 1

1. Gerry Badger, *The Genius of Photography: How Photography Has Changed Our Lives* (London: Quadrille, 2014), 20.
2. Lara Perry, 'The Carte De Visite in the 1860s and the Serial Dynamic of Photographic Likeness', *Art History* 35, no. 4 (2012): 732.
3. Cited in Jan von Brevern, 'Resemblance after Photography', *Representations* 123, Summer (2013): 2.
4. Cited in Alan Trachtenberg, 'Likeness as Identity: Reflections on the Daguerrean Mystique', in *The Portrait in Photography*, ed. Graham Clarke (London: Reaktion Books, 1992), 191.
5. See Perry, 'The Carte De Visite.'
6. Many nineteenth-century commentators observed that prior knowledge of a person was a necessary supplement to the photographic portrait. See ibid.
7. John Plunkett, 'Celebrity and Community: The Poetics of the *Carte-De-Visite*', *Journal of Victorian Culture* 8, no. 1 (2003): 68.
8. Rachel Teukolsky, 'Cartomania: Sensation, Celebrity, and the Democratized Portrait', *Victorian Studies* 57, no. 3 (2015): 464.

9. Teukolsky, 'Cartomania', 463.
10. Plunkett, 'Celebrity and Community', 69.
11. Teukolsky, 'Cartomania', 466.
12. Perry, 'The Carte De Visite', 738.
13. Stephen Burstow, 'The Carte De Visite and Domestic Digital Photography', *Photographies* 9, no. 3 (2016): 295.
14. Ibid., 300.
15. Annie Rudd, 'Victorians Living in Public: Cartes De Visite as 19th-Century Social Media', *Photography and Culture* 9, no. 3 (2017): 8.
16. Ibid., 4.
17. Ibid., 5.
18. Ibid.
19. Allan Sekula, 'The Body and the Archive', *October* 39 (1986): 7.
20. Ibid., 6; emphasis in original.
21. Tagg, *The Burden of Representation*, 64.
22. Nikolas Rose, *Governing the Soul: The Shaping of the Private Self* (London: Free Association Books, 1990), 5.
23. David Green, 'Veins of Resemblance: Photography and Eugenics', *The Oxford Art Journal* 7, no. 2 (1985): 8.
24. This is a particularly rich area of research. For a useful summary see Sarah Kember, 'Face Re-Cognition', *Photoworks* Autumn/Winter (2011/12). For more extended studies, see Suren Lalvani, *Photography, Vision and the Production of Modern Bodies* (Albany: State University of New York Press, 1996); Carrie A. Rentschler, 'The Physiognomic Turn', *International Journal of Communication* 4 (2010); Dana Seitler, 'Queer Physiognomies: Or, How Many Ways Can We Do the History of Sexuality?' *Criticism* 46, no. 1 (2004).
25. Shawn Michelle Smith, *American Archives: Gender, Race, and Class in Visual Culture* (Princeton, NJ: Princeton University Press, 1999), 86.
26. Sekula, 'The Body and the Archive', 12.
27. See Sekula for further details of Quetelet's ideas.
28. Ibid., 16.
29. Ibid.
30. John Tagg, 'The Archiving Machine; Or, the Camera and the Filing Cabinet', *Grey Room* no. 47, Spring (2012): 29.
31. Sarah Kember, 'Face Recognition and the Emergence of Smart Photography', *Journal of Visual Culture* 13, no. 2 (2014): 188.
32. Smith, *American Archives*, 86–7.
33. Green, 'Veins of Resemblance', 14.
34. Ibid.
35. Suzanne Bailey, 'Francis Galton's Face Project: Morphing the Victorian Human', *Photography and Culture* 5, no. 2 (2012): 194.
36. Sekula, 'The Body and the Archive', 14.
37. Nancy Armstrong, 'Monarchy in the Age of Mechanical Reproduction', *Nineteenth-Century Contexts* 22, no. 4 (2001): 504.

38. The series can be seen in full at www.eileenperrier.com/page7.htm
39. David Bate, *Photography: The Key Concepts* (Oxford and New York: Berg, 2009), 77.

Chapter 2

1. Julian Stallabrass, 'What's in a Face? Blankness and Significance in Contemporary Art Photography', *October* 122, Fall (2007).
2. Ibid., 71.
3. Stallabrass uses the term 'ethnographic portrait' rather than Tagg's designation of the subjugated portrait.
4. Stallabrass, 'What's in a Face?' 87.
5. Alison Dean, 'Intimacy at Work: Nan Goldin and Rineke Dijkstra', *History of Photography* 39, no. 2 (2015): 191.
6. Norman Bryson, 'Thomas Ruff: Spectacle and Surveillance', *Parkett*, no. 28 (1991): 93.
7. Stallabrass, 'What's in a Face?' 73.
8. Ibid., 87.
9. As von Zwehl has described the process of making *Untitled I*: 'I invited people to sleep in my room where I could wake them up myself at around 5am, taking their picture seconds later. The room was still dark, they had been told exactly where and how to sit and talking was not allowed', von Zwehl cited in Charlotte Cotton, 'Interview', in *Bettina Von Zwehl*, ed. David Chandler (Brighton: Photoworks, 2007), 70.
10. Bryson, 'Thomas Ruff', 94.
11. This is discussed in Chapter 1.
12. Lily Cho, 'Citizenship, Diaspora and the Bonds of Affect: The Passport Photograph', *Photography & Culture* 2, no. 3 (2009): 276.
13. Lily Cho, 'Intimacy among Strangers', *Interventions* 15, no. 1 (2013): 19.
14. Ben Burbridge, 'Exacting Photography: Self-Imaging and Its Frustration in Contemporary Art Photography', *re.bus* 5, Summer (2010).
15. Ibid., 14–15.
16. Joanna Lowry, 'Symptoms, Signs and Surfaces', in *Bettina Von Zwehl*, ed. David Chandler (Brighton: Photoworks, 2007), 36.
17. cited in Elizabeth Bronfen, *The Knotted Subject: Hysteria and Its Discontents* (Princeton, NJ: Princeton University Press, 1998), xi.
18. Ulrich Baer, 'Photography and Hysteria: Towards a Poetics of the Flash', *The Yale Journal of Criticism* 7, no. 1 (1994): 45. As a number of critics have observed, under Charcot, the camera not only documented but also played a fundamental part in producing a unique form of hysteria – *la grande hystérie*. Amongst others, see George Didi-Huberman, *Invention of Hysteria: Charcot and the Photographic Iconography of the Salpêtrière* (Cambridge and London: The MIT Press, 2003). Indeed, soon after his death in 1893 Charcot's findings began to be challenged not

only by medical rivals but also by some of his own interns who suggested that his patients had been coached in their performances.

19. Anne Golomb Hoffman, 'Archival Bodies', *American Imago* 66, no. 1 (2009): 12.
20. Ibid.
21. Gilbert, 'What Kind of Thing Is "Neoliberalism"?' 11.
22. Wendy Brown, *Undoing the Demos: Neoliberalism's Stealth Revolution* (New York: Zone, 2015), 10.
23. Jonathan Crary, *24/7: Late Capitalism and the Ends of Sleep* (London and New York: Verso, 2014), 10–11.
24. Burbridge, 'Exacting Photography', 15.
25. *Zoe Strauss: 10 Years*, ed. Peter Barberie (New Haven, CT and London: Philadelphia Museum of Art in association with Yale University Press, 2012).
26. Dean, 'Intimacy at Work', 178.
27. Nadar cited in ibid.
28. Liz Kotz, 'Aesthetics of Intimacy', in *The Passionate Camera*, 204–15, ed. Deborah Bright (London and New York: Routledge, 1998), 208.
29. Ibid., 207–8.
30. Ibid., 208.
31. Thea Traff, 'Zoe Strauss: 10 Years', *The New Yorker*, 4 October 2013, www.newyorker.com/culture/photo-booth/zoe-strauss-10-years
32. Miles Orvell, 'The Absolute Power of the Lens: Zoe Strauss and the Problem of the Street Portrait', *Afterimage* 40, no. 2 (2012): 11.
33. Ibid., 12.
34. Abigail Solomon-Godeau, 'Inside/Out', in *Public Information: Desire, Disaster, Document* (San Francisco, CA: San Francisco Museum of Modern Art, 1995), 49.
35. Abigail Solomon-Godeau, 'Who Is Speaking Thus? Some Questions About Documentary Photography', in *Photography at the Dock: Essays on Photographic History, Institutions, and Practices* (Minneapolis: University of Minnesota Press, 1991), 176.
36. Orvell, 'The Absolute Power of the Lens', 13.
37. Ibid.
38. Ibid., 12.
39. Sally Stein, 'How Do We Look? Counter-Intuitive Prompts and Probes in Zoe Strauss' Resurgent Social Documentary Photography', in *Zoe Strauss: 10 Years*, ed. Peter Barberie (New Haven, CT and London: Philadelphia Museum of Art in association with Yale University Press, 2012), 161.
40. As Clare Raymond has noted, Strauss documents the 'harsh, aching poverty that Americans tend to prefer not to recognize as their own', *Women Photographers and Feminist Aesthetics* (London and New York: Routledge, 2017), 173.
41. Beth A. Uzwiak, 'Make of This Whatever You Want: Violence and Intimacy in Zoe Strauss's I-95 Project', *Photography and Culture* (2018): 2; emphasis in original.
42. Ibid., 2.
43. Rose, *Governing the Soul*, 1.
44. Lauren Berlant, 'Intimacy: A Special Issue', *Critical Inquiry* 24, no. 2 (1998): 281.

45. In Berlant's words: 'The discourse world described by the public and the private has, historically, organized and justified other legally and conventionally based forms of social division (male and female, work and family, colonizer and colonized, friend and lover, hetero and homo, "unmarked" personhood versus racial-, ethnic-, and class-marked identities). ... The taken-for-grantedness of spatial taxonomies like public and private makes this cluster of taxonomic associations into facts within ordinary subjectivity as well.' Ibid., 283.
46. Ibid., 285.
47. Ibid.
48. Uzwiak, 'Make of This Whatever You Want', 17.
49. Raymond, *Women Photographers*, 174.
50. Ibid., 10.
51. Ibid., 12.
52. Dean, 'Intimacy at Work', 180.

Chapter 3

1. Catherine Zimmer, 'Surveillance Cinema: Narrative between Technology and Politics', *Surveillance and Society* 8, no. 4 (2011): 428.
2. David Lyon, *Surveillance after September 11* (Cambridge: Polity, 2003), 164.
3. David Lyon, *Surveillance Society: Monitoring Everyday Life* (Buckingham: Open University Press, 2001).
4. Mark Hayward, 'ATMs, Teleprompters and Photobooths: A Short History of Neoliberal Optics', *New Formations* 80/81 (2013).
5. K. F. Aas, '"The Body Does Not Lie": Identity, Risk and Trust in Technoculture', *Crime, Media, Culture* 2, no. 2 (2006): 150.
6. Ibid., 152.
7. Edward Welch, 'Stars of CCTV: Technology, Visibility and Identity in the Work of Sophie Calle and Annie Ernaux', *Nottingham French Studies* 48, no. 2 (2009): 60.
8. Hayward argues that the ATM was a key technological development in relation to surveillance and neoliberalism for the way in which it served to locate personal security and affective engagement within the same space. That is to say, the affective charge of these encounters is necessary for our engagement and not an anomalous side-effect. 'ATMs, Teleprompters and Photobooths'.
9. Sarah Hollenberg, 'Sophie Calle: Unfinished', *caa.reviews,* 5 November 2015: DOI: 10.3202/caa.reviews.2015.149
10. See for example Rachel Hall, 'Of Ziploc Bags and Black Holes: The Aesthetics of Transparency in the War on Terror', *The Communication Review* 10, no. 4 (2007).
11. Zara Dinnen and Sam McBean, 'The Face as Technology', *New Formations* 93 (2018): 124. See also, Kelly Gates, 'Identifying the 9/11 "Faces of Terror"', *Cultural Studies* 20, no. 4–5 (2006); 'Biometrics and Post-9/11 Technostalgia' *Social Text* 23,

no. 2 (2005); Kember, 'Face Recognition and the Emergence of Smart Photography', *Journal of Visual Culture* 13, no. 3 (2014).

12. Lisa Nakamura, 'The Socioalgorithmics of Race: Sorting It Out in Jihad Worlds', in *The New Media of Surveillance*, ed. Shoshana Magnet and Kelly Gates (New York: Routledge, 2009), 150; my emphasis.
13. Dinnen and McBean, 'The Face as Technology', 128.
14. Works from the series can be seen at www.zachblas.info/works/facial-weaponiza tion-suite/
15. Blas cited in Zach Blas and Jacob Gaboury, 'Biometrics and Opacity: A Conversation', *Camera Obscura: Feminism, Culture, and Media Studies* 31, no. 2 (2016): 156.
16. Zach Blas, 'Escaping the Face: Biometric Facial Recognition and the *Facial Weaponization Suite*', *Media-N* 9, no. 2 (2013). http://median.newmediacaucus.o rg/caa-conference-edition-2013/escaping-the-face-biometric-facial-recognition-an d-the-facial-weaponization-suite/
17. The examples cited by Blas are Nicholas O. Rule and Nalini Ambady, 'Brief Exposures: Male's Sexual Orientation Is Accurately Perceived at 50 ms', *Journal of Experimental Social Psychology* 44, no. 4 (2008): 1100–5; Joshua A. Tabak and Vivian Zayas, 'The Roles of Featural and Congural Face Processing in Snap Judgments of Sexual Orientation', *PLOS ONE* 7, no. 5 (2012): 1–7.
18. Blas cited in Blas and Gaboury, 'Biometrics and Opacity', 156.
19. Blas cited in Ibid., 158.
20. Blas proposes that these masks have utopic as well as practical functions and that they express 'ways to relate, be together, and live that no capitalist state or biometric can contribute to or foster' Ibid.
21. John Cheney-Lippold, 'A New Algorithmic Identity: Soft Biopolitics and the Modulation of Control', *Theory, Culture & Society* 28, no. 6 (2011): 165.
22. A useful definition of Big data and its effects is offered by Ball et al.:

    > Big data describes a range of socio-technical and commercial trends resulting in the storage, analysis and further usage of huge amounts of data generated by social networks and mobile devices. While both public and private sector organizations seek to capitalize on big data analytics to improve products and services, the data flows which feed big data originate in the mundane, everyday online activities of millions of people. This renders the everyday subject 'surveilled' by definition, yet it is difficult for the subject to comprehend exactly how to evade, resist or negotiate big data practices as – strictly speaking, in terms of embodied practices – there is nobody directly watching them.

    Kirstie Ball, MariaLaura Di Domenico and Daniel Nunan, 'Big Data Surveillance and the Body-Subject', *Body & Society* 22, no. 2 (2016): 58–9.
23. Tobias Matzner, 'Beyond Data as Representation: The Performativity of Big Data in Surveillance', *Surveillance and Society* 14, no. 2 (2016): 200.
24. Tyler Reigeluth, 'Why Data Is Not Enough: Digital Traces as Control of Self and Self-Control', *Surveillance and Society* 12, no. 2 (2014): 245.

25. See for example Lyndsey P. Beutin, 'Racialization as a Way of Seeing: The Limits of Counter-Surveillance and Police Reform', *Surveillance and Society* 15, no. 1 (2017).
26. Cheney-Lippold, 'A New Algorithmic Identity.'
27. Ibid., 170.
28. Ibid., 171.
29. Ibid., 177.
30. George Vasey, 'Erica Scourti', *Art Monthly* Issue 382, Dec.–Jan., (2014–15): 20.
31. For more on how the algorithmic organization of information through Google and sites like Amazon and Netflix has altered the way culture, as a category of experience, is now practised, experienced and understood see Ted Striphas, 'Algorithmic Culture', *European Journal of Cultural Studies* 18, no. 4–5 (2015).
32. Erica Scourti, 'Life in Adwords: March 2012', vimeo.com/album/1944360/video/39677781
33. Vasey, 'Erica Scourti', 20.
34. Eli Pariser, *The Filter Bubble: What the Internet Is Hiding from You* (Harmondsworth: Penguin, 2012).
35. As Rouvroy explains,

> The subject comes in the form of a myriad of data that link him or her to a multitude of profiles (as a consumer, a potential fraudster, a more or less trustable and productive employee and so on). All of them are related to him or her without inscribing him or her in any collective context (differently from the "classical" modes of categorisation, such as the ethnic profiling, that were adjusted on socially proved categorisations and therefore susceptible to give rise to collective actions)
>
> 'Algorithmic Governmentality: Radicalisation and Immune Strategy of Capitalism and Neoliberalism?' *La Deleuziana* 3 (2016): 34.

36. Vasey, 'Erica Scourti', 21.
37. 'Self 2 Selfie', *Art Monthly* Issue 371, Nov. (2013): 8.
38. Tanya Gayer, 'Archives and Algorithms Compressing Socio-Historical Distance', *Sightlines* (2016): 95.
39. Elahi is American Bangladeshi, thus the connection that was made relies not on data but on a common cultural conflation of religion with race. Carmen R Lugo-Lugo and Mary K. Bloodsworth-Lugo use the term 'the browning of terror' to describe this process in which issues such as race, religion, citizenship and immigration are merged to create a threatening other. '475° from September 11', *Cultural Studies* 24, no. 2 (2010).
40. Simon Hogue, 'Performing, Translating, Fashioning: Spectatorship in the Surveillant World', *Surveillance and Society* 14, no. 2 (2016): 179.
41. Matzner, 'Beyond Data as Representation', 206; my emphasis.
42. Jeremy Packer, 'Homeland Subjectivity: The Algorithmic Identity of Security', *Communication and Critical/Cultural Studies* 4, no. 2 (2007): 213.
43. Laurel Ahnert, 'The Surveillance Commodity, Unequal Exchange, and the (In)Visible Subject in Hasan Elahi's Tracking Transience', *Social Text* 35, no. 3, (2017): 10.

44. Dinnen and McBean, 'The Face as Technology', 127.
45. Nakamura, 'The Socioalgorithmics of Race', 153.
46. Lisa Nakamura, 'Cyberrace', *PMLA* 123, no. 5 (2008): 1677.
47. Ibid.
48. Gemma Killen, 'Archiving the Other or Reading Online Photography as Queer Ephemera', *Australian Feminist Studies* 32, no. 91–92 (2017): 70.
49. Ben Burbridge and Catherine Grant, 'Photography and Exhibitionism: An Introduction', http://eitherand.org/exhibitionism/very-brief-very-general-conversation-about-photogr/
50. Fu cited in Derek Conrad Murray, 'Notes to Self: The Visual Culture of Selfies in the Age of Social Media', *Consumption Markets & Culture* 18, no. 6 (2015): 504–5.
51. David Green, 'On Foucault: Disciplinary Power and Photography', in *The Camerawork Essays: Context and Meaning in Photography*, ed. Jessica Evans and Barbara Hunt (London: Rivers Oram, 1997), 129.
52. Ibid.

Part Two

1. Ann Bermingham, 'Landscape Imagery and Urban Culture in Early Nineteenth-Century Britain (Review)', *The Art Bulletin* 76, no. 2 (1994): 368.
2. Cited in David Marshall, 'The Problem of the Picturesque', *Eighteenth-Century Studies* 35, no. 3 (2002): 418; emphasis in original.
3. Koerner cited in Tacita Dean and Jeremy Millar, eds., *Place* (London: Thames & Hudson, 2005), 182.
4. Bate, *Photography*, 89.
5. W. J. T. Mitchell, 'Introduction', in *Landscape and Power*, ed. W. J. T. Mitchell (London and Chicago, IL: University of Chicago Press, 1994), 1; emphasis in original.
6. W. J. T. Mitchell, 'Imperial Landscape', in *Landscape and Power*, 14.
7. Mitchell, 'Introduction', 2.
8. Bate, *Photography*, 93.

Chapter 4

1. Bate, *Photography*, 96.
2. Gilpin cited in Geoffrey Batchen, *Burning with Desire: The Conception of Photography* (Cambridge, MA and London: The MIT Press, 1999), 72; emphasis in original.
3. In his 1794 book *Essay on the Picturesque*, Uvedale Price states that 'there are few words, whose meaning has been less accurately determined than that of the word picturesque' cited in Marshall, 'The Problem of the Picturesque', 415.

4. Gilpin cited in Batchen, *Burning with Desire*, 73.
5. Knight cited in Marshall, 'The Problem of the Picturesque', 429.
6. Knight cited in ibid.
7. In Knight's words: 'To all others, however acute soever may be their discernment, or how exquisite soever their sensibility, it is utterly imperceptible.' Knight cited in ibid.
8. John Tagg, *Grounds of Dispute: Art History, Cultural Politics and the Discursive Field* (Minneapolis: University of Minnesota Press, 1992), 118.
9. Michael Cataldi et al., 'Residues of a Dream World', *Theory, Culture & Society* 28, no. 7–8 (2012): 368.
10. Monk cited in Marshall, 'The Problem of the Picturesque', 435 note 44.
11. Mitchell, 'Imperial Landscape', 9.
12. Graham Clarke, *The Photograph* (Oxford: Oxford University Press, 1997), 55.
13. Jeffrey Auerbach, 'The Picturesque and the Homogenisation of Empire', *The British Art Journal* 5, no. 1 (2004).
14. Simon Pugh, 'Introduction', in *Reading Landscape: Country, City, Capital*, ed. Simon Pugh (Machester and New York: Manchester University Press, 1990), 5.
15. Jeffrey Auerbach, 'Art, Advertising, and the Legacy of Empire', *The Journal of Popular Culture* 35, no. 4 (2002).
16. Mitchell, 'Imperial Landscape', 18.
17. Mitchell, 'Introduction', 3.
18. Ibid., 9.
19. Mohini Chandra and Christopher Stewart, 'About Dark Pacific Sun', www.mohinichandra.com/about-dark-pacific-sun/
20. Sally Mann, *Deep South* (New York: Bulfinch, 2005), 13.
21. Vicki Goldberg, 'Sally Mann's Haunted South', *New York Times,* 29 March 2018, www.nytimes.com/2018/03/29/arts/design/sally-mann-a-thousand-crossings-review-national-gallery.html
22. Ayelet Carmi, 'Sally Mann's American Vision of the Land', *Journal of Art Historiography* 17, December (2017): 18.
23. Sally Mann, *Immediate Family* (New York: Aperture, 1992).
24. James Gibbons, 'Family, Landscape, and Race in Sally Mann's Photographs', *Hyperallergic,* 10 March 2018, hyperallergic.com/430901/sally-mann-a-thousand-crossings-national-gallery-of-art-washington-dc/
25. Ibid.
26. Mitchell, 'Introduction', 1; emphasis in original.
27. Mann cited in Suzanne Schuweiler, 'Sally Mann's South', *Southeastern College Art Conference Review*, 16, no. 3 (2013): 327.
28. Alison R. Hafera, 'Sally Mann: Emmett's Story (2007)', *American Suburb X* 23 November 2018, www.americansuburbx.com/2011/11/sally-mann-emmetts-story-2007.html
29. An interesting body of work to consider here is Josh Begley's *Officer Involved.* The work can be seen at theintercept.co/officer-involved/

30. Raymond, *Women Photographers and Feminist Aesthetics*, 156.
31. Ibid., 143.
32. Laura Elizabeth Shea, 'Sally Mann: A Thousand Crossings', *ASAP Journal,* 3 May 2018, http://asapjournal.com/sally-mann-a-thousand-crossings-laura-elizabeth-shea/
33. Carmi, 'Sally Mann's American Vision of the Land', 25.
34. Orvell, *American Photography*, 43.
35. Bate, *Photography*, 94.
36. Edmund Burke, 'A Philosophical Enquiry into the Origin of Our Ideas of the Sublime and Beautiful (1759)', in *The Sublime: A Reader in British Eighteenth-Century Aesthetic Theory*, ed. Andrew Ashfield and Peter de Bolla (Cambridge: Cambridge University Press, 1996), 131.
37. Ibid.
38. Shaw cited in Martyn Lee, 'The Sublime and Contemporary Popular Culture: The Radical Text in a Post-Political Era', *Journal for Cultural Research* 12, no. 3 (2008): 255–6.
39. David E. Nye, *American Technological Sublime* (Cambridge, MA and London: MIT Press, 1996), 3.
40. Ned O'Gorman, 'The Political Sublime: An Oxymoron', *Millennium: Journal of International Studies* 34, no. 3 (2006): 891–2.
41. O'Gorman, 'The Political Sublime', 905–6.
42. Nathan Stormer, 'Addressing the Sublime: Space, Mass Representation, and the Unpresentable', *Critical Studies in Media Communication* 21, no. 3 (2004): 213.
43. Ibid., 214.
44. As a number of critics have noted the subject position invoked is white, male and Western. Further, as Suvendrini Perera has observed 'the sublime, as a form of overcoming or elevating the power of reason over nature, is another enabling trope of European expansionism'. 'Torturous Dialogues: Geographies of Trauma and Spaces of Exception', *Continuum* 24, no. 1 (2010): 37.
45. The series can be seen in full at www.justinjamesking.com
46. Stormer, 'Addressing the Sublime', 234; emphasis in original.
47. Thomas Albdorf, *General View* (Jesi, Italy: Skinnerboox, 2017).
48. Albdorf cited in Susanna D'Aliesio, 'Thomas Albdorf's General View', *British Journal of Photography,* 15 May 2017, bjp-online.com/2017/05/photo-london-week-thomas-albdorfs-general-view/
49. Darren Campion, 'Thomas Albdorf: Almost as Good as Being There', in *General View*, ed. Thomas Albdorf (Jesi, Italy: Skinnerboox, 2017), 125–6.
50. Campion, 'Thomas Albdorf', 125.
51. In particular, positioning Yosemite as a sublime wilderness relied on the perception of Yosemite as empty. However, as Rebecca Solnit has observed, 'The West wasn't empty, it was emptied – literally by expeditions like the Mariposa Battalion, and figuratively by the sublime images of a virgin paradise created by so many painters, poets, and photographers' Solnit cited in Kevin Michael DeLuca and Anne Teresa Demo, 'Imaging Nature: Watkins, Yosemite, and the Birth of Environmentalism', *Critical Studies in Media Communication* 17, no. 3 (2000): 256. See also Martin

A. Berger, 'Overexposed: Whiteness and the Landscape Photography of Carleton Watkins', *Oxford Art Journal* 26, no. 1 (2003).

52. James Stinson, 'Re-Creating Wilderness 2.0: Or Getting Back to Work in a Virtual Nature', *Geoforum* 79 (2017): 174. For Stinson, Wilderness 2.0 describes the refiguring of nature that has taken place as a result of both technology and neoliberalism. As an example of the neoliberal logic underlying the promotion and use of Wilderness 2.0, Stinson cites Google's efforts to incorporate wilderness areas into Google Street View. Although Street View initially focused exclusively on urban streets, the project has subsequently been expanded to include rural and wilderness areas, allowing users to virtually explore iconic locations including the base camps at Everest, the Galapagos Islands and – of course – Yosemite, all from the comfort of their home computers or mobile devices.
53. Ibid., 180.
54. Ibid.
55. Ibid.
56. Campion, Ibid., 126.
57. Lukasz Zaremba, 'Mediating Visual Experience: Zbigniew Libera's Photographic Works and Google Street View Imagery', *InVisible Culture*, Issue 18 (2003): 13.
58. Laura Kurgan, *Close Up at a Distance: Mapping, Technology and Politics* (New York: Zone Books, 2013), 14.
59. Ibid.
60. Jason Farman, 'Mapping the Digital Empire: Google Earth and the Process of Postmodern Cartography,' *New Media & Society* 12, no. 3 (2010): 879.

Chapter 5

1. Wendy Cheng, '"New Topographics": Locating Epistemological Concerns in the American Landscape', *American Quarterly* 63, no. 1 (2011): 151.
2. John Beck, 'The Purloined Landscape: Photography and Power in the American West', *Tate Papers* 21, Spring (2014), www.tate.org.uk/research/publications/tate-papers/21/the-purloined-landscape-photography-and-power-in-the-american-west
3. Cheng, 'New Topographics', 152.
4. Britt Salvesen and Alison Nordstrom, 'Prologue', in *New Topographics* (Gottingen, Germany: Steidl, 2009), 9.
5. Cheng, 'New Topographics', 160.
6. Marc Augé, *Non-Places: An Introduction to Supermodernity*, trans. J. Howe (London: Verso, 1995).
7. Ibid., 77. It should be noted that non-place is not the opposite of place, both are in flux. In Augé's words, 'Place and non-place are rather like opposed polarities: the first is never completely erased, the second never totally completed; they are like palimpsests on which the scrambled game of identity and relations is ceaselessly rewritten' Ibid., 64.

8. Cited in Franziska Solte, 'Standard,' in *Standard* (Zürich: Verlag Scheidegger & Spiess AG, 2016), 13.
9. Augé, *Non-Places*, 101.
10. Ibid., 106.
11. Ibid., 103.
12. Ibid., 83.
13. Benedict Wells, 'The Foreign Home', in *Standard* (Zürich: Verlag Scheidegger & Spiess AG, 2016), 8.
14. Roger Eberhard, *Standard* (Zürich: Verlag Scheidegger & Spiess AG, 2016).
15. Solte, 'Standard', 13.
16. Edward Welch, 'Marc Augé, Jean Rolin and the Mapping of (Non-)Place in Modern France', *Irish Journal of French Studies* 9, no. 1 (2009): 56.
17. Kyle Chayka, 'Welcome to Airspace: How Silicon Valley Helps Spread the Same Sterile Aesthetic across the World', *The Verge*, 3 August 2016, www.theverge.com/2016/8/3/12325104/airbnb-aesthetic-global-minimalism-startup-gentrification
18. Ibid.
19. Jana Costas, 'Problematizing Mobility: A Metaphor of Stickiness, Non-Places and the Kinetic Elite', *Organization Studies* 34, no. 10 (2013): 1474.
20. Peter Merriman, 'Driving Places: Marc Augé, Non-Places, and the Geographies of England's M1 Motorway', *Theory, Culture & Society* 21, no. 4/5 (2004): 149.
21. Tim Cresswell, *On the Move: Mobility in the Modern Western World* (London: Routledge, 2006), 223.
22. Ibid., 224.
23. Sarah Sharma, 'Baring Life and Lifestyle in the Non-Place', *Cultural Studies* 23, no. 1 (2009): 129.
24. Ibid., 146.
25. Ibid.
26. Welch, 'Marc Augé, Jean Rolin and the Mapping of (Non-)Place in Modern France', 51.
27. Sharma, 'Baring Life and Lifestyle in the Non-Place', 139.
28. Ibid.
29. Huxley cited in Andreas Gefeller, 'Soma', www.andreasgefeller.com/soma/text
30. Ibid.: emphasis in original.
31. Alexandra Stara, '"Making Strange": The Photography of Steffi Klenz and Thomas Weinberger', *History of Photography* 37, no. 3 (2013): 353.
32. Jennifer Burris, 'The "Urban Photogénie" of *Architainment*', *The Journal of Aesthetics and Art Criticism* 69, no. 1 (2011): 99.
33. Ibid.
34. Sharma, 'Baring Life and Lifestyle in the Non-Place', 146.
35. As Sharma expresses it,

    > In fact it is not the non-place that displaces the local or creates asocial facelessness inasmuch as the theorist of non-place erases the local in these accounts of non-place. … What is forgotten in such conclusions is that invisibility and the experience of alienation are a direct result of certain people's labor and also by

the consumptive and cultural practices enacted by customers and theorists alike. Ibid., 134.

36. Andrew Wood has coined the term 'omnitopia' to describe the way in which geographically distinct spaces become part of a ubiquitous continuum. See "'The Best Surprise Is No Surprise'", *Space and Culture* 8, no. 4 (2016).
37. Trevor Paglen, 'Experimental Geography: From Cultural Production to the Production of Space', in *Critical Landscapes: Art, Space, Politics*, ed. Emily Eliza Scott and Kristen Swenson (Oakland, CA: University of California Press, 2015), 38.
38. Jill Dawsey, 'Trevor Paglen: Semiotics of the Hidden Empire', *Art Papers* 33, no. 5 (2009): 36.
39. Paglen, 'Experimental Geography', 38.
40. Ibid.
41. Paglen cited in John Beck, 'Signs of the Sky, Signs of the Times: Photography as Double Agent', *Theory, Culture & Society* 28, no. 7–8 (2011): 135.
42. Trevor Paglen, 'Goatsucker: Toward a Spatial Theory of State Secrecy', *Environment and Planning D: Society and Space* 28, no. 5 (2010): 760.
43. Ibid., 761.
44. Ibid.
45. Trevor Paglen, *Blank Spots on the Map: The Dark Geography of the Pentagon's Secret World* (Harmondsworth: Peguin, 2011).
46. Clare Birchall, 'Aesthetics of the Secret', *New Formations* 83 (2014): 36.
47. Gary Kafer, 'Documenting the Invisible: Political Agency in Trevor Paglen's Limit Telephotography', *Contemporaneity: Historical Presence in Visual Culture* 5, no. 1 (2016): 54.
48. Brian Wallis, 'Trevor Paglen Landing Site', *Aperture* 222, Spring (2016): 78.
49. Jack Z. Bratich, 'Adventures in the Public Secret Sphere', *Cultural Studies ↔ Critical Methodologies* 14, no. 1 (2013): 11.
50. Ibid.
51. Thomas Keenan, 'Disappearances: The Photographs of Trevor Paglen', *Aperture* 191, Summer (2008): 38.
52. Jayne Wilkinson, 'Art Documents: The Politics of Visibility in Contemporary Photography', *InVisible Culture* Issue 22, Spring (2015): http://ivc.lib.rochester.edu/art-documents-the-politics-of-visibility-in-contemporary-photography/
53. Keenan, 'Disappearances', 39.

Chapter 6

1. Deborah Bright, 'Of Mother Nature and Marlboro Men: An Inquiry into the Cultural Meanings of Landscape Photography', (1985): 2.
2. Magali Arriola, 'A Victim and a Viewer: Some Thoughts on Anticipated Ruins', *Afterall: A Journal of Art, Context and Enquiry* 12, Autumn/Winter (2005): 110.

3. For an account and critique of some of these debates see Andrew Emil Gansky, '"Ruin Porn" and the Ambivalence of Decline: Andrew Moore's Photographs of Detroit', *Photography and Culture* 7, no. 2 (2014).
4. David Lloyd, 'Ruination', *Third Text* 18, no. 3 (2004): 269.
5. Caitlin DeSilvey and Tim Edensor, 'Reckoning with Ruins', *Progress in Human Geography* 37, no. 4 (2012): 479.
6. Joel Meyerowitz, *Aftermath: World Trade Centre Archive* (New York and London: Phaidon, 2006).
7. László Munteán, 'Spectral Vestiges: Constructing the Ruins of the World Trade Center', *Americana* VII, no. 1 (2011): http://americanaejournal.hu/vol7no1/muntean
8. Liam Kennedy, 'Remembering September 11: Photography as Cultural Diplomacy', *International Affairs* 79, no. 2 (2003): 321.
9. Ibid., 320.
10. O'Gorman, 'The Political Sublime', 905.
11. See for example, François Debrix, 'The Sublime Spectatorship of War: The Erasure of the Event in America's Politics of Terror and Aesthetics of Violence', *Millennium: Journal of International Studies* 34, no. 3 (2006). Debrix similarly argues that the production of sublime spectatorship is an ideological exercise:

    > The aim of any ideology that seeks to make use of the sublime image is to gain control over the event, to decide its fate and presentation. The ideology of the sublime is successful when it can produce visual events that, by playing with the viewer's sense of shock and search for a pleasurable solution to the apparent trauma, reveal or reinforce what is already given, assured, and established ideologically or politically, 783.

12. O'Gorman, 'The Political Sublime', 905.
13. Weena Perry, '"Too Young and Vibrant for Ruins": Ground Zero Photography and the Problem of Contemporary Ruin', *Afterimage* 36, no. 3 (2008): 12.
14. Chris Vanderwees, 'Traces of the Virtual: Aesthetics, Affect, and the Event in Joel Meyerowitz's Photography of Ground Zero', *Photography and Culture* 10, no. 1 (2017): 22; my emphasis.
15. Kennedy, 'Remembering September 11', 320–1.
16. Perry, '"Too Young and Vibrant for Ruins"', 10.
17. Arriola, 'A Victim and a Viewer', 109.
18. Vanderwees, 'Traces of the Virtual', 30.
19. Jameson cited in ibid.
20. Claire Colebrook, 'Anti-Catastrophic Time', *New Formations* 92: Posthuman Temporalites(2017): 105; emphasis in original.
21. Ibid., 106.
22. Ibid., 103.
23. Zylinksa cited in Laura Benítez Valero, 'Joanna Zylinska: "We Need a New Way of Seeing the Anthropocene"', *CCCBLAB*, 24 April 2018, lab.cccb.org/en/joanna-zylinska-we-need-a-new-way-of-seeing-the-anthropocene/
24. Munteán, 'Spectral Vestiges'.

25. Marita Sturken, *Tourists of History: Memory, Kitsch and Comsumerism from Oklahoma City to Ground Zero* (Durham, NC: Duke University Press, 2007), 167.
26. As Gene Ray has observed in his writings on the sublime, 'As qualitative events of violence that actualise and demonstrate new genocidal potentials, the processes condensed in these two place-names [Auschwitz and Hiroshima] immediately expose as fraudulent the myth of automatic progress and thereby directly affect the very meaning of humanity.' Gene Ray, 'Hits: From Trauma and the Sublime to Radical Critique', *Third Text* 23, no. 2 (2009): 137.
27. Brian Dillon, 'Introduction: A Short History of Decay', in *Ruins: Documents of Contemporary Art* (London: Whitechapel and Cambridge, MA: MIT Press, 2011), 11.
28. Vanderwees, 'Traces of the Virtual', 31.
29. Joanna Zylinska, *Minimal Ethics for the Anthropocene*, ed. Tom Cohen and Claire Colebrook, Critical Climate Change (Ann Arbor: Open Humanities Press, 2014), 19.
30. Kathryn Yusoff, 'Anthropogenesis: Origins and Endings in the Anthropocene', *Theory, Culture & Society* 33, no. 2 (2015).
31. Nicholas Mirzoeff, 'Visualizing the Anthropocene', *Public Culture* 26, no. 2 (2014): 226–7.
32. Joanna Zylinska, 'Photography after the Human', *Photographies* 9, no. 2 (2016): 184.
33. Jodi Dean, 'A View from the Side: The Natural History Museum', *Cultural Critique* 94, Fall (2016).
34. Ibid., 75.
35. T. J. Demos, 'Welcome to the Anthropocene!', (2015), www.fotomuseum.ch/en/explore/stillsearching/articles/27011_welcome_to_the_anthropocene
36. The terms 'Capitalocene' and 'Colonialocene' have been suggested as alternative names for the current epoch as they identify the key contributory cause more directly. It is notable that the logic of inequality is also inscribed in the very profitable scientific and corporate solutions that have been proposed to combat Anthropocene.
37. Roger Luckhurst, 'Contemporary Photography and the Technological Sublime, or, Can There Be a Science Fiction Photography?' *Journal of the Fantastic In the Arts* 19, no. 2 (2008).
38. Zylinska, 'Photography after the Human', 174.
39. Tong Lam, 'Unreal Estate and China's Collective Unconscious', *Cross-Currents: East Asian History and Culture Review* 10, (2014): 112.
40. Ibid.
41. Jason McGrath, 'Apocalypse, or, the Logic of Late Anthropocene Ruins', *Cross-Currents: East Asian History and Culture Review* 10, (2014): 117.
42. Ibid.
43. Zylinska, 'Photography after the Human', 176.
44. 'iEarth (Artist's Statement)', www.joannazylinska.net/iearth/
45. Ibid.
46. T. J. Demos, *Decolonizing Nature: Contemporary Art and the Politics of Ecology* (Berlin: Sternberg Press, 2016), 14.
47. Ibid., 18.

48. Ibid., 19.
49. Mark Godfrey, 'The Artist as Historian', *October* 120, Spring (2007): 156.
50. Ibid.
51. Marija Grech, 'Where "Nothing Ever Was": Anthropomorphic Spectrality and the (Im)Possibility of the Post-Anthropocene', *New Formations* 95 (2018): 23.
52. Ibid., 35.
53. Ibid., 27.

Chapter 7

1. Images from the series were blown up on canvasses and exhibited at the Tate Modern for the exhibition *Performing for the Camera* (2016) and the Whitechapel Gallery for the exhibition *Electronic Superhighway* (2016). The Whitechapel additionally produced a limited edition of C-type print reverse mounted on glass.
2. Alastair Sooke, 'Is This the First Instagram Masterpiece?' *The Telegraph*, 18 January 2016, www.telegraph.co.uk/photography/what-to-see/is-this-the-first-instagra m-masterpiece/
3. Chris Dercon, 'Foreword', in *Performing for the Camera*, ed. Simon Baker and Fiontán Moran (London: Tate Publishing, 2016), 6.
4. Judith Butler, *Gender Trouble: Feminism and the Subversion of Identity* (New York: Routledge, 1999), 33.
5. Alan McKinlay, 'Performativity and the Politics of Identity: Putting Butler to Work', *Critical Perspectives on Accounting* 21, no. 3 (2010): 234.
6. Ibid., 236.
7. Judith Butler, *Bodies That Matter: On the Discursive Limits of 'Sex'* (New York: Routledge, 1993), 232.
8. Judith Butler, *Gender Trouble: Feminism and the Subversion of Identity* (New York: Routledge 1999), 175.
9. Elin Diamond, *Performance and Cultural Politics* (London: Routledge, 1996), 5.
10. Douglas Crimp, 'The Photographic Activity of Postmodernism', *October* 15, Winter (1980): 99.
11. For example, Megan Meagher has proposed that Sherman's work signalled a change from 1970s activism to 1980s postmodernism where the politics of identity was replaced by an exploration of identity as performative: 'While feminist art of the early 1970s placed an emphasis on women's experience and an authentic female identity, Sherman's work forces us to address the ways in which identities cannot be authentic but rather are always and only constructed.' 'Would the Real Cindy Sherman Please Stand Up? Encounters between Cindy Sherman and Feminist Art Theory', *Women: A Cultural Review* 13, no. 1 (2002): 32.
12. Jul-Ch'i Liu divides the feminist literature on Sherman's early works into three groups. The first views Sherman's performances as reproducing women's

objectification. The second argues that Sherman's performances are self-conscious parodies where stereotyped scenes are reproduced ironically in order to 'short-circuit' the male viewer's imaginary domination over the female body. Finally, there is a third group of critics propose a reading that recognises the dual nature of the work as both reinforcing and destabilizing female stereotypes. 'Female Spectatorship and the Masquerade: Cindy Sherman's Untitled Film Stills', *History of Photography* 34, no. 1 (2010).

13. Judith Butler, 'For a Careful Reading', in *Feminist Contentions: A Philosophical Exchange*, ed. Paul Kegan (New York: Routledge, 1995), 135.
14. A. Y. Jackson, 'Performativity Identified', *Qualitative Inquiry* 10, no. 5 (2004): 682; emphasis in original.
15. Ulman cited in Sooke, 'Is This the First Instagram Masterpiece?'
16. Just as Sherman's work was very different to the work of feminist artists who had preceded her, Ulman's work is markedly different from earlier forms of feminist internet art which presented gender as fluid.
17. Emma Maguire, *Girls, Autobiography, Media: Gender and Self-Mediation in Digital Economies* (Cham: Palgrave Macmillan, 2018): 197.
18. Tiqqun, *Preliminary Materials for a Theory of the Young Girl*, trans. Ariana Reines (Cambridge, MA; London: Semiotext(e), 2012).
19. See for example Catherine Driscoll, 'The Mystique of the Young Girl', *Feminist Theory* 14, no. 3 (2013); Jen Kennedy, 'The Young-Girl in Theory', *Women & Performance: A Journal of Feminist Theory* 25, no. 2 (2015); Nina Power, 'She's Just Not That into You', *Radical Philosophy* 177, Jan/Feb (2013).
20. Rosalind Gill, 'Post-Postfeminism? New Feminist Visibilities in Postfeminist Times', *Feminist Media Studies* 16, no. 4 (2016): 64.
21. Ibid., 11.
22. Mary Celeste Kearney, 'Sparkle: Luminosity and Post-Girl Power Media', *Continuum* 29, no. 2 (2015): 265.
23. As McCormack and Salmennieni note, 'The logics of late capitalism entail a shift from a fantasy of accumulation of experience … to an intensification of the present where one must be flexible, adaptable and preferably mobile. The past is not the guarantee of a future, and the present is where the self must be reworked, rethought, retrained, remobilized in yet another, multiply endless, direction.' Donna McCormack and Suvi Salmenniemi, 'The Biopolitics of Precarity and the Self', *European Journal of Cultural Studies* 19, no. 1 (2016): 8.
24. Ana Sofia Elias and Rosalind Gill, 'Beauty Surveillance: The Digital Self-Monitoring Cultures of Neoliberalism', *European Journal of Cultural Studies* 21, no. 1 (2018).
25. As Imogen Tyler has observed,

> In contemporary consumer culture, the pleasures of *narcissism as liberation* are more overtly marketed to women than ever before. In the 1990s, a new 'culture of pampering' emerged that encouraged women to compensate themselves for sexual inequality, and the difficulty of lives spent juggling the competing priorities of work and motherhood, through the consumption of scented candles

and bubble-bath .... The culture of pampering is antithetical to the feminist politics, promising personal solutions to public problems. 'Who Put the "Me" in Feminism?', *Feminist Theory* 6, no. 1 (2005): 38; emphasis in original.

26. Kearney, 'Sparkle', 265.
27. Angela McRobbie, 'Notes on the Perfect', *Australian Feminist Studies* 30, no. 83 (2015).
28. Ibid., 7.
29. Ibid., 9.
30. The makeover show is a key example of the way in which 'unacceptable' behaviour is regulated through shaming and correction. See for example Jessica Ringrose and Valerie Walkerdine, 'Regulating the Abject', *Feminist Media Studies* 8, no. 3 (2008).
31. Anne Burns, 'Self(ie)-Discipline: Social Regulation as Enacted through the Discussion of Photographic Practice', *International Journal of Communication* 9 (2015): 1716.
32. Sarah Gram, 'The Young-Girl and the Selfie', *.dpi: Feminist Journal of Art and Digital Culture* 28: Gender(ed) Cultures on the Internet (2013), dpi.studioxx.org/en/no/28-gendered-cultures-internet/young-girl-and-selfie
33. Amanda Rossie has suggested the term 'feedback' to be used instead of the term 'comments' as a way of indicating the disciplinary intent of these posts. Noting the way in which comments posted on social media carry a disciplinary force, Rossie writes the intent is 'to do something to the girls – whether that is support or encourage – or to make them feel something – shameful, validated, or desired. This is feedback meant to enact some kind of change upon the girls themselves', 'Moving Beyond "Am I Pretty or Ugly?" Disciplining Girls through YouTube Feedback', *Continuum* 29, no. 2 (2015): 233.
34. Rachel Dubrofsky has formulated this demand in terms of 'performing not-performing' see 'A Vernacular of Surveillance: Taylor Swift and Miley Cyrus Perform White Authenticity', *Surveillance & Society* 14, no. 2 (2016); Rachel E. Dubrofsky and Emily D. Ryalls, 'The Hunger Games: Performing Not-Performing to Authenticate Femininity and Whiteness', *Critical Studies in Media Communication* 31, no. 5 (2014).
35. Instagram Post, September 2, www.instagram.com/p/sc48slFV6l/?utm_source=ig_web_button_share_sheet
36. For example, 'ANNOYING'. 'That's right, cry. Im getting hott watcheing this / #crybitch! / It sounds like you're #cuttingyourself #lolol', *Instagram Post*, 8 August, www.instagram.com/p/rcBXSLlV-R/?utm_source=ig_web_button_share_sheet
37. Maguire, *Girls, Autobiography, Media*, 196.
38. It is notable here that Ulman's intention for the work was to raise questions about the female artist including how is a female artist supposed to look like? How is she supposed to behave? As Ulman explains, 'I had been this cliché of an arty girl. Which is so fetishized by certain people. So I thought, what if I transform myself into something that is *not* allowed in the art world?' Ulman cited in Ibid., 183; emphasis in original. As Maguire summarizes, 'Here, the sexism and elitism of the art world, as well as the sexist commodification of women artists, are made visible.' Ibid., 196.

Chapter 8

1. See for example Nadine Ehlers, '"Black Is" and "Black Ain't": Performative Revisions of Racial "Crisis"', *Culture, Theory and Critique* 47, no. 2 (2006); 'Retroactive Phantasies: Discourse, Discipline, and the Production of Race', *Social Identities* 14, no. 3 (2008); Catherine Rottenberg, '*Passing:* Race, Identification, and Desire', *Criticism* 45, no. 4 (2003); John T. Warren, 'Doing Whiteness: On the Performative Dimensions of Race in the Classroom', *Communication Education* 50, no. 2 (2001).
2. Ehlers, 'Retroactive Phantasies', 337; emphasis in original.
3. Rottenberg, '*Passing*', 437.
4. Warren, 'Doing Whiteness', 105.
5. Melissa Heer, 'Restaging Time: Photography, Performance and Anachronism in Shadi Ghadirian's *Qajar Series*', *Iranian Studies* 45, no. 4 (2012): 546.
6. Ibid., 538.
7. Ibid.
8. Judith Butler, 'Performativity, Precarity and Sexual Politics', *AIBR: Revista de Antropología Iberoamericana* 4, no. 3 (2009): x; emphasis in original.
9. Elizabeth Freeman, 'Packing History, Count(er)ing Generations', *New Literary History* 31, no. 4 (2000): 728.
10. Ibid; emphasis in original.
11. Ibid., 733.
12. Ibid., 734.
13. Ibid.
14. Sylvia Musto, 'Portraiture, Revolutionary Identity and Subjugation: Anne-Louis Girodet's *Citizen Belley*', *Canadian Art Review* 20, no. 1/2 (1993): 62.
15. Nicholas Mirzoeff, 'In and Out of Slavery', *The Unesco Courier* July/August (2001): 27–8.
16. Musto, 'Portraiture, Revolutionary Identity and Subjugation', 62.
17. Mirzoeff, 'In and Out of Slavery', 27.
18. Musto, 'Portraiture, Revolutionary Identity and Subjugation', 66.
19. Ibid., 69.
20. Rottenberg, '*Passing*', 444.
21. Ibid.
22. Ibid., 440.
23. Ibid.
24. Sean O'Hagan, 'Omar Victor Diop: "I Want to Reinvent the Heritage of African Studio Photography"', *The Guardian,* 11 July 2015, www.theguardian.com/artanddesign/2015/jul/11/mar-ictor-ioi-want-to-reinvent-great-heritage-of-african-studio-photography
25. Diop cited in Ibid.
26. Imogen Tyler, 'Designed to Fail: A Biopolitics of British Citizenship', *Citizenship Studies* 14, no. 1 (2010): 71.

27. Ibid.
28. Aihwa Ong, *Neoliberalism as Exception: Mutations in Citizenship and Sovereignty* (Durham, NC: Duke University Press, 2006), 6–7.
29. Les Back, Shamser Sinha and with Charlynne Bryan, 'New Hierarchies of Belonging', *European Journal of Cultural Studies* 15, no. 2 (2012).
30. Darrel Enck-Wanzer, 'Barack Obama, the Tea Party, and the Threat of Race: On Racial Neoliberalism and Born Again Racism', *Communication, Culture & Critique* 4, no. 1 (2011): 24.
31. Keith P. Feldman, 'The Globality of Whiteness in Post-Racial Visual Culture', *Cultural Studies* 30, no. 2 (2015): 293.
32. Joe Tompkins, '"A Postgame Interview for the Ages": Richard Sherman and the Dialectical Rhetoric of Racial Neoliberalism', *Journal of Sport and Social Issues* 40, no. 4 (2015): 293.
33. De Lissovoy, 'Conceptualizing the Carceral Turn', 742.
34. Feldman, 'The Globality of Whiteness in Post-Racial Visual Culture', 294.
35. Melamed cited in Tompkins, 'A Postgame Interview for the Ages', 296–7.
36. Roopali Mukherjee, 'Antiracism Limited', *Cultural Studies* 30, no. 1 (2014): 24.
37. Mark Sealy, 'Heni Talk Interviews Omar Victor Diop: Black Subjects in the Frame', 7 December 2018, www.jenkinsjohnsongallery.com/news/heni-talk-interviews-omar-victor-diop
38. McCormack and Salmenniemi, 'The Biopolitics of Precarity and the Self', 7.
39. Beth Buggenhagen, 'If You Were in My Sneakers: Migration Stories in the Studio Photography of Dakar-Based Omar Victor Diop', *Visual Anthropology Review* 33, no. 1 (2017): 40.
40. Priscilla Frank, 'Ghostly Photos Explore What — and Who — American History Forgets', *Huffington Post*, 13 December 2016, www.huffingtonpost.co.uk/entry/nona-faustine-photography_us_584eed9ce4b0bd9c3dfdcba6?guccounter=1
41. Alexandra Schwartz, 'A Living Monument to the Ghosts of American Slavery', *The New Yorker*, 28 December 2016, www.newyorker.com/culture/photo-booth/a-living-monument-to-the-ghosts-of-american-slavery
42. Susan Silas, 'Nona Faustine: White Shoes', 1 December 2015, theo-westenberger.tumblr.com/post/134358235279/nona-faustine-white-shoes
43. Danielle Moodie-Mills, 'Cultural Extermination and the Erasure of Blackness', *NBC News*, 27 July 2015, www.nbcnews.com/news/nbcblk/cultural-extermination-erasure-blackness-n395526
44. Henry Giroux, 'Beyond the Biopolitics of Disposability', 594.
45. Henry Giroux, 'Violence, Katrina, and the Biopolitics of Disposability', *Theory, Culture & Society* 24, no. 7–8 (2007): 308.
46. Ibid.
47. Henry Giroux, 'Spectacles of Race and Pedagogies of Denial: Anti-Black Racist Pedagogy under the Reign of Neoliberalism', *Communication Education* 52, no. 3 (2003): 206.
48. Ibid., 207.

49. Clorinde Peters, 'Visualizing Disposability: Photographing Neoliberal Conflict in the United States', *Afterimage* 44, no. 6 (2017): 10.
50. Ibid., 8.

Chapter 9

1. Petra Kuppers, 'Introduction', *Contemporary Theatre Review* 11, no. 3–4 (2001): 2.
2. Rosemarie Garland-Thomson, 'Seeing the Disabled: Visual Rhetorics of Disability in Popular Photography', in *The New Disability History*, ed. Paul K. Longmore and Lauri Umansky (New York and London: New York University Press, 2001), 347.
3. Rosemarie Garland-Thomson, 'The Story of My Work: How I Became Disabled', *Disability Studies Quarterly* 34, no. 2 (2014).
4. Garland-Thomson, 'Seeing the Disabled', 348. However, as Garland-Thompson has noted, because 'most of us are not born into disability but enter into it as we travel through life, we don't get acculturated the way most of us do in our race or gender.' 'Becoming Disabled', *International New York Times*, 20 August 2016, 9.
5. Kuppers, 'Introduction', 1.
6. George Pendle, 'Photography, but Not as We Know It', *The Economist: 1843*, 5 January 2016, www.1843magazine.com/culture/the-daily/photography-but-not-a s-we-know-it
7. Tobin Siebers, 'Disability as Masquerade', *Literature and Medicine* 23, no. 1 (2004): 1.
8. Ibid., 19.
9. Garland-Thomson, 'Seeing the Disabled', 348.
10. Ibid.
11. Hall cited in Amy L. Brandzel, 'The Subjects of Survival: The Anti-Intersectional Routes of Breast Cancer', *WSQ: Women's Studies Quarterly* 44, no. 1 and 2 (2016): 142.
12. Robert McRuer, 'Compulsory Able-Bodiedness and Queer/Disabled Existence', in *Disability Studies: Enabling the Humanities*, eds. Sharon L. Snyder, Brenda Jo Brueggemann and Rosemarie Garland-Thomson (New York: The Modern Languages Association of America, 2002), 97.
13. Garland-Thomson, 'Seeing the Disabled', 337.
14. Sarah Lochlann Jain, 'Living in Prognosis: Toward an Elegiac Politics', *Representations* 98, no. 1 (2007).
15. Alison Kafer, *Feminist, Queer, Crip* (Bloomington and Indianapolis: Indiana University Press, 2013), 3.
16. Garland-Thomson, 'Seeing the Disabled', 348.
17. Rosemarie Garland-Thomson, 'Staring at the Other', *Disability Studies Quarterly* 25, no. 4 (2005): np.
18. Garland-Thomson, 'Seeing the Disabled', 347.

19. Ibid., 349.
20. As Lindgren succinctly expressed it, Arbus's photographs have 'cast a long shadow on portraits of people with variant bodies' 'Looking at Difference: Laura Swanson's *Anti-Self-Portraits*, Diane Arbus's Portraits, and the Viewer's Gaze', *Journal of Literary & Cultural Disability Studies* 9, no. 3 (2015): 282.
21. Swanson cited in Ibid.
22. Ibid., 286.
23. Garland-Thomson, 'Seeing the Disabled', 347.
24. Amanda Cachia, 'Composing Dwarfism: Reframing Short Stature in Contemporary Photography', *Review of Disability Studies: An International Journal* 10, no. 3&4 (2014): 14.
25. Rosemarie Garland-Thomson, 'Misfits: A Feminist Materialist Disability Concept', *Hypatia* 26, no. 3 (2011): 592–3.
26. Ibid., 603.
27. Nadine Ehlers, 'The Scar Project', *Journal of Literary & Cultural Disability Studies* 9, no. 3 (2015): 332–3.
28. Jain, 'Living in Prognosis', 79.
29. Samantha King, 'Pink Diplomacy: On the Uses and Abuses of Breast Cancer Awareness', *Health Communication* 25, no. 3 (2010): 287.
30. Catherine Lord, *The Summer of Her Baldness: A Cancer Improvisation* (Austin: University of Texas Press, 2004).
31. Lynn Kohlman, *Lynn: Front to Back* (New York: Assouline, 2004).
32. Ehlers, 'The Scar Project', 342.
33. Stella Bolaki, 'Re-Covering the Scarred Body: Textual and Photographic Narratives of Breast Cancer', *Mosaic* 44, no. 2 (2011): 8.
34. Garland-Thomson, 'Seeing the Disabled', 347.
35. Bolaki, 'Re-Covering the Scarred Body', 11.
36. Jain, 'Living in Prognosis', 78.
37. Millar cited in Bolaki, 'Re-Covering the Scarred Body', 8.
38. Brandzel, 'The Subjects of Survival', 139.
39. Eve Kosofsky Sedgwick, 'White Glasses', *The Yale Journal of Criticism* 5, no. 3 (1992): 204; emphasis in original.
40. Bolaki, 'Re-Covering the Scarred Body', 13.
41. Jain, 'Living in Prognosis.'
42. Ibid., 89.
43. Ibid., 90.
44. Ibid.
45. The series can be seen in full at hannahlaycock.com/awakenings/
46. Stella Bolaki, 'Capturing the Worlds of Multiple Sclerosis: Hannah Laycock's Photography', *Medical Humanities* 43, no. 1 (2017): 49.
47. Ibid., 48.
48. Laycock cited in David Whelan, 'The Artists Explaining Their Multiple Sclerosis through Art', *Vice*, 23 November 2015, www.vice.com/en_uk/article/wd7kxw/a-hidden-disese-understanding-multiple-sclerosis-through-art-225

49. Kafer, *Feminist, Queer, Crip*, 25.
50. Ibid., 28.
51. Ibid.

Part Four

1. Joan Copjec, *Read My Desire: Lacan against the Historicists* (Cambridge and London: The MIT Press, 1995), 14.

Chapter 10

1. Chris Wiley, 'Lucas Blalock: Imperfect Grace', *Aperture*, no. 208 (2012): 32.
2. Anne Doran, 'Lucas Blalock', *Art in America*, 7 January 2012, www.artinamericamagazine.com/reviews/lucas-blalock/
3. Blalock cited in Giada De Agostinis, 'Studio Visit - Lucas Blalock', *Paper Journal*, 6 June 2017, paper-journal.com/studio-visit-lucas-blalock
4. Derek Hook, 'Lacan, the Meaning of the Phallus and the "Sexed" Subject' (London: LSE Reseach Online, 2006): 65.
5. Ibid.
6. Lacan cited in Ibid., 69.
7. Ibid. This will be discussed further in Chapter 11.
8. Alain Vanier, *Lacan* (New York: Other Press, 2000), 54–5.
9. Todd McGowan, *Capitalism and Desire: The Psychic Cost of Free Markets* (New York: Columbia University Press, 2016), 23.
10. Also written '*objet petit a*', Lacan specified that this term should remain untranslated as a marker of its status as an algebraic sign. Although a number of theorists do translate the term using 'object a', or 'object little a', I will be using the designation *objet a*.
11. Copjec, *Read My Desire*, 119; emphasis in original.
12. Vanier, *Lacan*, 64.
13. McGowan, *Capitalism and Desire*, 27.
14. McGowan gives the following example:

    When I desire to drink a can of Coca Cola, the particular can of Coca Cola is my object of desire. The object petit a is the enigmatic quality I attribute to Coca Cola that raises it above all other drinks and renders the particular can desirable. I don't pursue this object petit a – I pursue the particular can – and yet the object petit a serves as the engine for my desire. Ibid., 71–2.

15. Slavoj Žižek, *The Plague of Fantasies* (London and New York: Verso, 1997), 39.
16. Slavoj Žižek, *Looking Awry: An Introduction to Jacques Lacan through Popular Culture* (Cambridge and London: The MIT Press, 1992), 6; emphasis in original.

17. Jacques Lacan, 'Kant with Sade', *October* 51 (1989): 62.
18. Todd McGowan, 'Finding Ourselves on a *Lost Highway*: David Lynch's Lesson in Fantasy', *Cinema Journal* 39, no. 2 (2000): 61.
19. As Richard Feldstein has clarified, although *objet a* has no narrative or temporal dimension, we can, through fantasy, 'narrativize its lost quality' 'Subject of the Gaze for Another Gaze' in *Lacan, Politics, Aesthetics*, eds. Willy Apollon and Richard Feldstein (Albany: State University of New York Press, 1996), 58.
20. McGowan, *Capitalism and Desire*, 33.
21. Žižek cited in Yannis Stavrakakis, 'Objects of Consumption, Causes of Desire: Consumerism and Advertising in Societies of Commanded Enjoyment', *Gramma* 14 (2006): 93.
22. McGowan, *Capitalism and Desire*, 46.
23. Ibid., 36.
24. This is why successful adverts need not include the actual product and window shopping in which no products are actually bought can be satisfying.
25. Blalock cited in De Agostinis, 'Studio Visit.'
26. Blalock cited in Ibid.
27. Yannis Stavrakakis, *Lacan and the Political* (London and New York: Routledge, 1999), 46.
28. Copjec, *Read My Desire*, 131.
29. Parveen Adams, 'Bruce Nauman and the Object of Anxiety', *October* 83, Winter (1998): 96.
30. See for example Žižek, *Looking Awry*.
31. Adams, 'Bruce Nauman and the Object of Anxiety', 96.
32. Mladen Dolar, '"I Shall Be with You on Your Wedding-Night": Lacan and the Uncanny', *October* 58, Autumn (1991): 13.
33. Blalock cited in De Agostinis, 'Studio Visit.'
34. Lacan cited in McGowan, *Capitalism and Desire*, 277, note 18.
35. Ibid., 277 note 19.
36. Ibid., 179.

Chapter 11

1. Joan Copjec, 'The Sexual Compact', *Angelaki* 17, no. 2 (2012): 31.
2. Juliet Mitchell, *Psychoanalysis and Feminism: A Radical Reassessment of Freudian Psychoanalysis* (Harmondsworth: Penguin, 1975).
3. Laura Mulvey, 'Visual Pleasure and Narrative Cinema', *Screen* 3, no. 1 (1975).
4. Ibid., 6.
5. To offer a few examples: Tania Modleski, *The Women Who Knew Too Much* (London: Routledge, 1988); Kaja Silverman, *The Acoustic Mirror: The Female Voice in Psychoanalysis and Cinema* (Bloomington: Indiana University Press, 1988); Steven Cohan and Ina Rae Hark, eds., *Screening the Male: Exploring Masculinities*

in Hollywood Cinema (London: Routledge, 1993); Barbara Creed, *The Monstrous-Feminine: Film, Feminism, Psychoanalysis* (London: Routledge, 1993).

6. Respectively, *After Helmut Newton's 'Here They Come'* (1999), *Table 2* (1997-8) and *Headless Orange* (2000).
7. Mulvey, 'Visual Pleasure', 11; emphasis in original.
8. Heather Anderson, 'Performing Postfeminism: Escaping Identity Politics?' *Atlantis: Critical Studies in Gender, Culture & Social Justice/Études critiques sur le genre, la culture, et la justice* 30, no. 2 (2006): 121.
9. Ruth Rosengarten, 'Performing for the Camera 18 February–12 June 2016, Tate Modern (Review)', *Photography and Culture* 9, no. 2 (2016): 190.
10. Anderson, 'Performing Postfeminism', 121.
11. Ibid., 122.
12. Vivian L. Huang, 'Inscrutably, Actually: Hospitality, Parasitism, and the Silent Work of Yoko Ono and Laurel Nakadate', *Women & Performance: A journal of feminist theory* 28, no. 3 (2018), 194.
13. Although given generic names such as curator, writer and so on, the men in Stehli's piece are well known in their own right and easily recognizable. Adrian Searle has even written about his experience, "Why Do I Feel Naked?" *The Guardian*, 15 July 2000, www.theguardian.com/books/2000/jul/15/books.guardianreview4.
14. For example, Alice Anokhina's review states that 'ultimately, none of it appears to serve any purpose except to reiterate the gender dynamics everyone is already acutely aware of'. 'Laurel Nakadate's Outré Retrospective', *The London Word*, 21 November 2011, www.thelondonword.com/2011/11/laurel-nakadate-at-the-zabludowicz-collection/
15. Karen Rosenberg, 'Art in Review: Laurel Nakadate', *The New York Times*, 26 June 2009, archive.nytimes.com/query.nytimes.com/gst/fullpage-9C01E4D81630F935A15755C0A96F9C8B63.html
16. Regan McMahon, 'Artist Laurel Nakadate at Crossroads of Sex, Power', *SFGate*, 18 February 2011, www.sfgate.com/movies/article/Artist-Laurel-Nakadate-at-crossroads-of-sex-power-2475514.php
17. Ken Johnson, 'A Burgeoning Film Career Built on Random Encounters', *The New York Times*, 25 February 2011, www.nytimes.com/2011/02/25/arts/design/25nakadate.html
18. Prospero, 'The Art of Laurel Nakadate: Lust and Loneliness', *The Economist*, 13 July 2011, www.economist.com/prospero/2011/07/13/lust-and-loneliness
19. As Parveen Adams has stated, 'It is not the image of a woman as such that is crucial, but how the image organizes the way in which the image is looked at.' *The Emptiness of the Image: Psychoanalysis and Sexual Differences* (London and New York: Routledge, 1995), 2.
20. As Victor Burgin has noted, 'Many of Mulvey's followers have since shifted the ground from psychoanalysis to sociology, while nevertheless retaining a psychoanalytic terminology.' *In/Different Spaces: Place and Memory in Visual Culture* (Berkeley, LA and London: University of California Press, 1996), 57.

21. Joan Copjec, 'The Orthopsychic Subject: Film Theory and the Reception of Lacan', *October* 49, Summer (1989).
22. Among others, see Todd McGowan and Shelia Kunkle, eds., *Lacan and Contemporary Film* (New York: Other Press, 2004); Todd McGowan, 'Looking for the Gaze: Lacanian Film Theory and Its Vicissitudes', *Cinema Journal* 42, no. 3 (2003); Žižek, *Looking Awry: An Introduction to Jacques Lacan through Popular Culture*; Jennifer Friedlander, *Feminine Look: Sexuation, Spectatorship, Subversion* (Albany: State University of New York Press, 2008).
23. Jacques Lacan, 'The Mirror Stage as Formative of the *I* Function as Revealed in Psychoanalytic Experience', in *Écrits* (New York and London: W. W. Norton, 2006), 75-81.
24. Jacques Lacan, *The Four Fundamental Concepts of Psycho-Analysis* (New York and London: W. W. Norton, 1981).
25. Joan Copjec, *Imagine There's No Woman: Ethics and Sublimation* (Cambridge and London: The MIT Press, 2002), 216; emphasis in original.
26. Slavoj Žižek, '"I Hear You with My Ears"; or, the Invisible Master', in *Gaze and Voice as Love Objects*, ed. Renata Salecl and Slavoj Žižek (Durham, NC and London: Duke University Press, 1996), 90; emphasis in original.
27. Lacan, *The Four Fundamental Concepts of Psycho-Analysis*, 92.
28. Todd McGowan, *The Real Gaze: Film Theory after Lacan* (Albany: State University of New York Press, 2007), 7.
29. Margaret Iversen has theorized this difference in terms of stadium and punctum: 'Lacan's discussion of anamorphosis serves to illustrate the disparity between one's position as sovereign subject of sight (studium) and as object of the gaze (or the punctum).' 'What Is a Photograph?' *Art History* 17, no. 3 (1994): 457.
30. Hook, 'Lacan, the Meaning of the Phallus and the 'Sexed' Subject', 61.
31. Ibid., 62.
32. McGowan, *The Real Gaze*, 3.
33. Ibid.
34. Mulvey, 'Visual Pleasure', 18. The tactics advocated by Mulvey include strategies and techniques common to experimental and avant-garde film such as scratching the film, inserting text and experimenting with the printing and exposure of the film.
35. McGowan, *The Real Gaze*, 15.
36. Lacan cited in 'Lost on Mulholland Drive: Navigating David Lynch's Panegyric to Hollywood', *Cinema Journal* 43, no. 2 (2004): 80; translation McGowan's own.
37. Slavoj Žižek, *The Sublime Object of Ideology* (London and New York: Verso, 1995), 30.
38. Slavoj Žižek, *Tarrying with the Negative: Kant, Hegel, and the Critique of Ideology* (Durham, NC: Duke University Press, 1993), 117.
39. Jacques Lacan, *The Seminar. Book XX. Encore, On Feminine Sexuality, The Limits of Love and Knowledge, 1972-3,* Jacques-Alain Miller, ed., translated with notes Bruce Fink (New York: Norton, 1998).
40. Jennifer Friedlander, 'How Should a Woman Look? Scopic Strategies for Sexuated Subjects', *Journal for the Psychoanalysis of Culture and Society* 8, no. 1 (2003): 105.
41. Copjec, *Read My Desire*, 207.

42. As Copjec argues,

> The law of sexual difference is a law of unconscious necessity, which is to say, it is a law that *founds* culture and is *not a cultural law*. This means that *this law, which mandates that each subject make a choice as to his or her own sexual identity, does not define or even permit a fixed identity so much as it defines the mode in which the subject will come to question and challenge his or her own identity and the cultural laws that attempt to fix it*. The law that founds culture is not a constituent part of the culture it founds and maintains an antinomic relation to the latter. *Imagine There's No Woman*, 222; emphasis in original

Thus, as she summarizes elsewhere, 'Sex does not budge, and it is not heterosexist to say so. In fact, the opposite may be true. For it is by making it conform to the signifier that you oblige sex to conform to social dictates, to take on social content.' *Read My Desire*, 211.

43. John Gray, *Men Are from Mars, Women Are from Venus: A Practical Guide for Improving Communication and Getting What You Want in Your Relationships: How to Get What You Want in Your Relationships* (London: HarperThorsons, 1992).
44. Derek Hook, 'Restoring Universality to the Subject: Lacan's Kantian Logic of Sexuation', *Annual Review of Critical Psychology* 7 (2009): 159.
45. Copjec, *Read My Desire*, 235.
46. Hook, 'Restoring Universality to the Subject', 164.
47. As Copjec summarizes, 'One category does not complete the other, make up for what is lacking in the other. Were one to believe in the possibility of such a universe, one would believe in the sexual relation, with all its heterosexist implications', *Read My Desire*, 234.
48. Slavoj Žižek, *The Metastases of Enjoyment: Six Essays on Women and Causality* (London and New York: Verso, 2005), 155.
49. This is a theme throughout Nakadate's work. Perhaps the clearest expression of the non-relation is her video *Love Hotel* (2005) which shows Nakadate and an 'invisible' lover in several of Tokyo's pay-by-the hour hotel rooms. One reviewer notes the 'actual sight of one person having sex with nothing strips the act down to a succession of absurd and lonely gestures' Prospero, 'The Art of Laurel Nakadate'.
50. Rob Horning, 'You Know You're the Prettiest Girl', *The New Inquiry*, 1 July 2011, thenewinquiry.com/you-know-youre-the-prettiest-girl/
51. http://artfcity.com/2011/12/06/the-afc-guide-to-disliking-laurel-nakadate-without-hating-women/

Chapter 12

1. Peter Schjeldahl, 'Richard Prince's Instagrams', *The New Yorker*, 30 September 2014, www.newyorker.com/culture/culture-desk/richard-princes-instagrams
2. See for example Crimp, 'The Photographic Activity of Postmodernism'.

3. Douglas Eklund, *The Pictures Generation, 1974-1984* (New York: Metropolitan Museum of Art, 2009), 152.
4. Jerry Saltz, 'Richard Prince's Instagram Paintings Are Genius Trolling', *Vulture*, 23 September 2014, www.vulture.com/2014/09/richard-prince-instagram-pervert-troll-genius.html
5. Meghan M. Gallagher, 'Claiming Images: The Production and Preservation of Desire in Richard Prince's Re-Photography', *Scripps Senior Theses*. Paper 679. (2015): 48.
6. Cited in Lizzie Plaugic, 'The Story of Richard Prince and His $100,000 Instagram Art', *The Verge*, 30 May 2015, www.theverge.com/2015/5/30/8691257/richard-prince-instagram-photos-copyright-law-fair-use
7. Jodi Dean, 'Affective Networks', *Media Tropes* II, no. 2 (2010): 26; emphasis added.
8. Caitlin Dewey, '59 Percent of Links Shared on Social Media Have Never Been Clicked, Study Finds', *Independent*, 16 June 2016, www.independent.co.uk/life-style/gadgets-and-tech/59-percent-of-links-shared-on-social-media-have-never-actually-been-clicked-study-finds-a7086291.html
9. Dean, 'Affective Networks', 42.
10. Jodi Dean, 'The Real Internet', *International Journal of Žižek Studies* 4, no. 1 (2010): 16.
11. Cubitt cited in Paddy Johnson, 'Richard Prince Sucks: His Show of Instagram Printouts at Gagosian Isn't Just Bad, It's Sexist', *Artnet News*, 21 October 2014, news.artnet.com/market/richard-prince-sucks-136358
12. See Hito Steyerl's 'In Defense of the Poor Image', in *The Wretched of the Screen* (Berlin: Sternberg Press, 2012) for more on the politics of the poor quality digital image.
13. Jodi Dean, *Democracy and Other Neoliberal Fantasies: Communicative Capitalism and Left Politics* (Durham, NC and London: Duke University Press, 2009), 26.
14. Alex Needham, 'Richard Prince V Suicide Girls in an Instagram Price War', *The Guardian*, 27 May 2015, www.theguardian.com/artanddesign/2015/may/27/suicide-girls-richard-prince-copying-instagram
15. Dean, 'Affective Networks', 39.
16. Ibid., 21.
17. Derek Hook, 'What Is "Enjoyment as a Political Factor"?' *Political Psychology* 38, no. 4 (2017): 607; emphasis in original.
18. Ibid., 609.
19. Ibid., 605.
20. Sigmund Freud, *The Standard Edition of the Complete Psychological Works of Sigmund Freud*, trans. James and Alix Strachey (London: Hogarth Press and the Institute of Psychoanalysis, 1953-1974), vol. 13.
21. Ibid., 204–5.
22. Joan Copjec, 'The *Unvermögender* Other: Hysteria and Democracy in America', *New Formations* 14 (1991): 36.
23. Todd McGowan, *The End of Dissatisfaction? Jacques Lacan and the Emerging Society of Enjoyment* (New York: State University of New York Press, 2004), 16.
24. Ibid., 3.

25. Hook, 'What Is "Enjoyment as a Political Factor"?' 614.
26. Jodi Dean gives the following examples:

> The eternal feminine stolen by the Catholic Church in the best-seller, *The DaVinci Code*, or the powerful maternal, feminine essence appropriated by patriarchy in some versions of cultural feminism; the anti-Semitic vision of wealth to be had if not for the Jews; the sexual access to white women posited by white American racism toward black men; the fulfillment and sanctity that straight marriage would provide were it not under threat by same-sex couples; the prosperity, security, and freedom Americans would be enjoying had it not been stolen by fanatical Islamic fundamentalists according to the terms of the war on terror. 'Why Žižek for Political Theory?', *International Journal of Žižek Studies* 18–32 (2007): 22.

27. Žižek, *Tarrying with the Negative*, 203; emphasis in original.
28. Ibid., 202; emphasis in original.
29. Rob Reiner, *A Few Good Men*, 1992, Columbia Pictures USA.
30. Slavoj Žižek, 'Why Are Laibach and NSK Not Fascists?' *M'ARS* 3/4 (1993): www.nskstate.com
31. Žižek cited in Paul Kingsbury, 'Uneasiness in Culture, or Negotiating the Sublime Distances Towards the Big Other', *Geography Compass* 11, no. 6 (2017): 5.
32. Ibid.
33. McGowan, *The End of Dissatisfaction?*
34. Slavoj Žižek, *Enjoy Your Symptom! Jacques Lacan in Hollywood and Out* (London and New York: Routledge, 1992), 182.
35. Stavrakakis, 'Objects of Consumption', 101.
36. McGowan, *The End of Dissatisfaction?* 7.
37. Ibid., 37.
38. McGowan, *Capitalism and Desire*, 41. The Other is distinct from another person, thus the capital O. Some writers use the phrase 'the big Other' in order to make this distinction clear.
39. Lacan, *The Four Fundamental Concepts*, 235.
40. Jacques Lacan, *Écrits* (London: Tavistock Publications, 1977).
41. Slavoj Žižek, 'The Seven Veils of Fantasy', in *Key Concepts of Lacanian Psychoanalysis*, ed. Dany Nobus (New York: Other Press, 1999), 7.
42. Slavoj Žižek, *The Metastases of Enjoyment*, 177; emphasis in original.
43. McGowan, *Capitalism and Desire*, 43.
44. Ibid.
45. Ibid.
46. Dmitry Uzlaner, 'The Selfie and the Intolerable Gaze of the Other', *International Journal of Applied Psychoanalytic Studies* 14, no. 4 (2017): 287.
47. Ibid., 288.
48. Ibid.
49. Žižek, *The Plague of Fantasies*, 27; emphasis in original.

50. Ibid., 28.
51. Schjeldahl, 'Richard Prince's Instagrams'.
52. Hannah Jane Parkinson, 'Instagram, an Artist and the $100,000 Selfies – Appropriation in the Digital Age', *The Guardian*, 18 July 2015, www.theguardian.com/technology/2015/jul/18/instagram-artist-richard-prince-selfies
53. Johnson, 'Richard Prince Sucks'.

Chapter 13

1. Kerwin Lee Klein, 'On the Emergence of Memory in Historical Discourse', *Representations* 69, Winter (2000): 128; emphasis in original.
2. Shoshana Felman and Dori Laub, *Testimony: Crises of Witnessing in Literature, Psychoanalysis and History* (London and New York: Routledge, 1992).
3. Cathy Caruth, *Trauma: Explorations in Memory* (Baltimore and London: John Hopkins University Press, 1995); *Unclaimed Experience: Trauma, Narrative and History* (Baltimore, MD: John Hopkins University Press, 1996).
4. Caruth, *Trauma*, 5; emphasis in original.
5. Marianne Hirsch, 'Surviving Images: Holocaust Photographs and the Work of Memory', *The Yale Journal of Criticism* 14, no. 1 (2001): 9.
6. Ibid., 9; my emphasis.
7. Lisa Carstens, 'Sexual Politics and Confessional Testimony in *Sophie's Choice*', *Twentieth Century Literature* 47, no. 3 (2001): 299.
8. Debarati Sanyal, 'A Soccer Match in Auschwitz: Passing Culpability in Holocaust Criticism', *Representations* 79, no. 1 (2002): 12.
9. Anne Chapman, 'The Reality of Imagining the Holocaust: David Levinthal's *Mein Kampf*, *eSharp* 19: Reality/ Illusion (2012): 145.
10. Ibid.
11. Marianne Hirsch, *The Generation of Postmemory: Writing and Visual Culture after the Holocaust* (New York: Columbia University Press, 2012), 133.
12. Ibid., 134. In her discussion of *Mein Kampf*, Hirsch recognizes that Levinthal's work seeks to make us 'conscious of the uncomfortably tainted position we always occupy when we view perpetrator images' (147). However, she argues that the hyper-masculinized and hyper-feminized toy figures along with the eroticized staging of the power relationship between victim and perpetrator conflates the genocidal and the pornographic gaze causing a form of obfuscation that serves to grant the original perpetrator images a 'disturbing artistic and testimonial afterlife' (149).
13. Susannah Radstone, 'Social Bonds and Psychical Order: Testimonies', *Cultural Values* 5, no. 1 (2001): 61.
14. Ibid., 65.
15. Claudia Eppert, 'Entertaining History: (Un)Heroic Identifications, Apt Pupils, and an Ethical Imagination', *New German Critique* 86, Spring–Summer (2002): 8.

16. Ibid., 85. Indeed, as James Young has observed of Levinthal's work, 'at least part of what makes these images so unnerving for viewers is their suggestion that we, as viewers, may be no less complicit in the continuing degradation of victim'. *At Memory's Edge: After-Images of the Holocaust in Contemporary Art and Architecture* (New Haven and London: Yale University Press, 2000), 57–8.
17. Eppert, 'Entertaining History', 97.
18. Ibid., 86.
19. Gary Weissman, *Fantasies of Witnessing: Postwar Efforts to Experience the Holocaust* (Ithaca, NY and London: Cornell University Press, 2004), 209.
20. Nancy Weston, 'How to Remember', in *Absence/Presence: Essays and Reflections on the Artistic Memory of the Holocaust*, ed. Steve Feinstein (New York: Syracuse University Press, 2005), 43.
21. Ibid.
22. Lutz Koepnick, 'Photographs and Memories', *South Central Review* 21, no. 1 (2004): 95.
23. Alvin H. Rosenfeld, *The End of the Holocaust* (Indiana: Indiana University Press, 2011); Hilene Flanzbaum, *The Americanization of the Holocaust* (Baltimore and London: Johns Hopkins University Press, 1999); Peter Novick, *The Holocaust in American Life* (Boston and New York: Mariner Books, 1999).
24. Stella Setka, 'Bastardized History: How Inglourious Basterds Breaks through American Screen Memory', *Jewish Film & New Media* 3, no. 2 (2015): 142.
25. Sicher cited in Lucy Bond, 'Intersections or Misdirections? Problematising Crossroads of Memory in the Commemoration of 9/11', *Culture, Theory and Critique* 53, no. 2 (2012): 120.
26. Sanyal, 'A Soccer Match in Auschwitz', 20.
27. Michael Rothberg, *Multidirectional Memory: Remembering the Holocaust in the Age of Decolonization* (Stanford, CA: Stanford University Press, 2009), 16.
28. The work can be viewed at www.marcadelman.com/installation/
29. Adelman cited in Ben Valentine, 'Gays, Grinder, the Holocaust Memorial, and Art: An Interview with Marc Adelman', *Hyperallergic*, 21 December 2012, hyperallergic.com/62106/gays-grinder-the-holocaust-memorial-and-art-an-interview-with-marc-adelman/
30. Sophia Drakopoulou, '"We Can Remember It for You": Location, Memory, and Commodification in Social Networking Sites', *Sage Open* 7, no. 3 (2017): 8.
31. K. Anden-Papadopoulos, 'Citizen Camera-Witnessing: Embodied Political Dissent in the Age of 'Mediated Mass Self-Communication'', *New Media & Society* 16, no. 5 (2013): 754.
32. Ibid., 760.
33. Paul Frosh, 'The Gestural Image: The Selfie, Photography Theory, and Kinesthetic Sociability', *International Journal of Communication* 9 (2015).
34. Kate Douglas, 'Youth, Trauma and Memorialisation: The Selfie as Witnessing', *Memory Studies* (2017): 2–3; my emphasis.
35. Daniel Levy and Natan Sznaider, *The Holocaust and Memory in the Global Age*, trans. Assenka Oksiloff (Philadelphia, PA: Temple University Press, 2005).

36. Rothberg, *Multidirectional Memory*.
37. Alejandro Baer and Natan Sznaider, 'Ghosts of the Holocaust in Franco's Mass Graves: Cosmopolitan Memories and the Politics of "Never Again"', *Memory Studies* 8, no. 3 (2015): 329.
38. Ibid., 331.
39. Levy and Sznaider, *The Holocaust and Memory in the Global Age*, 4.
40. Rothberg, *Multidirectional Memory*, 6.
41. Adelman cited in Valentine, 'Gays, Grinder, the Holocaust Memorial, and Art'.
42. Rothberg, *Multidirectional Memory*, 5. Similarly, Arlene Stein has argued that 'historical memories are a potent symbolic resource for social movements, aiding the process of mobilization and the formation of collective identities. The Holocaust evokes a particularly powerful and disturbing set of images, associations, and emotions. It has therefore emerged as a common symbolic referent for contemporary social movements.' 'Whose Memories? Whose Victimhood? Contests for the Holocaust Frame in Recent Social Movement Discourse' In *Sociological Perspectives* 41, no. 3 (1998): 533.
43. Rothberg, *Multidirectional Memory*, 7; emphasis in original.

Chapter 14

1. Robert Shore, *Post-Photography* (London: Laurence King, 2014); Carles Guerra and Thomas Keenan, *Anti-Photojournalism* (Barcelona and Amsterdam: La Virreina and Foam, 2011); Julian Stallabrass, 'Sebastião Salgado and Fine Art Photojournalism', *New Left Review* 223, May–June (1997).
2. John Roberts has similarly argued that

   > we need to keep the objective demise of documentary culture separate from the more tendentious notion that documentary culture is the place where the truth-telling powers of photography were once secured politically through a commitment to a stable photographic realism, and then later eroded. For, it is precisely the confusion of the latter with the former that fuels much of the confused understanding of the political fate of the photodocument and documentary culture today.

   'Photography after the Photograph: Event, Archive, and the Non-Symbolic.' *Oxford Art Journal* 32, no. 2 (2009): 288.
3. Liam Kennedy, 'Photojournalism and Warfare in a Postphotographic Age', *Photography and Culture* 8, no. 2 (2015): 163.
4. Ibid., 162.
5. Stallabrass, 'Sebastião Salgado and Fine Art Photojournalism', 3.
6. Kennedy, 'Photojournalism and Warfare', 161.
7. Ariella Azoulay has also made a significant contribution to theorizing the practices of spectatorship through her concept of the 'civil contract of photography'. There

is, however, an idealism in Azoulay's work that is at odds with the tone found in the work of many contemporary artists who are using photography to engage with issues of violence and spectatorship. Therefore, I have not addressed Azoulay's writings in this chapter. For Azoulay's argument in full, see Ariella Azoulay, *The Civil Contract of Photography* (New York: Zone Books, 2008). For a recent application of Azoulay's argument see Chad Elias, 'Citizen Photography in Fouad Elkoury's Beyrouth Aller-Retour', *Photographies* 10, no. 3 (2017).

8. Lilie Chouliaraki, *The Ironic Spectator: Solidarity in the Age of Post-Humanitarianism* (Cambrigde and Maden: Polity Press, 2013).
9. See Thomas Keenan, 'Mobilizing Shame', *The South Atlantic Quarterly* 103, no. 2-3 (2004).
10. A number of critics have drawn attention to the privatization of politics that occurs under neoliberalism which, in Giroux's words, 'has eviscerated the space of democratic politics as well as the language in which it is affirmed and contested.' Henry Giroux, 'Beyond the Biopolitics of Disposability, 595.
11. Here it is interesting to note John Douglas Millar's point that, despite widespread claims of our contemporary desensitization to images of suffering, NGOs and charities are still able to mobilize vast sums of money. As such, Millar proposes that the problem to be addressed is 'not so much that images are not seen and in some sense acted upon (i.e. financially, the donation of money), but rather that they have become an emotional siphon emptied of radical potential.' 'Watching V Looking', *Art Monthly* 340, October (2010): 8.
12. Chouliaraki, *The Ironic Spectator*, 77: emphasis in original.
13. Judith Butler's work is also important here, see in particular *Frames of War: When Is Life Grievable?* (London: Verso, 2010).
14. Chouliaraki, *The Ironic Spectator*, 2.
15. Chouliaraki cited in Pierluigi Musarò, 'Tensions and Paradoxes of Humanitarianism. Dialogue with Lilie Chouliaraki', *International Review of Sociology* 27, no. 2 (2017): 283.
16. Christoph Bangert, *hello camel* (Berlin: Kehrer, 2016).
17. Christoph Bangert, *War Porn* (Berlin: Kehrer, 2014).
18. Bangert cited in Bruno Bayley, 'Photos of the Absurdity of Modern Warfare', *Vice*, 2 June 2016, www.vice.com/en_uk/article/avaw4j/cristoph-bangerts-hello-camel-captures-the-absurdity-of-modern-warfare.
19. David Campbell, 'Cultural Governance and Pictorial Resistance: Reflections on the Imaging of War', *Review of International Studies* 29, (2003); Fred Ritchin, *Bending the Frame: Photojournalism, Documentary, and the Citizen* (New York: Aperture, 2013).
20. Kennedy, 'Photojournalism and Warfare in a Postphotographic Age', 161.
21. Laurence Cornet, 'Overlooking the Realities of Conflict', *Photographic Museum of Humanity,* 13 September 2016, phmuseum.com/news/christoph-bangert-hello-camel.
22. Bangert cited in ibid.
23. Ibid.
24. Keenan, 'Mobilizing Shame', 442.

25. Lilie Chouliaraki, 'The Humanity of War: Iconic Photojournalism of the Battle Field, 1914–2012', *Visual Communication* 12, no. 3 (2013): 320.
26. Richard Mosse, *Infra* (New York: Aperture, 2012).
27. Rebecca Horne, 'Candy-Colored Congo Sees Waking Dreams Verge into Nightmares', *Wired* 7 February 2013, www.wired.com/2013/07/mosse-infrared/
28. Jessica Loudis, 'Infra', *Artforum International* April/May (2012): 25.
29. Aaron Rothman, 'Our Invisible Presence', *Places Journal* August (2012), doi.org/10.22269/120814
30. Susie Linfield, *The Cruel Radiance: Photography and Political Violence* (Chicago, IL and London: The University of Chicago Press, 2010).
31. Ibid., 133.
32. Ibid., 134.
33. Ibid., 135.
34. Roberts, 'Photography after the Photograph', 287.
35. Neelika Jayawardane, 'Queering the Congo', *Africa Is a Country,* 21 November 2011, africasacountry.com/2011/11/queering-the-congo/
36. Ibid.
37. Mary Walling Blackburn and A. B. Huber, 'The Flash Made Flesh', *Triple Canopy* Issue 11 (2011), www.canopycanopycanopy.com/issues/11/contents/the_flash_made_flesh
38. Susan Gibb, 'An Ongoing State of Conflict: Richard Mosse's *The Enclave*', *Art Monthly Australia* 269, May (2014): 21.
39. David Brancaleone, 'Richard Mosse's *Infra*: Conflict, Art and the Regime of the Documentary Image', *Enclave Review* 8, Summer (2013): 4.
40. For example, the aesthetic choices Mosse makes can be seen to place the debate over the ethics of documentary photography above the representation of the conflict in its singularity. This abstraction also be seen in the title of the work which privileges the medium Mosse uses over its subject and in the titling of the images where Mosse frequently draws on Western songs, literature and phrases which limits the possibilities for viewers to develop alternative interpretations to those that Mosse assigns to these images. Here the alternatives offered by the aesthetic choices might be seen to be ruined by enforced set of associations.
41. With regard to these debates in relation to Mosse's recent work see Daniel C. Blight's uncompromising critique 'Incoming: Photography, Contemporary Art, Whitness', *American Suburb X,* 23 March 2017, www.americansuburbx.com/2017/03/incoming-photography-contemporary-art-whiteness.html
42. These figures are cited in Brancaleone.
43. Gibb, 'An Ongoing State of Conflict', 25.
44. Keenan, 'Mobilizing Shame', 447.
45. Ibid.
46. Tirdad Zolghadr, 'Them and Us', *Frieze* Issue 96, Jan.–Feb., (2006): frieze.com/article/them-and-us
47. Antonio Denti, 'The Surviving Frame', *Lens Culture* (nd), www.lensculture.com/articles/antonio-denti-the-surviving-frame

48. Ibid.
49. 'The Surviving Frame', *Vimpt,* 12 December 2017, vimpt.com/2017/12/12/the-surviving-frame-antonio-denti/
50. Steyerl, 'In Defense of the Poor Image'.
51. Rebecca A. Adelman, 'Pixelizing Atrocity', *Philosophy of Photography* 4, no. 1 (2013).
52. Ibid., 39.
53. Ibid., 29.
54. Ibid.
55. Ibid., 28.
56. Chouliaraki cited in Musarò, 'Tensions and Paradoxes of Humanitarianism', 281.
57. Peters, 'Visualizing Disposability', 8.

Chapter 15

1. David Campany, 'Safety in Numbness: Some Remarks on Problems of "Late Photography"', in *Where Is the Photograph?* ed. David Green (Brighton: Photoforum/Photoworks, 2003).
2. Ibid., 127.
3. Ibid., 124.
4. Luc Delahaye cited in Bill Suillvan, 'The Real Thing: Photographer Luc Delahaye', *Artnet* (2003), www.artnet.com/magazine/features/sullivan/sullivan4-10-03.asp. They are, however, highly compatible with the gallery, and as Campany notes, there are a number of 'tired' applications of this aesthetic.
5. Roberts, 'Photography after the Photograph', 289–90; emphasis in original.
6. Campany, 'Safety in Numbness', 126.
7. Ibid., 132; emphasis in original.
8. See for example: Debbie Lisle, 'The Surprising Detritus of Leisure: Encountering the Late Photography of War', *Environment and Planning D: Society and Space* 29, no. 5 (2011); Jessica Neath, 'Empty Lands: Contemporary Art Approaches to Photographing Historical Trauma in Tasmania', *Journal of Australian Studies* 36, no. 3 (2012); Dong-Yeon Koh, '"Late Photography" in South Korea: Heungsoon Im, Onejoon Che, Suyeon Yun', *Photography and Culture* 8, no. 1 (2015); Simon Faulkner, 'Late Photography, Military Landscapes, and the Politics of Memory', *The Open Arts Journal*, Issue 3 (2014); Antonio Monegal, 'Picturing Absence: Photography in the Aftermath', *Journal of War & Culture Studies* 9, no. 3 (2016).
9. Frank Möller, 'From Aftermath to Peace: Reflections on a Photography of Peace', *Global Society* 31, no. 3 (2016): 18–19.
10. Lisle, 'The Surprising Detritus of Leisure', 883.
11. Ibid.
12. Ibid., 874.

13. Paul Lowe, 'The Forensic Turn: Bearing Witness and the Thingness of the Photograph', in *The Violence of the Image: Photography and International Conflict*, eds. Liam Kennedy and Caitlin Patrick (London: I. B. Tauris, 2014), 242.
14. Ibid., 243.
15. Kennedy, 'Photojournalism and Warfare', 167. As Norfolk himself has stated,

> In a gallery, I watch people look at the pictures, especially the fine details, and you can see their minds working, searching, thrown back upon their own critical resources for once, forced to reassess their expectations of what information the picture is going to give them. I'm endeavouring to set up a tension in the image between beauty and horror, two things that are normally separated in modern culture ... these two categories are kept apart, but I think it is more realistic to collide the two together. Norfolk cited in Lowe, 'The Forensic Turn', 244

16. Kennedy, 'Photojournalism and Warfare', 167.
17. Lowe, 'The Forensic Turn', 244.
18. Monegal, 'Picturing Absence', 263.
19. Faulkner, 'Late Photography', 123.
20. Ibid., 123; emphasis in original.
21. Rachel E. Cyr, 'The "Forensic Landscapes" of Srebrenica.', *Култура/Culture*, no. 5 (2014): 88.
22. Roberts, 'Photography after the Photograph', 292; emphasis in original.
23. Veronica Tello, 'The Aesthetics and Politics of Aftermath Photography', *Third Text* 28, no. 6 (2014): 559.
24. Imogen Tyler and Katarzyna Marciniak, 'Immigrant Protest: An Introduction', *Citizenship Studies* 17, no. 2 (2013): 153.
25. Imogen Tyler, '"Welcome to Britain": The Cultural Politics of Asylum', *European Journal of Cultural Studies* 9, no. 2 (2006): 195.
26. Tello, 'The Aesthetics and Politics of Aftermath Photography', 560.
27. Giorgio Agamben, *Homo Sacer: Soverign Power and Bare Life*, trans. Daniel Heller-Roazen (Stanford, CA: Stanford University Press, 1998).
28. Ibid., 175–6.
29. Ibid., 174.
30. Klaus Ronneberger, 'Bare Life or Just Existence?' in *Documenta Magazine* (Cologne: Tashen, 2007), 40.
31. Agamben, *Homo Sacer*, 168–9; emphasis in original.
32. As Anthony Downey notes, to suggest that the camps are the emblematic form for 'the political structure of modernity and the subject's relationship to power and politics is to go against another widely held belief: that such camps, in all their horror and abjectness, were not only fundamentally unrepeatable but were without historical precedent'. 'Zones of Indistinction: Giorgio Agamben's "Bare Life" and the Politics of Aesthetics', *Third Text* 23, no. 2 (2009): 114.
33. Agamben, *Homo Sacer*, 175.
34. Ibid.

35. Tello, 'The Aesthetics and Politics of Aftermath Photography', 561.
36. Ibid., 562.
37. Jenny Edkins, 'Sovereign Power, Zones of Indistinction, and the Camp', *Alternatives* 25, no. 1 (2000): 19.
38. Möller, 'From Aftermath to Peace', 3.
39. Dong-Yeon Koh, '"Late Photography" in South Korea', 83.
40. Faulkner, 'Late Photography', 124.
41. Koh, '"Late Photography" in South Korea', 105.
42. Ibid., 84.
43. Rebecca A. Adelman and Wendy Kozol, 'Ornamenting the Unthinkable: Visualizing Survival under Occupation', *WSQ: Women's Studies Quarterly* 44, no. 1 and 2 (2016): 173.
44. Ibid.
45. Ahlam Shibli, "Artist's Statement: *Occupation*", www.ahlamshibli.com/statement/occupation_en.htm
46. Ulrich Loock, "Ahlam Shibli's *Occupation*: Introduction", www.documenta14.de/en/south/25224_ahlam_shibli_s_occupation_introduction_by_ulrich_loock
47. Shibli explores this aspect of survival using a more traditional documentary approach in her extensive series *Trackers*. In this work Shibli records the lives of Palestinians of Bedouin descent who serve voluntarily in the Israeli army (IDF). As T. J. Demos has written of this work, 'The question conjured in these various images is how those persecuted in one context could go on to visit military violence and occupation on others elsewhere'. 'Disappearance and Precarity: On the Photography of Ahlam Shibli', in *Ahlam Shibli : Phantom Home*, ed. Museu d'Art Contemporani de Barcelona (MACBA) (Barcelona: MACBA, 2013), 22.
48. Möller, 'From Aftermath to Peace', 20.

Select Bibliography

Aas, K. F., '"The Body Does Not Lie": Identity, Risk and Trust in Technoculture', *Crime, Media, Culture* 2, no. 2 (2006): 143–58.

Adams, Parveen, *The Emptiness of the Image: Psychoanalysis and Sexual Differences* (London and New York: Routledge, 1995).

Adams, Parveen, 'Bruce Nauman and the Object of Anxiety', *October* 83, Winter (1998): 96–113.

Adams, Parveen, *Art: Sublimation or Symptom* (London: Karnac, 2003).

Adelman, Rebecca A., 'Pixelizing Atrocity', *Philosophy of Photography* 4, no. 1 (2013): 25–45.

Adelman, Rebecca A., '"Thank You for Our Flat Daddy": Photography, Imagination, and Citizenship as Child's Play', *Photography & Culture* 6, no. 1 (2015): 65–80.

Adelman, Rebecca A., and Wendy Kozol, 'Ornamenting the Unthinkable: Visualizing Survival under Occupation', *WSQ: Women's Studies Quarterly* 44, no. 1&2 (2016): 171–87.

Adler, Dan, 'The Apparatus: On the Photography of Thomas Ruff', *Art Journal* 75, no. 2 (2016): 66–87.

Agamben, Giorgio, *Homo Sacer: Sovereign Power and Bare Life* (Stanford: Stanford University Press, 1998).

Ahnert, Laurel, 'The Surveillance Commodity, Unequal Exchange, and the (In)Visible Subject in Hasan Elahi's Tracking Transience', *Social Text* 35, no. 3 (2017): 1–16.

Albdorf, Thomas. *General View* (Jesi, Italy: Skinnerboox, 2017).

Anden-Papadopoulos, K., 'Citizen Camera-Witnessing: Embodied Political Dissent in the Age of "Mediated Mass Self-Communication"', *New Media & Society* 16, no. 5 (2013): 753–69.

Anderson, Heather, 'Performing Postfeminism: Escaping Identity Politics?' *Atlantis: Critical Studies in Gender, Culture & Social Justice/Études critiques sur le genre, la culture, et la justice* 30, no. 2 (2006): 114–28.

Andrejevic, Mark, Alison Hearn, and Helen Kennedy, 'Cultural Studies of Data Mining: Introduction', *European Journal of Cultural Studies* 18, no. 4–5 (2015): 379–94.

Anokhina, Alice. 'Laurel Nakadate's Outré Retrospective', *The London Word*, 21 November 2011, www.thelondonword.com/2011/11/laurel-nakadate-at-the-zabludowicz-collection/

Apollon, Willy, and Richard Feldstein, eds., *Lacan, Politics, Aesthetics* (New York: State University of New York Press, 1996).

Armstrong, Nancy, 'Monarchy in the Age of Mechanical Reproduction', *Nineteenth-Century Contexts* 22, no. 4 (2001): 495–536.

Arriola, Magali, 'A Victim and a Viewer: Some Thoughts on Anticipated Ruins', *Afterall: A Journal of Art, Context and Enquiry* 12, Autumn/Winter (2005): 109–15.
Auerbach, Jeffrey, 'Art, Advertising, and the Legacy of Empire', *The Journal of Popular Culture* 35, no. 4 (2002): 1–23.
Auerbach, Jeffrey, 'The Picturesque and the Homogenisation of Empire', *The British Art Journal* 5, no. 1 (2004): 47–54.
Augé, Marc, *Non-Places: An Introduction to Supermodernity* (London: Verso, 1995).
Azoulay, Ariella, *The Civil Contract of Photography* (New York: Zone Books, 2008).
Back, Les, Shamser Sinha, and Charlynne Bryan, 'New Hierarchies of Belonging', *European Journal of Cultural Studies* 15, no. 2 (2012): 139–54.
Badger, Gerry, *The Genius of Photography: How Photography Has Changed Our Lives* (London: Quadrille, 2014).
Baer, Alejandro, and Natan Sznaider, 'Ghosts of the Holocaust in Franco's Mass Graves: Cosmopolitan Memories and the Politics of "Never Again"', *Memory Studies* 8, no. 3 (2015): 328–44.
Baer, Ulrich, 'Photography and Hysteria: Towards a Poetics of the Flash', *The Yale Journal of Criticism* 7, no. 1 (1994): 41–77.
Bailey, Suzanne, 'Francis Galton's Face Project: Morphing the Victorian Human', *Photography & Culture* 5, no. 2 (2012): 189–214.
Ball, Kirstie, MariaLaura Di Domenico, and Daniel Nunan, 'Big Data Surveillance and the Body-Subject', *Body & Society* 22, no. 2 (2016): 58–81.
Baker, Simon, and Fiontán Moran (eds.) *Performing for the Camera* (London: Tate Publishing, 2016).
Bangert, Christoph. *War Porn* (Berlin: Kehrer, 2014).
Bangert, Christoph. *hello camel* (Berlin: Kehrer, 2016).
Barst, Julie M., 'Transporting the Picturesque: Australia through the Claude Lorraine Glass', *European Romantic Review* 19, no. 2 (2008): 163–69.
Bassett, Caroline, 'Forms of Reconciliation: On Contemporary Surveillance', *Cultural Studies* 21, no. 1 (2007): 82–94.
Batchen, Geoffrey, *Burning with Desire: The Conception of Photography* (Cambridge, MA and London: The MIT Press, 1999).
Bate, David, *Photography: The Key Concepts* (Oxford and New York: Berg, 2009).
Bate, David, 'Introduction: Psychoanalysis and the Photographer', *Photographies* 10, no. 1 (2017): 3–11.
Bayley, Bruno. 'Photos of the Absurdity of Modern Warfare', *Vice*, 2 June 2016: www.vice.com/en_uk/article/avaw4j/cristoph-bangerts-hello-camel-captures-the-absurdity-of-modern-warfare.
Beck, John, 'Signs of the Sky, Signs of the Times: Photography as Double Agent', *Theory, Culture & Society* 28, no. 7–8 (2011): 123–39.
Beck, John, 'The Purloined Landscape: Photography and Power in the American West', *Tate Papers* 21, Spring (2014): www.tate.org.uk/research/publications/tate-papers/21/the-purloined-landscape-photography-and-power-in-the-american-west
Beck, John, 'High Formalism: The Aerial View and the Colour Field', *Photographies* 9, no. 2 (2016): 187–201.

Becker, Karin. 'Performing Photography: Performing the news', *Photographies*, 6, no. 1 (2013): 17–28.

Beckman, Karen, 'Telescopes, Transparency, and Torture: Trevor Paglen and the Politics of Exposure', *Art Journal* 66, no. 3 (2007): 62–67.

Berger, Martin A., 'Overexposed: Whiteness and the Landscape Photography of Carleton Watkins', *Oxford Art Journal* 26, no. 1 (2003): 3–23.

Berlant, Lauren, 'Intimacy: A Special Issue', *Critical Inquiry* 24, no. 2 (1998): 281–88.

Benítez Valero, Laura. 'Joanna Zylinska: "We Need a New Way of Seeing the Anthropocene"', *CCCBLAB*, 24 April 2018, http://lab.cccb.org/en/joanna-zylinska-we-need-a-new-way-of-seeing-the-anthropocene/

Bermingham, Ann, *Landscape and Ideology: The English Rustic Tradition, 1740–1860* (London: Thames and Hudson, 1987).

Bermingham, Ann. 'Landscape Imagery and Urban Culture in Early Nineteenth-Century Britain (Review)', *The Art Bulletin* 76, no. 2 (1994): 367–73.

Best, Susan, *Reparative Aesthetics: Witnessing in Contemporary Art Photography* (London and New York: Bloomsbury Academic, 2016).

Beutin, Lyndsey P., 'Racialization as a Way of Seeing: The Limits of Counter-Surveillance and Police Reform', *Surveillance and Society* 15, no. 1 (2017): 5–20.

Birchall, Clare, 'Aesthetics of the Secret', *New Formations* 83 (2014): 25–46.

Blackburn, Mary Walling, and A. B. Huber. 'The Flash Made Flesh', *Triple Canopy*, Issue 11 (2011): www.canopycanopycanopy.com/issues/11/contents/the_flash_made_flesh

Blas, Zach. 'Escaping the Face: Biometric Facial Recognition and the *Facial Weaponization Suite*', *Media-N* 9, no. 2 (2013): http://median.newmediacaucus.org/caa-conference-edition-2013/escaping-the-face-biometric-facial-recognition-and-the-facial-weaponization-suite/.

Blas, Zach, and Jacob Gaboury, 'Biometrics and Opacity: A Conversation', *Camera Obscura: Feminism, Culture, and Media Studies* 31, no. 2 (2016): 155–65.

Blight, Daniel C., 'Incoming: Photography, Contemporary Art, Whiteness', *American Suburb X*, 23 2017, www.americansuburbx.com/2017/03/incoming-photography-contemporary-art-whiteness.html

Bolaki, Stella, 'Re-Covering the Scarred Body: Textual and Photographic Narratives of Breast Cancer', *Mosaic* 44, no. 2 (2011): 1–17.

Bolaki, Stella, 'Capturing the Worlds of Multiple Sclerosis: Hannah Laycock's Photography', *Medical Humanities* 43, no. 1 (2017): 47–54.

Bolton, Richard, ed., *The Context of Meaning: Critical Histories of Photography* (Massachusetts: MIT Press, 1981).

Bond, Lucy, 'Intersections or Misdirections? Problematising Crossroads of Memory in the Commemoration of 9/11', *Culture, Theory and Critique* 53, no. 2 (2012): 111–28.

Brancaleone, David. 'Richard Mosse's *Infra*: Conflict, Art and the Regime of the Documentary Image', *Enclave Review* 8, Summer (2013): enclavereview.org/richard-mosses-infra-conflict-art-and-the-regime-of-the-documentary-image/

Brandzel, Amy L., 'The Subjects of Survival: The Anti-Intersectional Routes of Breast Cancer', *WSQ: Women's Studies Quarterly* 44, no. 1&2 (2016): 128–51.

Bratich, Jack Z., 'Adventures in the Public Secret Sphere', *Cultural Studies ↔ Critical Methodologies* 14, no. 1 (2013): 11–20.

Bright, Deborah, 'Of Mother Nature and Marlboro Men: An Inquiry into the Cultural Meanings of Landscape Photography' (1985): www.deborahbright.net/PDF/Bright-Marlboro.pdf

Bronfen, Elizabeth, *The Knotted Subject: Hysteria and Its Discontents* (Princeton, NJ: Princeton University Press, 1998).

Brown, Wendy, *Undoing the Demos: Neoliberalism's Stealth Revolution* (New York: Zone, 2015).

Bryson, Norman, 'Thomas Ruff: Spectacle and Surveillance', *Parkett* 28 (1991): 92–96.

Buggenhagen, Beth, 'If You Were in My Sneakers: Migration Stories in the Studio Photography of Dakar-Based Omar Victor Diop', *Visual Anthropology Review* 33, no. 1 (2017): 38–50.

Burbridge, Ben, 'Exacting Photography: Self-Imaging and Its Frustration in Contemporary Art Photography', *re.bus* 5, Summer (2010): www1.essex.ac.uk/arthistory/research/pdfs/rebus/rebus_issue_5.pdf

Burbridge, Ben, 'Paradise Lost: Exhibitionism and the Work of Nan Goldin', 2014: http://eitherand.org/exhibitionism/paradise-lost-exhibitionism-and-work-nan-goldin/

Burbridge, Ben, and Catherine Grant. 'Photography and Exhibitionism: An Introduction', 2014: http://eitherand.org/exhibitionism/very-brief-very-general-conversation-about-photogr/

Burgin, Victor. *In/Different Spaces: Place and Memory in Visual Culture* (Berkeley, LA and London: University of California Press, 1996).

Burke, Edmund. 'A Philosophical Enquiry into the Origin of Our Ideas of the Sublime and Beautiful (1759)'. In *The Sublime: A Reader in British Eighteenth-Century Aesthetic Theory*, edited by Andrew Ashfield and Peter de Bolla, 131–43. Cambridge: Cambridge University Press, 1996.

Burns, Anne, 'Self(ie)-Discipline: Social Regulation as Enacted through the Discussion of Photographic Practice', *International Journal of Communication* 9 (2015): 1716–33.

Burris, Jennifer, 'The "Urban Photogénie" of *Architainment*', *The Journal of Aesthetics and Art Criticism* 69, no. 1 (2011): 93–103.

Burstow, Stephen, 'The Carte De Visite and Domestic Digital Photography', *Photographies* 9, no. 3 (2016): 287–305.

Butler, Judith, 'Performative Acts and Gender Constitution: An Essay in Phenomenology and Feminist Theory', *Theatre Journal* 40, no. 4 (1988): 519–31.

Butler, Judith, *Bodies That Matter: On the Discursive Limits of 'Sex'* (New York: Routledge, 1993).

Butler, Judith. 'For a Careful Reading'. In *Feminist Contentions: A Philosophical Exchange*, edited by Paul Kegan, 127–44. New York: Routledge, 1995.

Butler, Judith, *Gender Trouble: Feminism and the Subversion of Identity* (New York: Routledge 1999).

Butler, Judith, 'Performativity, Precarity and Sexual Politics', *AIBR: Revista de Antropología Iberoamericana* 4, no. 3 (2009): i–xiii.

Butler, Judith, *Frames of War: When Is Life Grievable?* (London: Verso, 2010).

Cachia, Amanda, 'Composing Dwarfism: Reframing Short Stature in Contemporary Photography', *Review of Disability Studies: An International* Journal 10, no. 3&4 (2014): 6–19.

Campany, David. 'Safety in Numbness: Some Remarks on Problems of "Late Photography"'. In *Where Is the Photograph?* edited by David Green, 123–32. Brighton: Photoforum/Photoworks, 2003.

Campbell, David, 'Cultural Governance and Pictorial Resistance: Reflections on the Imaging of War', *Review of International Studies* 29, (2003): 57–73.

Campion, Darren, 'Thomas Albdorf: Almost as Good as Being There'. In *General View*, Thomas Albdorf, 120–27. Jesi, Italy: Skinnerboox, 2017.

Carmi, Ayelet, 'Sally Mann's American Vision of the Land', *Journal of Art Historiography* 17, December (2017): 1–26.

Carrabine, Eamonn, 'Seeing Things: Violence, Voyeurism and the Camera', *Theoretical Criminology* 18, no. 2 (2014): 134–58.

Carstens, Lisa. 'Sexual Politics and Confessional Testimony in *Sophie's Choice*', *Twentieth Century Literature* 47, no. 3 (2001): 293–324.

Caruth, Cathy, *Trauma: Explorations in Memory* (Baltimore and London: John Hopkins University Press, 1995).

Caruth, Cathy. *Unclaimed Experience. Trauma, Narrative and History* (Baltimore, MD: John Hopkins University Press, 1996).

Cataldi, Michael, David Kelley, Hans Kuzmich, Jens Maier-Rothe, and Jeannine Tang. 'Residues of a Dream World', *Theory, Culture & Society* 28, no. 7–8 (2012): 358–89.

Chandra, Mohini, and Christopher Stewart. 'About Dark Pacific Sun': www.mohini chandra.com/about-dark-pacific-sun/

Chapman, Anne, 'The Reality of Imagining the Holocaust: David Levinthal's *Mein Kampf*, *eSharp* 19: Reality/Illusion (2012): 141–57.

Chayka, Kyle. 'Welcome to Airspace: How Silicon Valley Helps Spread the Same Sterile Aesthetic across the World', *The Verge*, 3 August 2016, www.theverge.com/2016/8/3/12325104/airbnb-aesthetic-global-minimalism-startup-gentrification.

Cheney-Lippold, John. 'A New Algorithmic Identity: Soft Biopolitics and the Modulation of Control', *Theory, Culture & Society* 28, no. 6 (2011): 164–81.

Cheng, Wendy, '"New Topographics": Locating Epistemological Concerns in the American Landscape', *American Quarterly* 63, no. 1 (2011): 151–62.

Cho, Lily, 'Citizenship, Diaspora and the Bonds of Affect: The Passport Photograph', *Photography & Culture* 2, no. 3 (2009): 275–88.

Cho, Lily, 'Intimacy among Strangers', *Interventions* 15, no. 1 (2013): 10–23.

Chouliaraki, Lilie, 'The Humanity of War: Iconic Photojournalism of the Battle Field, 1914–2012', *Visual Communication* 12, no. 3 (2013): 315–40.

Chouliaraki, Lilie, *The Ironic Spectator: Solidarity in the Age of Post-Humanitarianism* (Cambrigde and Maden: Polity Press, 2013).

Chun, W. H. K., 'Introduction: Race and/as Technology; or, How to Do Things to Race', *Camera Obscura: Feminism, Culture, and Media Studies* 24, no. 1 (2009): 7–35.
Clarke, Graham. *The Photograph* (Oxford: Oxford University Press, 1997).
Clarke, Graham, *The Portrait in Photography* (London: Reaktion Books, 1992).
Codell, Julie F., 'Victorian Portraits: Re-Tailoring Identities', *Nineteenth-Century Contexts* 34, no. 5 (2012): 493–516.
Cohan, Steven, and Ina Rae Hark, eds., *Screening the Male: Exploring Masculinities in Hollywood Cinema* (London: Routledge, 1993).
Colebrook, Claire, *Death of the Posthuman: Essays on Extinction, Vol.* 1 (Ann Arbor: Open Humanities Press, 2014).
Colebrook, Claire, 'Anti-Catastrophic Time', *New Formations* 92: Posthuman Temporalites (2017): 102–19.
Copjec, Joan, 'The Orthopsychic Subject: Film Theory and the Reception of Lacan', *October* 49, Summer (1989): 53–71.
Copjec, Joan, 'The *Unvermögender* Other: Hysteria and Democracy in America', *New Formations* 14 (1991): 27–41.
Copjec, Joan, Read My Desire: *Lacan against the Historicists* (Cambridge and London: The MIT Press, 1995).
Copjec, Joan, *Imagine There's No Woman: Ethics and Sublimation* (Cambridge and London: The MIT Press, 2002).
Copjec, Joan, 'The Sexual Compact', *Angelaki* 17, no. 2 (2012): 31–48.
Cornet, Laurence. 'Overlooking the Realities of Conflict', *Photographic Museum of Humanity,* 13 September 2016, phmuseum.com/news/christoph-bangert-hello-camel.
Costas, Jana, 'Problematizing Mobility: A Metaphor of Stickiness, Non-Places and the Kinetic Elite', *Organization Studies* 34, no. 10 (2013): 1467–85.
Crary, Jonathan, *24/7: Late Capitalism and the Ends of Sleep* (London and New York: Verso, 2014).
Creed, Barbara , *The Monstrous Feminine: Film, Feminism, Psychoanalysis* (London: Routledge, 1993).
Cresswell, Tim, *On the Move: Mobility in the Modern Western World* (London: Routledge, 2006).
Crimp, Douglas, 'The Photographic Activity of Postmodernism', *October* 15, Winter (1980): 91–101.
Cyr, Rachel E., 'The "Forensic Landscapes" of Srebrenica', *Култура/Culture* no. 5 (2014): 81–92.
D'Aliesio, Susanna. 'Thomas Albdorf's General View', *British Journal of Photography,* 15 May 2017, www.bjp-online.com/2017/05/photo-london-week-thomas-albdorfs-general-view/
Dawsey, Jill, 'Trevor Paglen: Semiotics of the Hidden Empire', *Art Papers* 33, no. 5 (2009): 34–39.
De Agostinis, Giada. 'Studio Visit - Lucas Blalock', *Paper Journal,* 6 June 2017, http://paper-journal.com/studio-visit-lucas-blalock/
De Lissovoy, Noah, 'Conceptualizing the Carceral Turn: Neoliberalism, Racism, and Violation', *Critical Sociology* 39, no. 5 (2012): 739–55.

Dean, Alison, 'Intimacy at Work: Nan Goldin and Rineke Dijkstra', *History of Photography* 39, no. 2 (2015): 177–93.
Dean, Jodi, 'Why *Žižek* for Political Theory?' *International Journal of Žižek Studies* 1, no. 1 (2007): 18–32.
Dean, Jodi, *Democracy and Other Neoliberal Fantasies: Communicative Capitalism and Left Politics* (Durham and London: Duke University Press, 2009).
Dean, Jodi, 'Affective Networks', *Media Tropes* II, no. 2 (2010): 19–44.
Dean, Jodi, 'The Real Internet', *International Journal of Žižek Studies* 4, no. 1 (2010): 1–22.
Dean, Jodi, 'A View from the Side: The Natural History Museum', *Cultural Critique* 94, Fall (2016): 74–101.
Dean, Tacita, and Jeremy Millar, eds. *Place* (London: Thames & Hudson, 2005).
Deandrea, Pietro, 'The Spectralized Camp', *Interventions* 17, no. 4 (2014): 488–502.
Debrix, François, 'The Sublime Spectatorship of War: The Erasure of the Event in America's Politics of Terror and Aesthetics of Violence', *Millennium: Journal of International Studies* 34, no. 3 (2006): 767–91.
Debrix, François, 'Topologies of Vulnerability and the Proliferation of Camp Life', *Environment and Planning D: Society and Space* 33 (2015): 444–59.
DeLuca, Kevin, and Anne Demo, 'Imagining Nature and Erasing Class and Race: Carleton Watkins, John Muir, and the Construction of Wilderness', *Environmental History* 6, no. 4 (2001): 541–60.
DeLuca, Kevin, and Anne Demo, 'Imaging Nature: Watkins, Yosemite, and the Birth of Environmentalism', *Critical Studies in Media Communication* 17, no. 3 (2000): 241–60.
Demos, T. J. 'Disappearance and Precarity: On the Photography of Ahlam Shibli'. In *Ahlam Shibli: Phantom Home*, edited by Museu d'Art Contemporani de Barcelona (MACBA), 11–26. Barcelona: MACBA, 2013.
Demos, T. J. 'Welcome to the Anthropocene!' (2015): www.fotomuseum.ch/en/explore/stillsearching/articles/27011_welcome_to_the_anthropocene
Demos, T. J. *Decolonizing Nature: Contemporary Art and the Politics of Ecology* (England: Sternberg Press, 2016).
Demos, T. J., *Against the Anthropocene: Visual Culture and Environment Today* (London and Berlin: Sternberg Press, 2017).
Dennis, Kelly, 'Landscape and the West: Irony and Critique in New Topographic Photography', (2005): www.americansuburbx.com/2012/05/new-topographics-landscape-and-the-west-irony-and-critique-in-new-topographic-photography-2005.html
Dennis, Kelly, 'Eclipsing Aestheticism: Western Landscape Photography after Ansel Adams', *Miranda* 11, (2015): journals.openedition.org/miranda/6920
Denti, Antonio. 'The Surviving Frame', *Vimpt*, 12 December 2017, vimpt.com/2017/12/12/the-surviving-frame-antonio-denti/
Denti, Antonio. 'The Surviving Frame', *Lens Culture*, www.lensculture.com/articles/antonio-denti-the-surviving-frame
Dercon, Chris. 'Foreword'. In *Performing for the Camera*, edited by Simon Baker and Fiontán Moran, 7–9. London: Tate Publishing, 2016.

Dernbach, Rafael, 'Hacking the Vision Machine: Farocki's and Paglen's Detourning of Control Images', *Revista Teknokultura* 11, no. 2 (2014): 383–403.
DeSilvey, Caitlin, and Tim Edensor, 'Reckoning with Ruins', *Progress in Human Geography* 37, no. 4 (2012): 465–85.
Dewey, Caitlin. '59 Percent of Links Shared on Social Media Have Never Been Clicked, Study Finds', *Independent*, 16th June 2016, www.independent.co.uk/life-style/gadgets-and-tech/59-percent-of-links-shared-on-social-media-have-never-actually-been-clicked-study-finds-a7086291.html
Diamond, Elin, *Performance and Cultural Politics* (London: Routledge, 1996).
Didi-Huberman, Georges, *Invention of Hysteria: Charcot and the Photographic Iconography of the Salpetriere* (Cambridge and London: The MIT Press, 2003).
Dillon, Brian. 'Introduction: A Short History of Decay'. In *Ruins*, edited by Brian Dillon, 10–19. Documents of Contemporary Art: Whitechapel and M.I.T. Press, 2011.
Dillon, Brian, ed., *Ruins* (Whitechapel and M.I.T. Press, 2011).
Dinnen, Zara, and Sam McBean, 'The Face as Technology', *New Formations* 93, (2018): 122–37.
Dolar, Mladen, '"I Shall Be with You on Your Wedding-Night": Lacan and the Uncanny', *October* 58, (1991): 5–23.
Doran, Anne. 'Lucas Blalock', *Art in America*, 7 January 2012, www.artinamericamagazine.com/reviews/lucas-blalock/
Douglas, Kate, 'Youth, Trauma and Memorialisation: The Selfie as Witnessing', *Memory Studies* (2017): 1–16: doi.org/10.1177/1750698017714838.
Downey, Anthony, 'Zones of Indistinction: Giorgio Agamben's "Bare Life" and the Politics of Aesthetics', *Third Text* 23, no. 2 (2009): 109–25.
Drakopoulou, Sophia, '"We Can Remember It for You": Location, Memory, and Commodification in Social Networking Sites', *Sage Open* 7, no. 3 (2017): 1–13.
Driscoll, Catherine, 'The Mystique of the Young Girl', *Feminist Theory* 14, no. 3 (2013): 285–91.
Dubrofsky, Rachel E., 'Therapeutics of the Self: Surveillance in the Service of the Therapeutic', *Television and New Media* 8, no. 4 (2007): 263–84.
Dubrofsky, Rachel E., 'A Vernacular of Surveillance: Taylor Swift and Miley Cyrus Perform White Authenticity', *Surveillance & Society* 14, no. 2 (2016): 184–96.
Dubrofsky, Rachel E., and Emily D. Ryalls, '*The Hunger Games*: Performing Not-Performing to Authenticate Femininity and Whiteness', *Critical Studies in Media Communication* 31, no. 5 (2014): 395–409.
Eberhard, Roger. *Standard* (Zürich: Verlag Scheidegger & Spiess AG, 2016).
Edkins, Jenny, 'Sovereign Power, Zones of Indistinction, and the Camp', *Alternatives* 25, no. 1 (2000): 3–25.
Ehlers, Nadine, '"Black Is" and "Black Ain't": Performative Revisions of Racial "Crisis"', *Culture, Theory and Critique* 47, no. 2 (2006): 149–63.
Ehlers, Nadine, 'Retroactive Phantasies: Discourse, Discipline, and the Production of Race', *Social Identities* 14, no. 3 (2008): 333–47.
Ehlers, Nadine, 'The Scar Project', *Journal of Literary & Cultural Disability Studies* 9, no. 3 (2015): 331–47.

Eklund, Douglas, ed., *The Pictures Generation, 1974–1984* (New York: Metropolitan Museum of Art, 2009).

Elias, Ana Sofia, and Rosalind Gill, 'Beauty Surveillance: The Digital Self-Monitoring Cultures of Neoliberalism', *European Journal of Cultural Studies* 21, no. 1 (2018): 59–77.

Elias, Chad, 'Citizen Photography in Fouad Elkoury's Beyrouth Aller-Retour', *Photographies* 10, no. 3 (2017): 265–82.

Enck-Wanzer, Darrel, 'Barack Obama, the Tea Party, and the Threat of Race: On Racial Neoliberalism and Born Again Racism', *Communication, Culture & Critique* 4, no. 1 (2011): 23–30.

Eppert, Claudia, 'Entertaining History: (Un)Heroic Identifications, Apt Pupils, and an Ethical Imagination', *New German Critique* 86, Spring–Summer (2002): 71–101.

Farman, Jason 'Mapping the Digital Empire: Google Earth and the Process of Postmodern Cartography', *New Media & Society* 12, no. 3 (2010): 869–88.

Faulkner, Simon, 'Late Photography, Military Landscapes, and the Politics of Memory', *The Open Arts Journal* Issue 3 (2014): 121–36.

Feldman, Keith P. 'The Globality of Whiteness in Post-Racial Visual Culture', *Cultural Studies* 30, no. 2 (2015): 289–311.

Feldman, Susan, 'Reclaiming Sexual Difference: What Queer Theory Can't Tell Us About Sexuality', *Journal of Bisexuality* 9, no. 3–4 (2009): 259–78.

Feldstein, Richard, 'Subject of the Gaze for Another Gaze'. In *Lacan, Politics, Aesthetics*, edited by Willy Apollon and Richard Feldstein, 45–64. Albany: State University of New York Press.

Feldstein, Richard, Bruce Fink, and Marie Jaanus. eds. *Reading Seminar XI: Lacan's Four Fundamentals of Psychoanalysis* (New York: State University of New York Press, 1995).

Feldstein, Richard, Bruce Fink, and Marie Jaanus. eds. *Reading Seminars I and II: Lacan's Return to Freud* (New York: State University of New York Press, 1996).

Felman, Shoshana, and Dori Laub, *Testimony: Crises of Witnessing in Literature, Psychoanalysis and History* (London and New York: Routledge, 1992).

Finn, Jonathan, 'Photographing Fingerprints: Data Collection and State Surveillance', *Surveillance and Society* 3, no. 1 (2005): 21–44.

Finn, Jonathan, *Capturing the Criminal Image: From Mug Shot to Surveillance Society* (Minneapolis and London University of Minnesota Press, 2009).

Flanzbaum, Hilene. *The Americanization of the Holocaust* (Baltimore and London: Johns Hopkins University Press, 1999).

Foster, Hal, 'Death in America', *October* 75, Winter (1996): 37–59.

Foster, Hal, 'Obscene, Abject, Traumatic', *October* 78, Fall (1996): 107–24.

Foster, Hal, Bad New Days: *Art, Criticism, Emergency* (London and New York: Verso, 2015).

Foucault, Michel and Colin Gordon, eds. *Power-knowledge: Selected Interviews and Other Writings, 1972–77* (New York and London: Harvester Wheatsheaf, 1980).

Frank, Priscilla. 'Ghostly Photos Explore What — and Who — American History Forgets', *Huffington Post*, 13 December 2016, www.huffingtonpost.co.uk/entry/nona-faustine-photography_us_584eed9ce4b0bd9c3dfdcba6?guccounter=1provided.

Freeman, Elizabeth, 'Packing History, Count(er)ing Generations', *New Literary History* 31, no. 4 (2000): 727–44.
Freud, Sigmund, *The Standard Edition of the Complete Psychological Works of Sigmund Freud*, 24 volumes, translated by James and Alix Strachey (London: The Hogarth Press and the Institute of Psychoanalysis, 1953–74).
Friedlander, Jennifer, 'How Should a Woman Look? Scopic Strategies for Sexuated Subjects', *Journal for the Psychoanalysis of Culture and Society* 8, no. 1 (2003): 99–108.
Friedlander, Jennifer, Feminine Look: *Sexuation, Spectatorship, Subversion* (Albany: State University of New York Press, 2008).
Frosh, Paul, 'The Gestural Image: The Selfie, Photography Theory, and Kinesthetic Sociability', *International Journal of Communication* 9, (2015): 1607–28.
Gansky, Andrew Emil, '"Ruin Porn" and the Ambivalence of Decline: Andrew Moore's Photographs of Detroit', *Photography & Culture* 7, no. 2 (2014): 119–39.
Garland-Thomson, Rosemarie. 'Seeing the Disabled: Visual Rhetorics of Disability in Popular Photography'. In *The New Disability History*, edited by Paul K. Longmore and Lauri Umansky, 335–74. New York and London: New York University Press, 2001.
Garland-Thomson, Rosemarie, 'Staring at the Other', *Disability Studies Quarterly* 25, no. 4 (2005): http://dsq-sds.org/article/view/610/787
Garland-Thomson, Rosemarie, 'Misfits: A Feminist Materialist Disability Concept', *Hypatia* 26, no. 3 (2011): 591–609.
Garland-Thomson, Rosemarie, 'The Story of My Work: How I Became Disabled', *Disability Studies Quarterly* 34, no. 2 (2014).
Garland-Thomson, Rosemarie. 'Becoming Disabled', *International New York Times*, 20 August 2016, 9.
Gallagher, Meghan M. 'Claiming Images: The Production and Preservation of Desire in Richard Prince's Re-Photography', *Scripps Senior Theses.* Paper 679 (2015): scholarship.claremont.edu/scripps_theses/679/
Gates, Kelly, 'Biometrics and Post-9/11 Technostalgia', *Social Text*, 23, no. 2 (2005): 35–53.
Gates, Kelly, 'Identifying the 9/11 "Faces of Terror"', *Cultural Studies* 20, no. 4–5 (2006): 417–40.
Gayer, Tanya, 'Archives and Algorithms Compressing Socio-Historical Distance', *Sightlines*, 2016: www.academia.edu/30100662/Archives_and_Algorithms_Compressing_Socio-historical_Distance
Gibb, Susan. 'An Ongoing State of Conflict: Richard Mosse's *The Enclave*', *Art Monthly Australia* 269, May (2014): 20–25.
Gibbons, James. 'Family, Landscape, and Race in Sally Mann's Photographs', *Hyperallergic*, March 10, 2018, hyperallergic.com/430901/sally-mann-a-thousand-crossings-national-gallery-of-art-washington-dc/
Gibson, Ross, 'Narrative Hunger: GIS Mapping, Google Street View and the Colonial Prospectus', *Cultural Studies Review* 20, no. 2 (2014): 250–65.
Gilbert, Jeremy, 'What Kind of Thing Is "Neoliberalism?"' *New Formations* 80/81 (2013): 7–22.

Gill, Rosalind, 'Post-Postfeminism?: New Feminist Visibilities in Postfeminist Times', *Feminist Media Studies* 16, no. 4 (2016): 610–30.

Gill-Peterson, Julian, 'Sexting Girls: Technological Sovereignty and the Digital', *Women & Performance: A journal of feminist theory* 25, no. 2 (2015): 143–56.

Ginzburg, Carlo, 'Family Resemblances and Family Trees: Two Cognitive Metaphors', *Critical Inquiry* 30, no. 3 (2004): 537–56.

Giroux, Henry, 'Spectacles of Race and Pedagogies of Denial: Anti-Black Racist Pedagogy under the Reign of Neoliberalism', *Communication Education* 52, no. 3 (2003): 191–211.

Giroux, Henry, 'Violence, Katrina, and the Biopolitics of Disposability', *Theory, Culture & Society* 24, no. 7–8 (2007): 305–09.

Giroux, Henry, 'Beyond the Biopolitics of Disposability: Rethinking Neoliberalism in the New Gilded Age', *Social Identities* 14, no. 5 (2008): 587–620.

Godfrey, Mark, 'The Artist as Historian', *October* 120, Spring (2007): 140–72.

Goldberg, Vicki. 'Sally Mann's Haunted South', *New York Times*, 29 March 2018, www.nytimes.com/2018/03/29/arts/design/sally-mann-a-thousand-crossings-review-national-gallery.html

Gonzalez, J., 'The Face and the Public: Race, Secrecy, and Digital Art Practice', *Camera Obscura: Feminism, Culture, and Media Studies* 24, no. 1 (2009): 37–65.

Goodyear, Anne Collins, 'Digitization, Genetics, and the Defacement of Portraiture', *American Art* 23, no. 2 (2009): 28–31.

Gram, Sarah, 'The Young-Girl and the Selfie', *.dpi: Feminist Journal of Art and Digital Culture* 28: Gender(ed) Cultures on the Internet (2013): dpi.studioxx.org/en/no/28-gendered-cultures-internet/young-girl-and-selfie

Grant, Catherine, 'Fans of Feminism: Re-Writing Histories of Second-Wave Feminism in Contemporary Art', *Oxford Art Journal* 34, no. 2 (2011): 265–86.

Grant, Catherine, and Lori Waxman, eds. *Girls! Girls! Girls! In Contemporary Art* (Bristol: Intellect, 2011).

Gray, John. *Men Are from Mars, Women Are from Venus: A Practical Guide for Improving Communication and Getting What You Want in Your Relationships: How to Get What You Want in Your Relationships* (London: HarperThorsons, 1992).

Grech, Marija. 'Where "Nothing Ever Was": Anthropomorphic Spectrality and the (Im) Possibility of the Post-Anthropocene', *New Formations* 95, (2018): 22–36.

Green, David, 'Veins of Resemblance: Photography and Eugenics', *The Oxford Art Journal* 7, no. 2 (1985): 3–16.

Green, David. 'On Foucault: Disciplinary Power and Photography'. In *The Camerawork Essays: Context and Meaning in Photography*, edited by Jessica Evans and Barbara Hunt, 119–31. London: Rivers Oram, 1997.

Green, David, ed., *Where Is the Photograph?* (Brighton: Photoforum/Photoworks, 2003).

Guerra, Carles, and Thomas Keenan, *Anti-Photojournalism* (Barcelona and Amsterdam: La Virreina and Foam, 2011).

Gustafsson, Henrik, 'Foresight, Hindsight and State Secrecy in the American West: The Geopolitical Aesthetics of Trevor Paglen', *Journal of Visual Culture* 12, no. 1 (2013): 148–64.

Hacking, Ian, *Rewriting the Soul: Multiple Personality and the Sciences of Memory* (Princeton, NJ: Princeton University Press, 1998).
Hadley, Bree, 'Cheats, Charity Cases and Inspirations: Disrupting the Circulation of Disability-Based Memes Online', *Disability & Society* 31, no. 5 (2016): 676–92.
Hafera, Alison R. 'Sally Mann: Emmett's Story (2007)', *American Suburb X*, 23 November 2018, http://www.americansuburbx.com/2011/11/sally-mann-emmetts-story-2007.html
Hall, Kimberly Ann, 'The Authenticity of Social-Media Performance: Lonelygirl15 and the Amateur Brand of Young-Girlhood', *Women & Performance: a Journal of Feminist Theory* 25, no. 2 (2015): 128–42.
Hall, Rachel, 'Of Ziploc Bags and Black Holes: The Aesthetics of Transparency in the War on Terror', *The Communication Review* 10, no. 4 (2007): 319–46.
Hamilton, Peter, and Roger Hargreaves, *The Beautiful and the Damned: The Creation of Identity in Nineteenth Century Portraiture* (Aldershot: Lund Humphries, 2001).
Hariman, Robert, and John Louis Lucaites, *The Public Image: Photography and Civic Spectatorship* (Chicago and London: University of Chicago Press, 2016).
Hawker, Rosemary, 'Repopulating the Street: Contemporary Photography and Urban Experience', *History of Photography* 37, no. 3 (2013): 341–52.
Hayward, Mark, ATMs, Teleprompters and Photobooths: A Short History of Neoliberal Optics', *New Formations* 80/81 (2013): 194–208.
Heer, Melissa, 'Restaging Time: Photography, Performance and Anachronism in Shadi Ghadirian's *Qajar Series*', *Iranian Studies* 45, no. 4 (2012): 537–48.
Hirsch, Marianne. 'Projected Memory: Holocaust Photographs in Personal and Public Fantasy'. In *Acts of Memory: Cultural Recall in the Present*, edited by Mieke Bal, Jonathan Crewe and Leo Spitzer, 2–23. Hanover and London: University of New England Press, 1999.
Hirsch, Marianne, 'Surviving Images: Holocaust Photographs and the Work of Memory', *The Yale Journal of Criticism* 14, no. 1 (2001): 5–37.
Hirsch, Marianne, *The Generation of Postmemory: Writing and Visual Culture after the Holocaust* (New York: Columbia University Press, 2012).
Hoffman, Anne Golomb, 'Archival Bodies', *American Imago* 66, no. 1 (2009): 5–40.
Hogue, Simon. 'Performing, Translating, Fashioning: Spectatorship in the Surveillant World', *Surveillance and Society* 14, no. 2 (2016): 168–83.
Hollenberg, Sarah. 'Sophie Calle: Unfinished' *caa.reviews*, 5 November 2015, DOI: 10.3202/caa.reviews.2015.149
Hook, Derek, 'Lacan, the Meaning of the Phallus and the "Sexed" Subject' (London: LSE Research Online, 2006): http://eprints.lse.ac.uk/960/
Hook, Derek, 'Restoring Universality to the Subject: Lacan's Kantian Logic of Sexuation', *Annual Review of Critical Psychology* 7 (2009): 151–67.
Hook, Derek, 'What Is "Enjoyment as a Political Factor?"' *Political Psychology* 38, no. 4 (2017): 605–20.
Horne, Rebecca. 'Candy-Colored Congo Sees Waking Dreams Verge into Nightmares', *Wired*, 7 February 2013, www.wired.com/2013/07/mosse-infrared/
Horning, Rob. 'You Know You're the Prettiest Girl', *The New Inquiry*, 1 July 2011, thene winquiry.com/you-know-youre-the-prettiest-girl/

Hornsey, Richard, 'Francis Bacon and the Photobooth: Facing the Homosexual in Post-War Britain', *Visual Culture in Britain* 8, no. 2 (2007): 83–103.

Hostetler, Lisa, Joanna Marsh, and Dave Hickey, *David Levinthal: War, Myth, Desire* (Rochester, New York and Heidelberg, Berlin: George Eastman Museum and Kehrer Verlag, 2018).

Huang, Vivian L., 'Inscrutably, Actually: Hospitality, Parasitism, and the Silent Work of Yoko Ono and Laurel Nakadate', *Women & Performance: A Journal of Feminist Theory* 28, no. 3 (2018): 187–203.

Imperato, Alessandro, 'Boundaries of Representation: Holocaust Manipulation, Digital Imaging and the Real', *drain magazine*, 2005, www.drainmag.com/contentFEBRUARY/RELATED_ESSAYS/boundaries.htm.

Iversen, Margaret, 'What Is a Photograph?' *Art History* 17, no. 3 (1994): 450–63.

Jackson, A. Y. 'Performativity Identified', *Qualitative Inquiry* 10, no. 5 (2004): 673–90.

Jain, Sarah Lochlann, 'Living in Prognosis: Toward an Elegiac Politics', *Representations* 98, no. 1 (2007): 77–92.

Jayawardane, Neelika. 'Queering the Congo', *Africa Is a Country*, 21 November 2011, africasacountry.com/2011/11/queering-the-congo/

Jeandrée, Philipp, 'The Limits of the Visible: The Politics of Contingency in the Photographic Work of Trevor Paglen', *Critical Studies* 2, no. 1 (2016): 84–95.

Johnson, Ken. 'A Burgeoning Film Career Built on Random Encounters', *The New York Times*, 25 February 2011, www.nytimes.com/2011/02/25/arts/design/25nakadate.html

Johnson, Paddy. 'Richard Prince Sucks: His Show of Instagram Printouts at Gagosian Isn't Just Bad, It's Sexist', *Artnet News*, 21 October 2014, news.artnet.com/market/richard-prince-sucks-136358

Jones, Alison, 'Jemima Stehli: On All Fours Naked in High Heels – a Critical Position?' *Women: A Cultural Review* 10, no. 3 (1999): 297–307.

Kafer, Alison, *Feminist, Queer, Crip* (Bloomington and Indianapolis: Indiana University Press, 2013).

Kafer, Gary, 'Documenting the Invisible: Political Agency in Trevor Paglen's Limit Telephotography', *Contemporaneity: Historical Presence in Visual Culture* 5, no. 1 (2016): 53–71.

Kafer, Gary, 'Reimagining Resistance: Performing Transparency and Anonymity in Surveillance Art', *Surveillance and Society* 14, no. 2 (2016): 227–39.

Kearney, Mary Celeste, 'Sparkle: Luminosity and Post-Girl Power Media', *Continuum* 29, no. 2 (2015): 263–73.

Keenan, Thomas, 'Mobilizing Shame', *The South Atlantic Quarterly* 103, no. 2/3 (2004): 435–49.

Keenan, Thomas, 'Disappearances: The Photographs of Trevor Paglen', *Aperture* 191, Summer (2008): 36–43.

Kember, Sarah, 'Face Re-Cognition', *Photoworks* Autumn/Winter (2011/12): 50–5.

Kember, Sarah, 'Face Recognition and the Emergence of Smart Photography', *Journal of Visual Culture* 13, no. 2 (2014): 182–99.

Kennedy, Jen, 'The Young-Girl in Theory', *Women & Performance: A Journal of Feminist Theory* 25, no. 2 (2015): 175–94.
Kennedy, Liam, 'Remembering September 11: Photography as Cultural Diplomacy', *International Affairs* 79, no. 2 (2003): 315–26.
Kennedy, Liam, '"A Compassionate Vision": Larry Burrows's Vietnam War Photography', *Photography and Culture* 4, no. 2 (2011): 179–94.
Kennedy, Liam, 'Photojournalism and Warfare in a Postphotographic Age', *Photography and Culture* 8, no. 2 (2015): 159–71.
Killen, Gemma, 'Archiving the Other or Reading Online Photography as Queer Ephemera', *Australian Feminist Studies* 32, no. 91–92 (2017): 58–74.
King, Samantha, 'Pink Diplomacy: On the Uses and Abuses of Breast Cancer Awareness', *Health Communication* 25, no. 3 (2010): 286–9.
Kingsbury, Paul. 'Uneasiness in Culture, or Negotiating the Sublime Distances Towards the Big Other', *Geography Compass* 11, no. 6 (2017): 1–11.
Klein, Kerwin Lee, 'On the Emergence of Memory in Historical Discourse', *Representations* 69, Winter (2000): 127–50.
Koepnick, Lutz, 'Photographs and Memories', *South Central Review* 21, no. 1 (2004): 94–129.
Koh, Dong-Yeon, '"Late Photography" in South Korea: Heungsoon Im, Onejoon Che, Suyeon Yun', *Photography & Culture* 8, no. 1 (2015): 81–106.
Kohlman, Lynn. *Lynn: Front to Back* (New York: Assouline, 2004).
Kotz, Liz. 'Aesthetics of Intimacy'. In *The Passionate Camera*, edited by Deborah Bright, 204–15. London and New York: Routledge, 1998.
Krause, Valentina Rozas, 'Cruising Eisenman's Holocaust Memorial', *Anos 90 – Revista do Programa de Pós-Graduação em História da Universidade Federal do Rio Grande do Sul* 22, no. 42 (2015): doi.org/10.22456/1983-201X.52481
Kuppers, Petra, 'Deconstructing Images: Performing Disability', *Contemporary Theatre Review* 11, no. 3–4 (2001). 25–40.
Kuppers, Petra, 'Introduction', *Contemporary Theatre Review* 11, no. 3–4 (2001): 1–4.
Kurgan, Laura, *Close up at a Distance: Mapping, Technology and Politics* (New York: Zone Books, 2013).
Lacan, Jacques, *The Four Fundamental Concepts of Psycho-Analysis* (1964) (New York and London: W. W. Norton, 1981).
Lacan, Jacques, 'Kant with Sade', *October* 51 (1989): 55–75.
Lacan, Jacques, *Écrits* (1977) (New York and London: W. W. Norton, 2006)
Jacques Lacan, *The Seminar. Book XX. Encore, On Feminine Sexuality, The Limits of Love and Knowledge, 1972-3*, edited by Jacques-Alain Miller, translated with notes by Bruce Fink (New York: Norton, 1998).
Lacan, Jacques. 'The mirror Stage as Formative of the *I* Function as Revealed in Psychoanalytic Experience', Translated by Bruce Fink. In *Écrits*, 75–81. New York and London: W. W. Norton, 2006.
Lalvani, Suren, 'Photography, Epistemology and the Body', *Cultural Studies* 7, no. 3 (1993): 442–65.

Lalvani, Suren, *Photography, Vision and the Production of Modern Bodies* (Albany: State University of New York Press, 1996).

Lam, Tong, 'Unreal Estate and China's Collective Unconscious', *Cross-Currents: East Asian History and Culture Review* 10 (2014): 110–12.

Lamm, Kimberly, 'Texting Girls: Images, Sounds, and Words in Neoliberal Cultures of Femininity', *Women & Performance: A Journal of Feminist Theory* 25, no. 2 (2015): 111–27.

Lauer, J., 'Surveillance History and the History of New Media: An Evidential Paradigm', *New Media & Society* 14, no. 4 (2011): 566–82.

Lee, Martyn, 'The Sublime and Contemporary Popular Culture: The Radical Text in a Post-Political Era', *Journal for Cultural Research* 12, no. 3 (2008): 253–67.

Lee, Pamela M, 'Open Secret', *Artforum International* 49, no. 9 (2011): 220–29.

Levy, Daniel, and Natan Sznaider, *The Holocaust and Memory in the Global Age* (Philadelphia, PA: Temple University Press, 2005).

Lindgren, Kristin, 'Looking at Difference: Laura Swanson's *Anti-Self-Portraits*, Diane Arbus's Portraits, and the Viewer's Gaze', *Journal of Literary & Cultural Disability Studies* 9, no. 3 (2015): 277–94.

Linfield, Susie, *The Cruel Radiance: Photography and Political Violence* (Chicago and London: The University of Chicago Press, 2010).

Lisle, Debbie, 'Gazing at Ground Zero: Tourism, Voyeurism and Spectacle', *Journal for Cultural Research* 8, no. 1 (2004): 3–21.

Lisle, Debbie, 'Sublime Lessons: Education and Ambivalence in War Exhibitions', *Millennium: Journal of International Studies* 34, no. 3 (2006): 841–62.

Lisle, Debbie, 'The Surprising Detritus of Leisure: Encountering the Late Photography of War', *Environment and Planning D: Society and Space* 29, no. 5 (2011): 873–90.

Liu, Jui-Ch'i, 'Female Spectatorship and the Masquerade: Cindy Sherman's Untitled Film Stills', *History of Photography* 34, no. 1 (2010): 79–89.

Lloyd, David, 'Ruination', *Third Text* 18, no. 3 (2004): 263–72.

Lloyd, Moya, 'Performativity, Parody, Politics', *Theory, Culture & Society* 16, no. 2 (1999): 195–213.

Loock, Ulrich. 'Ahlam Shibli's *Occupation*: Introduction', www.documenta14.de/en/south/25224_ahlam_shibli_s_occupation_introduction_by_ulrich_loock.

Lord, Catherine. *The Summer of Her Baldness: A Cancer Improvisation* (Austin: University of Texas Press, 2004).

Loudis, Jessica. '*Infra*', *Artforum International* April/May (2012): 25.

Lowe, Paul. 'The Forensic Turn: Bearing Witness and the Thingness of the Photograph'. In *The Violence of the Image: Photography and International Conflict*, edited by Liam Kennedy and Caitlin Patrick, 226–54. London: I. B. Tauris, 2014.

Lowry, Joanna. 'Symptoms, Signs and Surfaces'. In *Bettina Von Zwehl*, edited by David Chandler, 36–41. Brighton: Photoworks, 2007.

Luckhurst, Roger, 'Contemporary Photography and the Technological Sublime, or, Can There Be a Science Fiction Photography?' *Journal of the Fantastic In the Arts* 19, no. 2 (2008): 181–95.

Lugo-Lugo, Carmen R., and Mary K. Bloodsworth-Lugo, '475 from September 11', *Cultural Studies* 24, no. 2 (2010): 234–55.

Lury, Celia, *Prosthetic Culture: Photography, Memory and Identity* (London and New York: Routledge, 1998).

Lyon, David, *The Electronic Eye: The Rise of Surveillance Society* (Cambridge: Polity Press, 1994).

Lyon, David, *Surveillance Society: Monitoring Everyday Life* (Buckingham: Open University Press, 2001).

Lyon, David, *Surveillance after September 11* (Cambridge: Polity, 2003).

Maguire, Emma, *Girls, Autobiography, Media: Gender and Self-Mediation in Digital Economies* (Cham: Palgrave Macmillan, 2018).

Maimon, Vered, 'Precarious Marks: Thomas Ruff's Jpegs', *Oxford Art Journal* 37, no. 2 (2014): 173–92.

Mann, Sally. *Immediate Family* (New York: Aperture, 1992).

Mann, Sally. *Deep South* (New York: Bulfinch, 2005).

Marshall, David, 'The Problem of the Picturesque', *Eighteenth-Century Studies* 35, no. 3 (2002): 413–37.

Matzner, Tobias, 'Beyond Data as Representation: The Performativity of Big Data in Surveillance', *Surveillance and Society* 14, no. 2 (2016): 197–210.

McCormack, Donna, and Suvi Salmenniemi, 'The Biopolitics of Precarity and the Self', *European Journal of Cultural Studies* 19, no. 1 (2016): 3–15.

McGowan, Todd, 'Finding Ourselves on a *Lost Highway*: David Lynch's Lesson in Fantasy', *Cinema Journal* 39, no. 2 (2000): 51–73.

McGowan, Todd, 'Looking for the Gaze: Lacanian Film Theory and Its Vicissitudes', *Cinema Journal* 42, no. 3 (2003): 27–47.

McGowan, Todd, 'Lost on Mulholland Drive: Navigating David Lynch's Panegyric to Hollywood', *Cinema Journal* 43, no. 2 (2004): 67–89.

McGowan, Todd, *The End of Dissatisfaction? Jacques Lacan and the Emerging Society of Enjoyment* (New York: State University of New York Press, 2004).

McGowan, Todd, *The Real Gaze: Film Theory after Lacan* (Albany: State University of New York Press, 2007).

McGowan, Todd, *Capitalism and Desire: The Psychic Cost of Free Markets* (New York: Columbia University Press, 2016).

McGowan, Todd, and Shelia Kunkle, eds. *Lacan and Contemporary Film* (New York: Other Press, 2004).

McGrath, Jason, 'Apocalypse, or, the Logic of Late Anthropocene Ruins', *Cross-Currents: East Asian History and Culture Review* 10 (2014): 113–19.

McKinlay, Alan, 'Performativity and the Politics of Identity: Putting Butler to Work', *Critical Perspectives on Accounting* 21, no. 3 (2010): 232–42.

McMahon, Regan. 'Artist Laurel Nakadate at Crossroads of Sex, Power', *SFGate*, 18 February, 2011, www.sfgate.com/movies/article/Artist-Laurel-Nakadate-at-crossroads-of-sex-power-2475514.php

McRobbie, Angela, 'Young Women and Consumer Culture', *Cultural Studies* 22, no. 5 (2008): 531–50.

McRobbie, Angela, 'Notes on the Perfect', *Australian Feminist Studies* 30, no. 83 (2015): 3–20.

McRuer, Robert. 'Compulsory Able-Bodiedness and Queer/Disabled Existence'. In *Disability Studies: Enabling the Humanities*, edited by Sharon L. Snyder, Brenda Jo Brueggemann and Rosemarie Garland-Thomson, 88–99. New York: The Modern Languages Association of America, 2002.

Meagher, Michelle, 'Would the Real Cindy Sherman Please Stand Up? Encounters between Cindy Sherman and Feminist Art Theory', *Women: A Cultural Review* 13, no. 1 (2002): 18–36.

Meagher, Michelle 'Improvisation within a Scene of Constraint: Cindy Sherman's Serial Self-Portraiture', *Body & Society* 13, no. 4 (2007): 1–19.

Meagher, Michelle, 'Telling Stories About Feminist Art', *Feminist Theory* 12, no. 3 (2011): 297–316.

Merriman, Peter, 'Driving Places: Marc Augé, Non-Places, and the Geographies of England's M1 Motorway', *Theory, Culture & Society* 21, no. 4/5 (2004): 145–67.

Meyerowitz, Joel *Aftermath: World Trade Centre Archive* (New York and London: Phaidon, 2006).

Millar, John Douglas. 'Watching V Looking', *Art Monthly* 340, October (2010): 7–10.

Millett, Ann, 'Performing Amputation: The Photographs of Joel-Peter Witkin', *Text and Performance Quarterly* 28, no. 1–2 (2008): 8–42.

Mitchell, Juliet. *Psychoanalysis and Feminism: A Radical Reassessment of Freudian Psychoanalysis* (Harmondsworth: Penguin, 1975).

Mitchell, W. J. T., ed *Landscape and Power* (Chicago and London University of Chicago Press, 1994).

Mirzoeff, Nicholas, 'In and out of Slavery', *The Unesco Courier* July/August, (2001): 26–28.

Mirzoeff, Nicholas, 'Visualizing the Anthropocene', *Public Culture* 26, no. 2 (2014): 213–32.

Modleski, Tania. *The Women Who Knew Too Much* (London: Routledge, 1988).

Möller, Frank, 'From Aftermath to Peace: Reflections on a Photography of Peace', *Global Society* 31, no. 3 (2016): 315–35.

Monegal, Antonio, 'Picturing Absence: Photography in the Aftermath', *Journal of War & Culture Studies* 9, no. 3 (2016): 252–70.

Moodie-Mills, Danielle. 'Cultural Extermination and the Erasure of Blackness', *NBC News*, 27 July 2015, www.nbcnews.com/news/nbcblk/cultural-extermination-erasure-blackness-n395526.

Mosse, Richard. *Infra* (New York: Aperture, 2012).

Mukherjee, Roopali, 'Antiracism Limited', *Cultural Studies* 30, no. 1 (2014): 47–77.

Mulvey, Laura, 'Visual Pleasure and Narrative Cinema', *Screen* 3, no. 1 (1975): 6–18.

Munteán, László, 'Spectral Vestiges: Constructing the Ruins of the World Trade Center', *Americana* VII, no. 1 (2011): http://americanaejournal.hu/vol7no1/muntean

Murray, Derek Conrad, 'Notes to Self: The Visual Culture of Selfies in the Age of Social Media', *Consumption Markets & Culture* 18, no. 6 (2015): 490–516.

Musarò, Pierluigi, 'Tensions and Paradoxes of Humanitarianism. Dialogue with Lilie Chouliaraki', *International Review of Sociology* 27, no. 2 (2017): 280–86.
Musto, Sylvia, 'Portraiture, Revolutionary Identity and Subjugation: Anne-Louis Girodet's *Citizen Belley*', *Canadian Art Review* 20, no. 1/2 (1993): 60–71.
Nahm, Kee-Yoon, 'Subvert/Reinscribe', *Performance Research* 21, no. 3 (2016): 92–102.
Nakamura, Lisa, 'Cyberrace', *PMLA* 123, no. 5 (2008): 1673–82.
Nakamura, Lisa. 'The Socioalgorithmics of Race: Sorting It out in Jihad Worlds'. In *The New Media of Surveillance*, edited by Shoshana Magnet and Kelly Gates, 149–61. New York: Routledge, 2009.
Neath, Jessica, 'Empty Lands: Contemporary Art Approaches to Photographing Historical Trauma in Tasmania', *Journal of Australian Studies* 36, no. 3 (2012): 309–25.
Needham, Alex. 'Richard Prince V Suicide Girls in an Instagram Price War', *The Guardian*, 27 May 2015, www.theguardian.com/artanddesign/2015/may/27/suicide-girls-richard-prince-copying-instagram.
Nobus, Danny, ed., *Key Concepts of Lacanian Psychoanalysis* (New York: Other Press, 1999).
Novick, Peter. *The Holocaust in American Life* (Boston and New York: Mariner Books, 1999).
Nye, David E., *American Technological Sublime* (Cambridge, MA and London: MIT Press, 1996).
O'Gorman, Ned, 'The Political Sublime: An Oxymoron', *Millennium: Journal of International Studies* 34, no. 3 (2006): 889–915.
O'Hagan, Sean. 'Omar Victor Diop: "I Want to Reinvent the Heritage of African Studio Photography"', *The Guardian*, 11 July 2015, www.theguardian.com/artanddesign/2015/jul/11/mar-ictor-ioi-want-to-reinvent-great-heritage-of-african-studio-photography
Ong, Aihwa, *Neoliberalism as Exception: Mutations in Citizenship and Sovereignty* (Durham, NC: Duke University Press, 2006).
Orvell, Miles, *American Photography* (Oxford: Oxford University Press, 2003).
Orvell, Miles, 'The Absolute Power of the Lens: Zoe Strauss and the Problem of the Street Portrait', *Afterimage* 40, no. 2 (2012): 10–13.
Packer, Jeremy, 'Homeland Subjectivity: The Algorithmic Identity of Security', *Communication and Critical/Cultural Studies* 4, no. 2 (2007): 211–15.
Paglen, Trevor, 'Goatsucker: Toward a Spatial Theory of State Secrecy', *Environment and Planning D: Society and Space* 28, no. 5 (2010): 759–71.
Paglen, Trevor, *Blank Spots on the Map: The Dark Geography of the Pentagon's Secret World* (Harmondsworth: Penguin, 2011).
Paglen, Trevor. 'Experimental Geography: From Cultural Production to the Production of Space'. In *Critical Landscapes: Art, Space, Politics*, edited by Emily Eliza Scott and Kristen Swenson, 34–42. Oakland, CA: University of California Press, 2015.
Pariser, Eli. *The Filter Bubble: What the Internet Is Hiding from You* (Harmondsworth: Penguin, 2012).

Parkinson, Hannah Jane. 'Instagram, an Artist and the $100,000 Selfies – Appropriation in the Digital Age', *The Guardian*, 18 July 2015, www.theguardian.com/technology/2015/jul/18/instagram-artist-richard-prince-selfies

Peck, Julia, 'Vibrant Photography: Photographs, Actants and Political Ecology', *Photographies* 9, no. 1 (2016): 71–89.

Pendle, George. 'Photography, but Not as We Know It', *The Economist: 1843*, January 5 2016, www.1843magazine.com/culture/the-daily/photography-but-not-as-we-know-it

Perera, Suvendrini, 'Torturous Dialogues: Geographies of Trauma and Spaces of Exception', *Continuum* 24, no. 1 (2010): 31–45.

Perry, Lara, 'The Carte De Visite in the 1860s and the Serial Dynamic of Photographic Likeness', *Art History* 35, no. 4 (2012): 728–49.

Perry, Weena, '"Too Young and Vibrant for Ruins": Ground Zero Photography and the Problem of Contemporary Ruin', *Afterimage* 36, no. 3 (2008): 8–12.

Peters, Clorinde, 'Visualizing Disposability: Photographing Neoliberal Conflict in the United States', *Afterimage* 44, no. 6 (2017): 6–11.

Plaugic, Lizzie. 'The Story of Richard Prince and His $100,000 Instagram Art', *The Verge*, 30 May 2015, www.theverge.com/2015/5/30/8691257/richard-prince-instagram-photos-copyright-law-fair-use

Plunkett, John, 'Celebrity and Community: The Poetics of the *Carte-De-Visite*', *Journal of Victorian Culture* 8, no. 1 (2003): 55–79.

Power, Nina. 'She's Just Not That into You', *Radical Philosophy* 177, Jan/Feb (2013): www.radicalphilosophy.com/reviews/individual-reviews/rp177-shes-just-not-that-into-you

Prospero. 'The Art of Laurel Nakadate: Lust and Loneliness', *The Economist*, 13 July 2011, www.economist.com/prospero/2011/07/13/lust-and-loneliness

Pugh, Simon, *Reading Landscape: Country, City, Capital* (Manchester and New York: Manchester University Press, 1990).

Radstone, Susannah. 'Social Bonds and Psychical Order: Testimonies', *Cultural Values* 5, no. 1 (2001): 59–78.

Ray, Gene, *Terror and the Sublime in Art and Critical Theory: From Auschwitz to September 11* (New York and Hampshire: Palgrave MacMillian, 2005).

Ray, Gene, 'HITS: From Trauma and the Sublime to Radical Critique', *Third Text* 23, no. 2 (2009): 135–49.

Raymond, Claire, *Women Photographers and Feminist Aesthetics* (London and New York: Routledge, 2017).

Reigeluth, Tyler, 'Why Data Is Not Enough: Digital Traces as Control of Self and Self-Control', *Surveillance and Society* 12, no. 2 (2014): 243–54.

Reiner, Rob. *A Few Good Men* (Los Angeles, CA: Columbia Pictures, 1992).

Rentschler, Carrie A., 'Witnessing: US Citizenship and the Vicarious Experience of Suffering', *Media, Culture and Society* 26, no. 2 (2004): 296–304.

Rentschler, Carrie A., 'The Physiognomic Turn', *International Journal of Communication* 4 (2010): 231–36.

Ringrose, Jessica, and Valerie Walkerdine, 'Regulating the Abject', *Feminist Media Studies* 8, no. 3 (2008): 227–46.

Ritchin, Fred. *Bending the Frame: Photojournalism, Documentary, and the Citizen* (New York: Aperture, 2013).

Roberts, John, 'Photography after the Photograph: Event, Archive, and the Non-Symbolic', *Oxford Art Journal* 32, no. 2 (2009): 283–98.

Roberts, John, '"Pointing To": Ostension, Trauma and the Photographic Document', *Parallax* 16, no. 2 (2010): 87–94.

Ronneberger, Klaus. 'Bare Life or Just Existence?' In *Documenta Magazine* no. 2 (Cologne: Tashen, 2007).

Rosamond, Emily, 'Technologies of Attribution: Characterizing the Citizen-Consumer in Surveillance Performance', *International Journal of Performance Arts and Digital Media* 11, no. 2 (2015): 148–64.

Rose, Nikolas, *Governing the Soul: The Shaping of the Private Self* (London: Free Association Books, 1990).

Rose, Nikolas, *The Politics of Life Itself: Biomedicine, Power, and Subjectivity in the Twenty-First Century* (Princeton, NJ; Oxford: Princeton University Press, 2009).

Rosenberg, Karen. 'Art in Review: Laurel Nakadate', *The New York Times*, 26 June 2009, archive.nytimes.com/query.nytimes.com/gst/fullpage-9C01E4D81630F935A15755C0A96F9C8B63.html

Rosenfeld, Alvin H. *The End of the Holocaust* (Indiana: Indiana University Press, 2011).

Rosengarten, Ruth. 'Performing for the Camera 18 February–12 June 2016, Tate Modern (Review)', *Photography and Culture* 9, no. 2 (2016): 190.

Rosler, Martha. 'In, around, and Afterthoughts (on Documentary Photography)'. In *The Context of Meaning: Critical Histories of Photography*, edited by Richard Bolton, 303–25. Cambridge, MA: MIT Press, 1981.

Rossie, Amanda, 'Moving Beyond 'Am I Pretty or Ugly?' Disciplining Girls through YouTube Feedback', *Continuum* 29, no. 2 (2015): 230–40.

Rothberg, Michael, *Multidirectional Memory: Remembering the Holocaust in the Age of Decolonization* (Stanford: Stanford University Press, 2009).

Rothberg, Michael, 'From Gaza to Warsaw: Mapping Multidirectional Memory', *Criticism* 53, no. 4 (2011): 523–48.

Rothman, Aaron. 'Our Invisible Presence', *Places Journal* August (2012): doi.org/10.22269/120814

Rottenberg, Catherine, '*Passing*: Race, Identification, and Desire', *Criticism* 45, no. 4 (2003): 435–52.

Rouvroy, Antoinette, 'The Digital Regime of Truth: From the Algorithmic Governmentality to a New Rule of Law', *La Deleuziana* 3 (2016): 6–27.

Rouvroy, Antoinette, 'Algorithmic Governmentality: Radicalisation and Immune Strategy of Capitalism and Neoliberalism?' *La Deleuziana* 3 (2016): 30–36.

Rudd, Annie, 'Victorians Living in Public: Cartes De Visite as 19th-Century Social Media', *Photography and Culture* 9, no. 3 (2017): 1–23.

Rule, Nicholas O. and Nalini Ambady. 'Brief Exposures: Male's Sexual Orientation Is Accurately Perceived at 50 ms', *Journal of Experimental Social Psychology* 44, no. 4 (2008): 1100–5.

Salecl, Renata and Slavoj Žižek, eds., *Gaze and Voice as Love Objects* (Durham, NC and London: Duke University Press, 1996).
Saltz, Jerry. 'Richard Prince's Instagram Paintings Are Genius Trolling', *Vulture*, 23 September 2014, www.vulture.com/2014/09/richard-prince-instagram-pervert-troll-genius.html
Salvesen, Britt, and Alison Nordstrom, eds., *New Topographics* (Gottingen, Germany: Steidl, 2009).
Sanyal, Debarati, 'A Soccer Match in Auschwitz: Passing Culpability in Holocaust Criticism', *Representations* 79, no. 1 (2002): 1–27.
Scott, Emily Eliza, and Kristen Swenson, eds., *Critical Landscapes: Art, Space, Politics* (Oakland, CA: University of California Press, 2015).
Schjeldahl, Peter. 'Richard Prince's Instagrams', *The New Yorker*, 30 September 2014, www.newyorker.com/culture/culture-desk/richard-princes-instagrams
Schulenburg, Alexander Hugo "Island of the Blessed': Eden, Arcadia and the Picturesque in the Textualizing of St Helena', *Journal of Historical Geography*, 29, no. 4 (2003): 535–53.
Schuweiler, Suzanne 'Sally Mann's South', *Southeastern College Art Conference Review* 16, no. 3 (2013): 325–36.
Schwartz, Alexandra. 'A Living Monument to the Ghosts of American Slavery', *The New Yorker*, 28 December 2016, www.newyorker.com/culture/photo-booth/a-living-monument-to-the-ghosts-of-american-slavery
Sealy, Mark. 'Heni Talk Interviews Omar Victor Diop: Black Subjects in the Frame', 7 December 2018, www.jenkinsjohnsongallery.com/news/heni-talk-interviews-omar-victor-diop
Searle, Adrian. 'Why Do I Feel Naked?' *The Guardian*, 15 July 2000, www.theguardian.com/books/2000/jul/15/books.guardianreview4
Sedgwick, Eve Kosofsky. 'White Glasses', *The Yale Journal of Criticism* 5, no. 3 (1992): 193–208.
Seitler, Dana, 'Queer Physiognomies: Or, How Many Ways Can We Do the History of Sexuality?', *Criticism* 46, no. 1 (2004): 71–102.
Sekula, Allan, 'The Body and the Archive', *October* 39 (1986): 3–64.
Senior, Emily, 'The Colonial Picturesque and the Medical Utility of Landscape Aesthetics', *Journal for Eighteenth-Century Studies* 36, no. 4 (2013): 505–17.
Setka, Stella, 'Bastardized History: How Inglourious Basterds Breaks through American Screen Memory', *Jewish Film & New Media* 3, no. 2 (2015): 141–69.
Sharma, Sarah, 'Baring Life and Lifestyle in the Non-Place', *Cultural Studies* 23, no. 1 (2009): 129–48.
Shea, Laura Elizabeth. 'Sally Mann: A Thousand Crossings', *ASAP Journal*, 3 May 2018, http://asapjournal.com/sally-mann-a-thousand-crossings-laura-elizabeth-shea/
Shibli, Ahlam. 'Artist's Statement: *Occupation*', www.ahlamshibli.com/statement/occupation_en.htm
Shore, Robert, *Post-Photography* (London: Laurence King, 2014).
Siebers, Tobin, 'Disability as Masquerade', *Literature and Medicine* 23, no. 1 (2004): 1–22.

Silas, Susan. 'Nona Faustine: White Shoes', 1 December 2015, theo-westenberger.tumblr.com/post/134358235279/nona-faustine-white-shoes.

Silverman, Kaja. *The Acoustic Mirror: The Female Voice in Psychoanalysis and Cinema* (Bloomington: Indiana University Press, 1988).

Smith, Shawn Michelle, *American Archives: Gender, Race, and Class in Visual Culture* (Princeton, NJ: Princeton University Press, 1999).

Snyder, Sharon L., Brenda Jo Brueggemann and Rosemarie Garland-Thomson, eds., *Disability Studies: Enabling the Humanities* (New York: The Modern Languages Association of America, 2002).

Solomon-Godeau, Abigail. *Photography at the Dock: Essays on Photographic History, Institutions, and Practices* (Minneapolis: University of Minnesota Press, 1991).

Solomon-Godeau, Abigail. 'Who Is Speaking Thus? Some Questions About Documentary Photography', In *Photography at the Dock: Essays on Photographic History, Institutions, and Practices*, 169–83. Minneapolis: University of Minnesota Press, 1991.

Solomon-Godeau, Abigail. 'Inside/Out'. In *Public Information: Desire, Disaster, Document*, 48–61. San Francisco Museum of Modern Art, 1995.

Solte, Franziska. 'Standard', In *Standard*, 12–13. Zürich: Verlag Scheidegger & Spiess AG, 2016.

Sooke, Alastair. 'Is This the First Instagram Masterpiece?' *The Telegraph*, 18 January 2016, www.telegraph.co.uk/photography/what-to-see/is-this-the-first-instagram-masterpiece/

Soutter, Lucy. *Why Art Photography?* (London and New York: Routledge, 2013).

Stallabrass, Julian, 'Sebastião Salgado and Fine Art Photojournalism', *New Left Review* 223, May–June (1997): 131–3.

Stallabrass, Julian, 'What's in a Face? Blankness and Significance in Contemporary Art Photography', *October* 122, Fall (2007): 71–90.

Stallabrass, Julian, 'War/Photography: Images of Armed Conflict and Its Aftermath', *Photography & Culture* 7, no. 2 (2014): 223–28.

Stara, Alexandra, '"Making Strange": The Photography of Steffi Klenz and Thomas Weinberger', *History of Photography* 37, no. 3 (2013): 353–59.

Stavrakakis, Yannis, *Lacan and the Political* (London and New York: Routledge, 1999).

Stavrakakis, Yannis, 'Objects of Consumption, Causes of Desire: Consumerism and Advertising in Societies of Commanded Enjoyment', *Gramma* 14 (2006): 83–106.

Stein, Arlene, 'Whose Memories? Whose Victimhood? Contests for the Holocaust Frame in Recent Social Movement Discourse', *Sociological Perspectives* 41, no. 3 (1998): 519–40.

Stein, Sally. 'How Do We Look? Counter-Intuitive Prompts and Probes in Zoe Strauss' Resurgent Social Documentary Photography'. In *Zoe Strauss: 10 Years*, edited by Peter Barberie 156–69. New Haven and London: Philadelphia Museum of Art in association with Yale University Press, 2012.

Stevenson, Sara, 'Robert Louis Stevenson and the Portrait Photographers', *History of Photography* 37, no. 2 (2013): 235–42.

Steyerl, Hito. 'In Defense of the Poor Image', In *The Wretched of the Screen*, 31–45. Berlin: Sternberg Press, 2012.
Steyerl, Hito. *The Wretched of the Screen* (Berlin: Sternberg Press, 2012).
Stinson, James, 'Re-Creating Wilderness 2.0: Or Getting Back to Work in a Virtual Nature', *Geoforum* 79 (2017): 174–87.
Stormer, Nathan, 'Addressing the Sublime: Space, Mass Representation, and the Unpresentable', *Critical Studies in Media Communication* 21, no. 3 (2004): 212–40.
Striphas, Ted, 'Algorithmic Culture', *European Journal of Cultural Studies* 18, no. 4–5 (2015): 395–412.
Sturken, Marita, *Tourists of History: Memory, Kitsch and Consumerism from Oklahoma City to Ground Zero* (Durham, NC: Duke University Press, 2007).
Suillvan, Bill, 'The Real Thing: Photographer Luc Delahaye', *Artnet*, 2003, www.artnet.com/magazine/features/sullivan/sullivan4-10-03.asp
Szorenyi, Anna, 'Distanced Suffering: Photographed Suffering and the Construction of White in/vulnerability', *Social Semiotics* 19, no. 2 (2009): 93–109.
Tabak, Joshua A. and Vivian Zayas. 'The Roles of Featural and Congural Face Processing in Snap Judgments of Sexual Orientation', *PLOS ONE* 7, no. 5 (2012): 1–7.
Tagg, John, *The Burden of Representation: Essays on Photographies and Histories* (Basingstoke: MacMillan, 1988).
Tagg, John, *Grounds of Dispute: Art History, Cultural Politics and the Discursive Field* (Minneapolis: University of Minnesota Press, 1992).
Tagg, John, 'The Archiving Machine; or, the Camera and the Filing Cabinet', *Grey Room* no. 47, Spring (2012): 24–37.
Tello, Veronica, 'The Aesthetics and Politics of Aftermath Photography', *Third Text* 28, no. 6 (2014): 555–62.
Teukolsky, Rachel, 'Cartomania: Sensation, Celebrity, and the Democratized Portrait', *Victorian Studies* 57, no. 3 (2015): 462–75.
Tiqqun, *Preliminary Materials for a Theory of the Young Girl,* translated by Ariana Reines (Cambridge, MA and London: Semiotext(e), 2012).
Tompkins, Joe, '"A Postgame Interview for the Ages": Richard Sherman and the Dialectical Rhetoric of Racial Neoliberalism', *Journal of Sport and Social Issues* 40, no. 4 (2015): 291–314.
Trachtenberg, Alan. 'Likeness as Identity: Reflections on the Daguerrean Mystique'. In *The Portrait in Photography*, edited by Graham Clarke, 173–93. London: Reaktion Books, 1992.
Traff, Thea. 'Zoe Strauss: 10 Years', *The New Yorker*, 4 October 2013, www.newyorker.com/culture/photo-booth/zoe-strauss-10-years
Tyler, Imogen, 'Who Put the "Me" in Feminism?' *Feminist Theory* 6, no. 1 (2005): 25–44.
Tyler, Imogen, '"Welcome to Britain": The Cultural Politics of Asylum', *European Journal of Cultural Studies* 9, no. 2 (2006): 185–202.
Tyler, Imogen, 'Designed to Fail: A Biopolitics of British Citizenship', *Citizenship Studies* 14, no. 1 (2010): 61–74.
Tyler, Imogen, and Katarzyna Marciniak, 'Immigrant Protest: An Introduction', *Citizenship Studies* 17, no. 2 (2013): 143–56.

Ulman, Amalia. *Excellences & Perfections* (Instagram Update, July 8, 2014) (#itsjustdifferent), 2015: www.instagram.com/p/qNDFxGlV6N/?utm_source=ig_web_button_share_sheet.

Ulman, Amalia. *Excellences & Perfections* (Instagram Update, August 8, 2014) www.instagram.com/p/rcBXSLlV-R/?utm_source=ig_web_button_share_sheet

Ulman, Amalia. *Excellences & Perfections* (Instagram Update, September 2, 2014) (Meditating before a long day of work). www.instagram.com/p/sc48slFV6l/?utm_source=ig_web_button_share_sheet.

Ulman, Amalia. *Excellences & Perfections* (Munich, London, New York: Prestel Verlag, 2018).

Uzlaner, Dmitry, 'The Selfie and the Intolerable Gaze of the Other', *International Journal of Applied Psychoanalytic Studies* 14, no. 4 (2017): 282–94.

Uzwiak, Beth A., 'Make of This Whatever You Want: Violence and Intimacy in Zoe Strauss's I-95 Project', *Photography & Culture* 11, no. 1 (2018): 1–21.

Valentine, Ben. 'Gays, Grinder, the Holocaust Memorial, and Art: An Interview with Marc Adelman', *Hyperallergic*, 21 December 2012, hyperallergic.com/62106/gays-grinder-the-holocaust-memorial-and-art-an-interview-with-marc-adelman/

Vanderwees, Chris, 'Traces of the Virtual: Aesthetics, Affect, and the Event in Joel Meyerowitz's Photography of Ground Zero', *Photography & Culture* 10, no. 1 (2017): 19–36.

Vanier, Alain, *Lacan* (New York: Other Press, 2000).

von Brevern, Jan, 'Resemblance after Photography', *Representations* 123, no. 1 (2013): 1–22.

Vasey, George. 'Self 2 Selfie', *Art Monthly* Issue 371, November (2013): 5–8.

Vasey, George. 'Erica Scourti', *Art Monthly* Issue 382, December–January (2014–15): 20–21.

Wallis, Brian, 'Trevor Paglen Landing Site', *Aperture* 222, Spring (2016): 78–87.

Warren, John T., 'Doing Whiteness: On the Performative Dimensions of Race in the Classroom', *Communication Education* 50, no. 2 (2001): 91–108.

Warren-Crow, Heather, 'Gossip Girl Goes to the Gallery', *Performance Research* 18, no. 5 (2013): 108–19.

Weissman, Gary, *Fantasies of Witnessing: Postwar Efforts to Experience the Holocaust* (Ithaca, NY and London: Cornell University Press, 2004).

Welch, Edward, 'Stars of CCTV: Technology, Visibility and Identity in the Work of Sophie Calle and Annie Ernaux', *Nottingham French Studies* 48, no. 2 (2009): 55–67.

Welch, Edward, 'Marc Augé, Jean Rolin and the Mapping of (Non-)Place in Modern France', *Irish Journal of French Studies* 9, no. 1 (2009): 49–68.

Wells, Benedict. 'The Foreign Home', In *Standard*, 7–9. Zürich: Verlag Scheidegger & Spiess AG, 2016.

Wells, Liz, *Land Matters: Landscape Photography, Culture and Identity* (London and New York: I. B. Tauris).

Weston, Nancy. 'How to Remember', In *Absence/Presence: Essays and Reflections on the Artistic Memory of the Holocaust*, edited by Steve Feinstein, 39–54. New York: Syracuse University Press, 2005.

Whelan, David. 'The Artists Explaining Their Multiple Sclerosis through Art', *Vice*, 23 November 2015, www.vice.com/en_uk/article/wd7kxw/a-hidden-disese-understanding-multiple-sclerosis-through-art-225

Wiley, Chris. 'Lucas Blalock: Imperfect Grace', *Aperture*, 208, Fall (2012): 32–35.

Wilkinson, Jayne, 'Art Documents: The Politics of Visibility in Contemporary Photography', *InVisible Culture* Issue 22, Spring (2015): http://ivc.lib.rochester.edu/art-documents-the-politics-of-visibility-in-contemporary-photography/

Wolthers, Louise, 'Self-Surveillance and Virtual Safety', *Photographies* 6, no. 1 (2013): 169–76.

Wood, Andrew, 'The Best Surprise Is No Surprise', *Space and Culture* 8, no. 4 (2016): 399–415.

Wood, Kelly, 'In Favour of Heroines: Lincoln Clarkes's Vancouver Photographs', *Philosophy of Photography* 4, no. 2 (2013): 217–41.

Wright, Elizabeth and Edmond Wright, eds., *The Žižek Reader* (Oxford: Blackwell, 2000).

Young, James E. *At Memory's Edge: After-Images of the Holocaust in Contemporary Art and Architecture* (New Haven and London: Yale University Press, 2000).

Yusoff, Kathryn, 'Anthropogenesis: Origins and Endings in the Anthropocene', *Theory, Culture & Society* 33, no. 2 (2015): 3–28.

Zaremba, Lukasz, 'Mediating Visual Experience: Zbigniew Libera's Photographic Works and Google Street View Imagery', *InVisible Culture*, Issue 18 (2003): http://ivc.lib.rochester.edu/category/issues/archives/issue-18/

Zimmer, Catherine, 'Surveillance Cinema: Narrative between Technology and Politics', *Surveillance and Society* 8, no. 4 (2011): 427–40.

Žižek, Slavoj, *Looking Awry: An Introduction to Jacques Lacan through Popular Culture* (Cambridge and London: The MIT Press, 1992).

Žižek, Slavoj, *Enjoy Your Symptom! Jacques Lacan in Hollywood and Out* (London and New York: Routledge, 1992).

Žižek, Slavoj. 'Why Are Laibach and NSK Not Fascists?' *M'ARS* 3/4 (1993): www.nskstate.com.

Žižek, Slavoj, *Tarrying with the Negative: Kant, Hegel, and the Critique of Ideology* (Durham, NC: Duke University Press, 1993).

Žižek, Slavoj, *The Sublime Object of Ideology* (London and New York: Verso, 1995).

Žižek, Slavoj. '"I Hear You with My Ears"; or, the Invisible Master', In *Gaze and Voice as Love Objects*, edited by Renata Salecl and Slavoj Žižek, 90–126. Durham and London: Duke University Press, 1996.

Žižek, Slavoj, *The Plague of Fantasies* (London and New York: Verso, 1997).

Žižek, Slavoj, 'The Big Other Doesn't Exist', *Journal of European Psychoanalysis* no. 5, Spring-Fall (1997): www.psychomedia.it/jep/number5/zizek.htm

Žižek, Slavoj. 'The Seven Veils of Fantasy'. In *Key Concepts of Lacanian Psychoanalysis*, edited by Dany Nobus, 190–218. New York: Other Press, 1999.

Žižek, Slavoj. 'Fantasy as a Political Category: A Lacanian Approach'. In *The Žižek Reader*, edited by Elizabeth Wright and Edmond Wright, 87–101. Oxford: Blackwell, 2000.

Žižek, Slavoj, *The Metastases of Enjoyment: Six Essays on Women and Causality* (London and New York: Verso, 2005).
Žižek, Slavoj and Renata Salecl, eds., *Gaze and Voice as Love Objects* (Durham and London: Duke University Press, 1996).
Zolghadr, Tirdad 'Them and Us', *Frieze*, Issue 96, Jan–Feb (2006): frieze.com/article/them-and-us
Zylinska, Joanna. 'iEarth (Artist's Statement)', www.joannazylinska.net/iearth/
Zylinska, Joanna, *Minimal Ethics for the Anthropocene* (Ann Arbor: Open Humanities Press, 2014).
Zylinska, Joanna, 'On Life, Movement and Stoppage: Agency and Ethics in the Anthropocene', *Leonardo* 48, no. 2 (2015): 180–81.
Zylinska, Joanna, 'Photography after the Human', *Photographies* 9, no. 2 (2016): 167–86.

Index

Note: Page numbers in **bold** denote figures